D1637050

THE
SMART
PARENTING
REVOLUTION

THE
SMART
PARENTING
REVOLUTION

A POWERFUL NEW APPROACH
TO UNLEASHING YOUR CHILD'S POTENTIAL

DAWNA MARKOVA, PH.D.

BALLANTINE BOOKS • NEW YORK

This book is intended as a reference volume only, not as a medical manual. The information given here is designed to help you make informed decisions about your child's intellectual development and behavior. It is not intended as a treatment or substitute for medical treatment. The names and identifying characteristics of all children and parents mentioned have been changed.

Published in the United States by Ballantine Books, an imprint of The Random House Publishing Group, a division of Random House, Inc., New York.

BALLANTINE and colophon are registered trademarks of Random House, Inc.

LIBRARY OF CONGRESS CATALOGING-IN-PUBLICATION DATA
Markova, Dawna
    The SMART parenting revolution: a powerful new approach
to unleashing your child's potential / Dawna Markova.
        p.   cm.
    Includes bibliographical references.
    ISBN 0-345-48245-X (alk. paper)
    1. Child psychology.   2. Self-actualization (Psychology) in children
3. Success in children.   4. Learning ability.   5. Child rearing.   6. Parenting.   I. Title.
HQ772.M258 2005
649'.6—dc22   2005045754

Printed in the United States of America on acid-free paper

www.ballantinebooks.com

9 8 7 6 5 4 3 2 1

FIRST EDITION

Graphic conceptualization: Angela McArthur
Graphic design: John Vieceli
Book design: Diane Hobbing of Snap-Haus Graphics

To David and Angie

you are my dreams, you are my prayers, you are my next step

FOREWORD

By the co-authors of The Spiritual Dimension of Leadership, *Dr. Paul D. Houston, executive director of the American Association of School Administrators, and Dr. Stephen L. Sokolow, executive director of the Center for Empowered Leadership*

We (Paul and Steve) both are parents and grandparents as well as lifelong teachers and leaders in public education. In all of those roles we wanted the same thing for the children we served as we did for our own children and grandchildren—the gift of empowerment. We also wanted to learn who we were and where we fit in the world. We wanted to learn what we had to offer and how to best use the innate gifts and talents we had been given. That's what all people want. But how do we go about it? That's what this remarkable book you now hold in your hands is about—discovering our innate gifts, and then cultivating and sharing them. At a deeper level this book is about making the world better by bringing out the best in each and every parent's child—bringing out the best in your child.

Gifts come in all shapes and sizes. Some are innate, waiting for us to discover them and give them a means of expression. Others are already on the outside for us to see and feel. When you first think about gifts, it is usually about something that you have received that was meaningful to you. Then you might think about something you have given to someone else. But the true power of giving resides in the intention of the giver, and this is the gift you get to share with yourself.

There was a teacher who was working on an isolated island in the South Pacific. There were few things of worth on the island, but it was known for a special kind of shell that could be found on a remote beach. The teacher commented to her class that someday she hoped to walk to that beach so she could have one of the shells. A few days later, one of the students came in and placed one of the shells on the teacher's desk. The teacher was touched but told the student, "You shouldn't have walked that long distance just to give me this shell." The child replied, "But, teacher, the walk was part of the gift."

As educators we have always loved that story, for it is the task of teachers and parents to make that long walk on behalf of our children. But what constitutes the right path?

When we first met Dawna Markova, it was quickly apparent that she was a gift to us from the universe. Dawna is an incredibly talented woman whose engaging life force exudes a powerful radiance. She is a natural storyteller, and we wanted to hear her story. We wanted to know everything about her. Instead, she focused on us, on what we were doing, shedding light on our story. As she did so, we were uplifted and empowered. It was as if she were holding up a magic mirror, reflecting back to us the best that was in us. She also showered us with gifts of books, poems, and prayers—even a crystal bowl. But the real gift was the gift of her presence, of her being. Being around Dawna leads you to understand that with her, the gift is in the walk. She makes life special by giving her shells to others.

Dawna has brought her poetry and passion to the world. She has inspired hundreds of thousands to give to others through the Random Acts of Kindness movement that she helped spawn. And now she is embarking on her greatest walk—to help the world understand the innate gifts that our children bring to us.

We all have a mother, the person who brought us into this world, the person from whom we first learned love and trust, and in whose eyes we first learned to see ourselves. Dawna Markova is the embodiment of the Universal Mother, the universal nurturer who helps us to become our best self. She has an abundance of love and wisdom and a burning passion to help each of us reach our fullest potential. She empowers us and helps us to identify and nurture our unique spark, our unique gifts and talents. This extraordinary woman of wisdom is our teacher and guide, a role model who can show us how to be the parents we want to be and how to create for our children what we most want for them—the opportunity to be who they really are and add their special strand to the evolving fabric of life.

This book is a living prayer, a blessing to every parent and every child, and to life itself.

CONTENTS

THE
SMART
PARENTING
REVOLUTION

INTRODUCTION:
LIVING AS IF YOUR LIFE MATTERS

It cannot be easy being my son. I have been embarrassing him on a daily basis for the last thirty-eight years. Not on purpose, mind you. It just seems that the more I live who I am meant to be, the more I embarrass him. I know that beginning this book by writing about him will cause David embarrassment. He is a quiet and private person with a mother whose path calls her to speak to the entire world about how it can be worthy of its children. He is a superb athlete whose mother, fondly known as Klara Klutz, almost did not graduate college because there was not one physical education course she could pass.

When I was a public school teacher, he was continually embarrassed by people's expectations that he would be the best student in any class. When I was a psychotherapist, he was embarrassed by people's expectations that he would be sane and well balanced, a nearly impossible task for any hormonally challenged adolescent. When I was an adviser to corporate leaders, he was embarrassed by my inability to understand a ledger sheet. I was meant, it seems, to rock the world but not a cradle.

The most embarrassing moment in the last year must have been last February when he and I were meeting in the Pentagon with James L. Jones, the supreme allied commander of the NATO forces. David was immaculately dressed and I'm sure that when we sat down at the general's massive mahogany desk with various photographs of military leaders from Dwight David Eisenhower to Wesley Clark on the wall, surrounded by multicolored flags and things starched and shiny, David must have been wondering what humiliating experience his incurably defiant, former hippie mother had in store for him.

On the desk was a pile of all the carefully prepared papers and brochures he had sent the general explaining the project we were there to discuss. David had given me a list of pithy four-letter words I was *not* to use when talking to the general about why we wanted his support creating a million-child SmartWired pilot program that would help military families unleash the potential in their children. I had promised to be appropriate in my speech. Still, David has known me for thirty-eight years and, as I said, never known me not to embarrass him somehow.

He seemed fine when I pulled a small box out of my briefcase, explaining I had brought a gift for General Jones. We had been through three security searches— what evil thing could I possibly have in that innocent little cardboard box? General

Jones is six foot five and then some. When he opened the box and took out a brown
bullet-shaped object, it almost disappeared in his huge weathered hands. David sat
up, alert, as if waiting for sirens to go off. General Jones smiled. Even as I explained
to him that it was an acorn from a California live oak, I could almost hear David's
subvocalization, "She gives one of the world's most important military leaders an
acorn? What is she doing? Is she crazy? She's gotten even more bizarre since she
moved to California than she was when she lived in that little cabin in Utah!"

I told General Jones that I had recently moved to California because I had been
diagnosed with emphysema and couldn't breathe in Utah's altitude. I recounted
how we had bought an old house in a grove of oak trees, and how, when I was
walking among them, I picked up one of the acorns and decided to bring it to him.
General Jones smiled kindly. I could almost hear David grinding his teeth.

I went on to explain that several things made me want to bring it. One was that
each acorn, as small as it was, developed into a unique, immense tree, with a root
system beneath the surface that was equally immense. I told him that many people would not pay attention to such a small thing, but that someone who could see
deeply would understand the power and potential packed into that small nut, and
how each acorn carries all the tree's great knowledge compressed into a tiny core.
The general rolled the acorn around in his palm as I spoke, looking at it, into it,
rather than at me. "It is just like a child. In spite of all this potential, the acorn can
do nothing by itself. It holds all possibility, but it also holds the frustration of an
unlived life. It holds the fury of the tiny infant who cries because it cannot reach
what it sees, cannot do what it imagines."

I paused, passion rising in my throat like sap in a tree. David was clenching and
unclenching his fingers.

General Jones, however, was touching the acorn with his large index finger as if
he were stroking the cheek of an infant. I took that as a good sign, and went on to
explain that I brought him the acorn because throughout history there has been the
notion that nature speaks through the voice of an oak tree to ears that can listen.

I paused to take a breath and General Jones began to speak, still looking at the
acorn. In slow and gentle words, he told us of his four children and, particularly, of
the last one, his only daughter. When he held her, he could feel that she was a miracle, that she had a unique and great gift inside her. Then he looked up, first at me,
then at David. "I was right, in that moment. She has grown that gift and shared it
with us and our entire family every day of her life."

I looked at David. He was breathing easily. He realized the general had understood exactly what I was talking about and why we were there asking for his support.

I spoke into the silence. "I want every child to grow up in the arms of someone who recognizes in them what you did in your daughter, General Jones. The oaks behind our house are so huge they barely move in the strongest wind. They are so steady that they seem to connect what is above with what is below. It takes a large, deep network of roots underneath each oak tree to hold it up. We want to create the conditions that you did for your daughter as a network of roots for all the children of the world. It's a big dream. We need to help families see beyond what appears to be one fragile little acorn among thousands of others, to what their children might become someday. Each acorn needs a champion, and we want to tap into the huge system that can grow, nourish, and support them."

David was breathing slow and easy. General Jones turned to him and said simply, "How can I help?"

Making the Most of the Moments We Have

> *"The entire society suffers from attention deficit disorder—big time—and from its most prevalent variant—attention deficit hyperactivity disorder. And it is getting worse by the day. Learning how to refine our ability to pay attention and to sustain attention may no longer be a luxury but a lifeline back to what is most meaningful in our lives, what is easily missed, ignored, denied or run through so quickly that it could not possibly be noticed."*
>
> JON KABBAT-ZINN, SCIENTIST AND AUTHOR

I'm sure that after my last book—*I Will Not Die an Unlived Life: Reclaiming Purpose and Passion*—was published, David was embarrassed by people expecting him to be a flaming paragon of determination and intention, trying to decide whether to accept the Nobel Prize for medicine or literature. But if that is so, they never read the book.

In its beginning I wrote, "Each of us is here to give something that only we can offer, and when we avoid knowing ourselves, we end up living numb, passionless lives, disconnected from our soul's true purpose." Near the end I wrote:

I understand that life is not a spectator sport, that we are not its victims, but its co-creators. I also understand that children call us forth into what Martin Luther King, Jr., named "soul force," the strength of the heart to love even in the face of the most difficult circumstances. . . . We forget that the source of the energy is from a spring greater than we can even imagine. It is by spilling over, ultimately, that we are the most fulfilled. When I am empty and think I need to feel loved, what I really need may be to express love out into the world in some way that is meaningful to me.

When *I Will Not Die an Unlived Life* was published, neither David nor I were flaming paragons of anything other than ourselves. I didn't even know what I was going to do or write next. I left my six-month mountaintop retreat hanging between two questions as if they were the bar of a trapeze: "What if I could travel back and forth with grace and ease between my inner and outer worlds, between analytic and intuitive thinking? What if I could help the world conspire in the expansion of children's gifts rather than diminishing them because they learn differently?"

Over the last four years, I assumed that I would write a book entitled *Divided No More* about living what author and educator Parker Palmer calls "the integrated life." I imagined I would flow effortlessly back and forth between my oh-so-profound inner world and my oh-so-meaningful outer life.

I now understand why humor, humility, and humus all come from the same root. I experienced all three as I flew frenetically back and forth to Europe every month, consulting to corporations that were lost in their frenzy to increase the mythical bottom line. Eventually, my body found its own bottom line and screamed "No," as it always does when I am being blown off course. I was forced to stop traveling. I began to write a book about freedom, and then discovered how difficult it was to find when stumbling around on an oxygen leash.

In the nine months since Andy and I decided to move to sea level and this oak grove in northern California, we have been involved with David and several colleagues midwifing SmartWired, a worldwide movement dedicated to the recognition of children as resources to be developed, rather than problems to be solved. Instead of a silent mountaintop where I could hear each snowflake fall, I am surrounded by the mind-numbing chaos of house renovation. I could not, would not, take time off to write this book as I did my last. I am riding the crest of what will probably be the last big wave of my life to help make the world worthy of its children, and I cannot leisurely go out and make poems in the snow.

This is a time when everything, everywhere, is going so fast that we can barely catch our collective breath. It is a time when breath is all important to me, when I have to go slow enough to notice and enjoy every breath that is available. I am learning to reflect in the time I have. My breath is teaching me to rest in the place between each inhale and each exhale, and then again in the place between each exhale and each inhale. Whenever I can, between hammers banging and nail guns popping, between phone calls and terrorist attacks, between tsunamis and torrents of e-mail, I rest, and breathe, and write.

This book insists on being about helping parents understand that each of us bears a potential that asks to be lived. It invites them to champion their children's discovery of the gifts that hide in their differences. It presumes that in the liberation of these gifts, children can develop a genuine sense of orientation in the world and a passionate connection to it.

Potential isn't about something abstract. It is an imperative we feel from the inside out. It manifests in actions we must do despite challenges or difficulties. It is what connects us to one another and to the larger world. Potential reveals itself to you. It's there all the time, as the stars are in the brightness of noon, but it's only during the dark of night that the constellations become apparent. It is in the darkness of the challenges one faces that potential appears. Plato said we must notice this "call" as a prime fact of human existence and align our lives with it, recognizing that difficulties and challenges are necessary to its realization.

We are as subject to potential as we would be to a strong wind in a sailboat. It appears when we have become impatient with the too small story in which we have been cocooned. I believe that parents are the most passionate and impatient part of our population. We want a bigger story for our children than the one they are currently finding on TV screens or computer monitors. We want them to thrive, not just survive.

If you ask most parents what they want for their children, they will invariably say, "I want them to be happy." But "happy" is a placeholder for a constellation of positive emotional states. When parents think of happiness, they may initially think of wanting their children to feel good. Current research, however, indicates that two equally important aspects of happiness are having something to look forward to and the well-being that is associated with engaging and embracing the world in a positive way.

Neuroscientists have learned over the past decade that the brain is highly plastic. It rewires itself in response to experience and relationships. We can, therefore, create experiences and conditions for our children that actually help increase the possibility that they will engage with the world in a positive way, and have something to look forward to. That is why, above all else, I have written this book now.

In this frenzied time, books are getting smaller and smaller because people are too busy to even read the newspaper. Our collective attention span is shrinking so much that I'm amazed we're reading anything larger than matchbooks. It is a time of hyperspeed, when things are going faster and wider and shallower; a time that demands what my friend Linda Stone calls "continual partial attention."

This book isn't a short, fast read. We all have the capacity to go fast and shallow, to multitask at hyperspeed. And if we don't have it, our children certainly do, and we're trying to keep up with them. But we also have and need to develop the balancing capacity of going slow and deep. Without it, we have no way of discovering the importance of our lives. We become lost in a meaning void—as do our children. If we want to give our children the best we can offer, if we want to bring out the best they have to offer, we owe them nothing less than developing, and helping them develop, the capacity to know how to go slow and deep as well as fast and wide.

This book is big and meant to be read slowly and deeply. In a time that demands continual partial attention, you must learn to gather your distracted attention as if you were a shepherd and your attention a flock scattered all over the hillside. The gift I have given myself as I wrote this book is the same gift you can give your children—the quality and direction of your own attention.

We can only live our purpose if we live *on purpose* rather than allowing our lives to just happen to us. Purpose is about being inspired by your own possibility and conspiring with others to make a better world inside and outside your own skin. Passion is the fire that results from realizing that you have a purpose, that your presence does matter to the rest of us, that you do and can make a difference.

I wanted to write this as a book to help parents find the gifts in their children. The book refused. It would not be a guide for what parents could do *to* their children. It insisted on being a guide for how parents could engage *with* their children. It is meant to help you both diminish whatever interferes with the growth of potential in your lives and to enhance whatever helps its emergence.

The more vital your own life is, the more vital your children's will be. If you make the most of the moments you have, your children will as well. If you miss your moments, if you allow them to fill up with "stuff" like dry sand filling your footprints on the beach, your children will follow you and do the same.

This book doesn't focus on how to fix what's wrong with you or your child or how to avoid conflict between you. It asks you to connect with your child on the journey, to realize, to make real, who each of you is and to live your life as if your moments matter. They are all you really have to share.

This book is about connecting: connecting with your own life, connecting with your child, connecting each of you to your unique gifts, connecting with others in support of developing those gifts. We are coming to learn that the brain itself is a social organ based on connection. It is estimated that the theoretical number of different patterns of connection possible in a single brain is forty quadrillion. Nobel laureate and neurologist Gerald Edelman tells us that where there is no connection there is no life, and the connections within the brain are made stronger or weaker according to use. We develop a unique brain suited to our particular needs, and it changes as our environment, experiences, and relationships change. This is why we can learn—and unlearn—throughout our lives. The more we repeat the same actions and thoughts, the more fixed the circuits in the brain for that particular activity become. If you don't exercise brain circuits, the connections will slowly weaken and be lost. Which is the good news and the bad. As with our muscles, we can strengthen our neural pathways through experience—brain exercise, if you will—or we can let them wither. Use it or lose it. New experiences can create new connections, and habitual connections that no longer serve us will weaken with lack of use.

The deep innate resources that lie waiting for us are folded into our brains, bodies, minds, genes, and our relationships with one another. We cultivate them when we are motivated to do so. Oftentimes, that motivation comes when we experience a life-threatening disease or trauma. The desire to develop these capacities also comes at parenthood, when evolutionary intelligence gathers itself and, like a wave of passion swelling in us, carries us forward, wanting us to make the most of the moments we have. We ask ourselves, "How do I craft the story of my life so my child will be inspired by it? How can I help my child find his or her place in this vast world?"

Potential, though incredibly powerful, cannot be mapped. Curiosity, intuition, daring, compassion, and passion keep us searching for it. The search itself is inspiring and revolutionary. We diminish or expand our lives according to how we conceive of them. How you imagine your life will strongly affect how you raise your children.

In essence, this book supports you in doing three things: giving open, curious attention to what can be possible for both you and your child; recognizing and utilizing the unique resources your child brings to the world; and developing those resources by forming supportive alliances and creating connective environments.

Someone told me once that embarrassment occurs just before enlightenment. If this is so, then David must be very close to being enlightened. For the past two decades, it has been embarrassing for me to realize that I am leaving him a world in worse condition than the one that was passed on to me. I am beginning to understand that neither he nor I will ever wipe the sweat off our satisfied brows and say, "At last! We have realized our purpose!" Perhaps both of us are in this world at this time, when life has become crowded with irrelevance and criticism, to help each other search for and follow the intuitive gravitational pull that comes when we are living our lives as if our moments mattered.

This book is dedicated to two questions that cannot be answered by any one of us but can be held in the imagination of all of us:

What if every child in the world were seen as a valued resource to be developed rather than a problem to be solved?

How can we give our children the best by unleashing the potential that is within them?

In support of that quest, I offer this book, this approach, and the following blessing to be whispered to your child each night:

You Are Our Dreams and Prayers
> *You are completely unique.*
> *There is no other like you.*
> *You can always learn.*
> *Trust your own mind.*
> *Go after your greatest dreams.*
> *You do make a difference.*
> *The world needs the gifts that only you can bring.*

SECTION ONE

Finding the Spot of Grace

When I was little and still afraid of the dark, I used to stay up very late reading with my flashlight under a tent of blankets. One night, my grandmother came to visit our house. She crawled in with me and told me the following story:

"Let's imagine, my darling, that you could float on the darkness the way you learned to float on a lake: comfortably, looking up into the wide sky."

I, of course, stretched out next to her and gave Grandma the flashlight. I didn't even notice when she turned it off, because her warm hand was resting on my forehead and I was following her singsong words in my mind.

"While we're floating here in the darkness, you can notice how it gets deliciously quiet, so quiet that all you can hear is the sound of your own breath. Now, imagine that you see something in the distance. It's moving closer, very, very slowly. All at once, you see that it is an immense crystal bowl. It glows because it is made of light."

When Grandma started telling stories like this, they became real and all there was.

"For a moment, everything is perfect and still, but suddenly, as you watch, the bowl shatters into a thousand different shards of light that fly everywhere, piercing everything that is alive on the earth."

I held my breath until she continued.

"Every living being on this planet has one of those tiny sparks of light hidden inside. One is inside of you and one is inside of me."

Grandma stopped. She knew that when we got to a waiting place like this in a story, I'd ask a question. Sure enough, one bubbled up.

"Why, Grandma? Why do we each have a spark of light inside?"

Her hand caressed my forehead for several long minutes before she answered.

"Because, my darling, each of us, whether we know it or not, is supposed to find that special light to shine in the darkness. It is called the 'spot of grace.' We're supposed to help other people find their spot of grace, too, because when everyone does, the bowl will be made whole again."

"What if someone has a light that's too little, Grandma? And how come no one talks about the spot of grace?"

Her lips kissed my warm forehead. She whispered, "Everyone's spot of grace is different and just right for them. Many people don't know about the bowl or that little spark of light because they don't have a grandma like you do. So when you grow up, it will be your job to tell them this story so they can find their own. When you do, your spot of grace will shine even brighter."

Chapter One

Blaming the Victim: Disconnecting Children from Their Own Future

"Education is the kindling of a flame, not the filling of a vessel."
—SOCRATES

When we hold an infant in our arms, we all feel it—that gaping awe and amazement as we look at the prints at the ends of those tiny fingers. At that moment, it is as if a door inside our hearts opens—we feel a wave of wonder at the miracle of this child's uniqueness and potential. My grandmother would have said that we are recognizing their spot of grace.

Before you read further, I'd like to invite you to pause and bring that moment alive again—the sensations, smells, sounds. Where were you? Who else was there? What time of year was it? What was your deepest wish in that moment? If you could have given that child a blessing, what would it have been? What did you dream for that infant? What was your commitment as a parent? And those who stand behind you—grandparents, great-grandparents, great-great-grandparents—what do you imagine were their dreams and prayers for this tiny bundle of possibility?

In that first moment and a thousand times since, you've probably asked yourself how you could best cultivate this being so that he or she could blossom as fully as possible. You are not alone. Parents and guardians throughout history have felt what you felt. They have whispered fiercely, tenderly, lovingly, "I want my child to succeed, to be who he or she is meant to be in this world, to be happy, to know he or she makes a difference. I want to give my child the best I possibly can."

How does the door close? How do we all forget? Rather than cherishing all that potential, we come to see Martin as "hyperactive" instead of energetic. We think of Sally as "inattentive" instead of imaginative. We label George "oppositional" rather than independent. How do we develop a handicap of trust that limits our perception of the unique island of brilliance on which each child stands? How does our attention shift from what might be natural resources that need to be developed to what could be deficits that need to be fixed? How do we learn to limit what could be possible for our children instead of learning to champion their innate gifts?

This happens gradually, but as they go through school, we shift our focus to what's wrong with them and how it can be fixed. This is not unique to parents. As a culture, we are experiencing a crisis of understanding that results from the way we have learned to think about our children and the challenges they face. When I was in graduate school studying clinical psychology, I was meticulously trained in the history of pathology. I could sit down with anyone and within thirty minutes, while carrying on a polite conversation, diagnose their particular neurosis down to the numerical classification code. (No wonder, at cocktail parties, when I told people I was a psychologist, they quickly moved away!)

After several years, although proficient in categorizing what was wrong with every person I met, I found myself skilled in knowing how to help someone become sick or crazy. I also found myself feeling removed, remote, and isolated from the very children I wanted to help. My supervisors commended my "professional objectivity."

I was not atypical. Since 1947, more than $30 billion has been invested in research that follows this deficit model. "The neurochemistry of depression is much better known than that of happiness, mostly because the former has been studied more intensively and for much longer." As author Dacher Keltner said in the January 17, 2005, issue of *Time* magazine, "Until a decade ago, 90 percent of emotion research focused on the negative, so there are still all these questions about positive states."

A recent search of psychological literature revealed 50,000 articles on depression, but only 400 on joy. When my daughter-in-law, Angie, searched the Internet, she found three times as many sites dedicated to learning disabilities as to learning abilities; 746 that track failures, 127 that track successes; 42,020 sites were focused on "What's Wrong with Me?" and 90 sites were dedicated to "What's Right About Me?"

We have made significant progress in many areas of individual treatment, especially those using psychotropic drugs. We have gained great proficiency in focusing on individual pathology and dysfunction. However, since this deficit model locates the problem "inside" the individual person and considers meeting the needs of at-risk youth largely a task for professionals, it fosters what could be called a "them" strategy: Since the deficit is inside us (or our children or both), the solution must be outside in "them"—the experts, the schools, the government, the drugs. If they don't fix the problem, we have someone else to blame: them. This model results in continually dedicating more resources to design more medications, treatment programs, and fixes for the "special needs" children who we categorize according to their pathologies. In October 2003, *Time* magazine reported that fifteen million prescriptions were written for antidepressants for children and teens. A conservative estimate states that 5 percent of American children today are being medicated for ADD/ADHD, while in England the figure is about 0.3 percent. Are we raising Generation Rx?

What effect has this deficit focus had? In the past two decades, "in the midst of unprecedented material affluence, large and growing numbers of U.S. children and adolescents are failing to flourish. In particular, more and more young people are suffering from mental illness, emotional distress, and behavioral problems," says the Commission on Children at Risk, a group of thirty-three high-profile children's doctors, research scientists, and mental health and youth service professionals, in their report "Hardwired to Connect."

The report continues, "Scholars at the National Research Council in 2002 estimated that at least one of every four adolescents in the U.S. is currently at serious risk of not achieving productive adulthood."

In the time it takes me to stare out the window and sip my iced tea, four teenagers tumble through my mind: Curtis, twelve, who doesn't like to talk a whole lot but is completely at ease break-dancing in front of an audience of two hundred adults; Max, who has to be forced to sit and do homework but can't wait to volunteer for the Special Olympics; Tiffany, who is considered a troublemaker because she tells it like it is even when it's not "appropriate"; Latisha, who pushes wheelchairs in an airport after school while dreaming of being a clothes designer. Which one out of these four?

Reluctantly, I return to reading the report: "Despite increased ability to treat depression, the current generation of young people is more likely to be depressed and anxious than was its parent's generation. . . . About 20% of students report having seriously considered suicide in the past year. . . . Death rates overall since the 1950's have dropped by 50%, but homicide rates among U.S. youth rose by more than 130%. . . . Suicide rates rose by nearly 140%. . . ."

More children come to mind: Clayton, ten, whose teacher says he's below grade level, while he secretly draws pictures any artist would envy; Seth, eight, who hypertexts from one imaginary world to another while his parents consider which medication to put him on because he can't pay attention in creative writing class; Pedro, sixteen, who dreams of playing in a heavy metal band while the other kids mock his crooked teeth and skinny arms; Marc, fourteen, who just got kicked out of school for smoking pot and is being sent to boarding school in the fall. Which one of these four?

There is a tightness in the center of my chest, but I go on reading: "We are increasing our capacity to rescue children who are drowning in the river, but steadily losing ground when it comes to keeping children out of the river in the first place. . . . Treating pathology is not the same as positive youth development. The former focuses on illness and emphasizes the need to direct help to a few of us, the latter focuses on health and emphasizes the need to shift probabilities for most of us."

What would another way of thinking about children's challenges be? If a student drops out of school, the deficit model would have us ask: What's wrong with this child? What's wrong with his parents? What's his problem? A different way of thinking would begin with a very different kind of question: What are this youth's strengths, gifts, and talents? Are they being utilized in school? At home? When has he been successful in the past? How can he use what he's good at to deal with the challenges he's facing? What are the energizing and engaging forces available to him? Who does this youth have mentoring and supporting him? What conditions would make it possible for this youth to make a positive difference to his community? It would ask you, the parent or guardian, what do you cherish and appreciate about your child? How can we all nurture that? How could you do more of that?

This kind of inquiry expands our thinking, broadens our attention, connects us to possibilities, widens our options of response, and shifts responsibility for this youth's health and development where it belongs—to all of us. The strategies that result are "us" focused: They require something from all of us. Together, we have the capacity it takes to support our children in this revolution.

What is required to accomplish this is a shift in perception. We must help ourselves and one another change the way we see our children, ourselves, and our responsibilities. To do this we must change the stories we tell ourselves. We have done this before. In my lifetime, we have unwoven the stories that define how we see women. My mother believed that the only way she could fulfill her role as a woman successfully was to get married (once), have children (two), bake chocolate chip cookies in the oven of her own house in the suburbs (with three bedrooms). Similarly, we have unwoven the stories of what it means to be a family, a man, what it means to work.

What remains to be seen is how we reweave those stories. If our children are to have the kind of future we dream for them, it is clear we must change the way we think about them.

Giving Your Child the Best in a Crazy, Beautiful, Complex World

"Young people are resources to be developed, not problems to be solved."
—MICHAEL RESNICK, PH.D, PROFESSOR OF PEDIATRICS,
UNIVERSITY OF MINNESOTA

I have written this book because I believe in "us strategies." I believe that passionate parents can help their children live up to their potential rather than down to their deficits. I believe all of us can give children the best by bringing out the best in them.

I could not have written this book when I was a parent. I had to wait until I was a grandparent, until I had seen enough and done enough and struggled enough to realize that my granddaughter cannot flourish unless all grandchildren do. Now I can say to you, dear reader, what my grandmother said to my parents, "What you must do is help your children love to learn and find their spot of grace. In this way they will be able to develop their gifts and share them with the rest of us. You must help them recognize and honor the different gifts of others who are also unique. We need them all." This is what each of us can do so our children will feel as if they matter and as if they belong to this crazy, beautiful, complex world.

When I was twenty years old, I rode the New York City subway every day from Columbia University, where I was a graduate student in psychology, to Harlem, where I was a brand-new first-grade teacher. It was my first year in charge of a classroom. I was assigned thirty-five youngsters, many of whom came to school with rat bites on their faces. Though I had made lesson plans in advance for the first six months, I was completely unprepared for the task ahead of me. My education classes at college had taught me how to color and cut out fall leaves and hang them on the windows of the classroom. I had been carefully instructed in the making of Easter bunnies by drawing two yellow circles on a green sheet of construction paper and attaching a cotton ball with white glue. I had no idea how to make sense of the lives of these six- and seven-year-olds or how to "teach" them anything that was relevant to them. My lesson plans were all about phonically decoding Sally, Dick, and Jane. I didn't have the vaguest idea how to decipher the squiggling, giggling, squirming, craving little minds that surrounded me.

What saved me (and them) was that I was young, energetic, and then, as now, a "learning junkie." On my endless subway rides, I became totally captivated by a book called *A Man's Search for Meaning*, written by Dr. Victor Frankl, a man who had survived years in Nazi concentration camps by believing in what he called "personal freedom." He clearly couldn't change the events that were happening to him, but he realized that no one could take away his right to determine the meaning he placed on those events. In Frankl's case, he chose to believe that he was experiencing the camps so that after the war he would be able to teach the world about the human need for meaning. It was choosing that belief that saved his soul and gave his life the meaning he needed in order to survive.

Meanwhile, the students in my classroom had more labels in their cumulative folders than the cans in the local supermarket: educably retarded, severely learning disabled, seriously unmotivated, troublemaker, and of course the ever-present "slow learner." Each of these labels carried an implied story that could imprison them for the rest of their lives. The more experienced teachers in the crumbling school gave me another limiting story, warning me that I had better start by "holding a tight rein," because once I let it get slack, "they'll have you up against the wall and take over the classroom."

What the other teachers didn't know is that I was, then and still am now, incurably defiant. I chose to believe that those kids were born to learn, and that it was my task to support every one to succeed in doing just that. Mr. Stewart, the principal, warned me at the end of every day that I was a "naïve white girl." And I was. But I was burning with the fierce belief that each child in that classroom had a spot of grace buried in him or her somewhere, and I was determined to find it.

I rode the subway the first morning of the school year imagining Victor Frankl as one guardian angel and my grandmother as the other. Under my arm I carried the thick red manual of state and federal education regulations. If only I had been given an operator's manual to each child along with the classroom register and standardized test scores! Lulled into a wide-minded state by the rocking of the train and my own desperation, an idea began to form in my mind.

That day, I covered the cracked yellow walls of my classroom with sheets of newsprint, one for each child. First thing as they came in, I hugged each one and asked him or her to draw a picture of something they were good at or smart about. They sprawled all over the room, bellies pressed into the ground, crayons strewn everywhere. The room began to hum as if it were a beehive. They spent the rest of the day telling stories about what they loved, what they were good at, what successes they'd had over the summer, what helped them imagine, and what helped them concentrate. The hum became a buzz and then the bell rang, signaling it was time to go home. Without being asked they lined up at the door waiting. I bent down and hugged each one, and put a letter in each of their little hands. They were requests to the parents and guardians for help. Mr. Stewart had told me not to expect anything from them, but defiant as I was, I invited them to write something positive about how their children learned, about their successes, how they overcame frustration; about their resources; about what they knew "worked" with their children. The next morning, all but two sent back responses.

The idea grew as if it were yeasted bread dough. I invited other people to add to the growing newsprint on the walls—the janitor, school bus drivers, siblings, after school babysitters, grandparents. I implored anyone I could find who might know anything about how a child learned to include it on his or her list.

Maps began to emerge for each child—a pattern of successes, lists of interests, descriptions of talents, and more. The maps became instructional guidebooks— a way to keep track of each student's skills, talents, interests, and strengths. If I needed ideas for motivating a child, I'd read his or her chart. At the end of the first month of school, I knew more about what worked with each child than I did from the endless batteries of standardized tests that filled their cumulative folders. Every child knew that there was something of worth inside him or her, something that only they could contribute to the world. It was and is my belief that knowing about that spot of grace could help them create meaning from the dark places in their lives.

I typed up the operating manuals and sent them home, used them as the basis of each parent-teacher conference, added to them each quarter, and finally added the information to each child's cumulative folder. Oftentimes it was the only positive information in there.

I continued to create these "Smart Guides" for the next fourteen years that I remained in education as a classroom teacher, a learning specialist, and eventually a school psychologist. I stuffed them in as many cumulative folders as I could. In the endless meetings and conferences I attended, I persisted, asking, "Yes, I understand that you think Johnny is (disabled, retarded, gifted, bad tempered, oppositional, dyslexic . . .), but please, please tell me how he *is* smart, what can he do well, how does he learn easily?" My questions frequently were met by an awkward silence, the clearing of throats, the shifting of eyes.

I eventually left education, or, to quote my friend author Parker Palmer, I became an "educator at large," but my passion for discovering the gifts inside each individual carried me forward. My commitment to foster those gifts so they can be shared with the rest of us has been my compass for forty years.

What Is Required Is a Shift in Thinking

"You can find problems everywhere when you start looking. You can thus create a sense that it's all insurmountable. But if we could construct a world in which something is possible, we can talk about that in such a way that we might be able to achieve it together."
—KENNETH GERGEN, PROFESSOR OF PSYCHOLOGY,
SWARTHMORE COLLEGE

I haven't been alone these past four decades. There have been other explorers following the same magnetic north. They are leading a quiet, profound revolution, a positive and significant shift in how we think about human beings. In 1998, the president of the American Psychological Association, Martin Seligman, initiated a new emphasis in the field of psychology now referred to as "positive psychology." Its focus is on strengths and building the best in life. The basic assumption is that goodness and excellence are not illusions, but are authentic states and modes of being that can be analyzed and achieved. Rather than trying to replace existing psychological work, Seligman refocused on three points: positive experiences, such as joy, fulfillment, happiness; positive individual traits, such as talents, values, and interests; and positive institutions or communities, such as families, schools, and businesses.

This movement has expanded into organizations through the work of David Cooperrider at Case Western Reserve University in developing a new approach to organizational change that is called "appreciative inquiry." AI focuses on finding the best in people, their organizations, and the relevant world around them. It involves the art and practice of asking questions that identify past examples of peak performance, spectacular successes, and positive aspirations for the future. By exploring the conditions that account for the successes of the past, organizations are helped to craft a vision for the future they believe can be possible.

Business and industry has aimed a large percentage of its corporate training toward strengthening deficits. It also uses such personality tests as the Myers-Briggs Type Indicator (MBTI) for assessment. Recently, this strategy has been criticized by psychologist Annie Murphy Paul, who states in her book, *The Cult of Personality*, that such assessments consign people to narrow categories and cause ill-informed decisions to be made about hiring and promotion. The Gallup Organization, however, has been part of the new asset-focused revolution by teaching corporations to identify and match employees' talents to the appropriate task. Much of their research has demonstrated that getting people into jobs that capitalize on their *thinking* strengths rather than their personalities can create positive employee engagement, which in turn significantly relates to desired organizational outcomes such as productivity, profit, customer service, safety, and retention. Gallup describes these "signature strengths" as an individual's inherent and unique mental capacities—such as focus, analysis, empathy, future orientation—that can be developed and give the person energy when used. Gallup found that the most successful companies were those that supported people developing these signature strengths rather than trying to overcome their weaknesses.

The stunning implication of Gallup's research is that not everyone can do everything, and trying to make everyone learn to do everything only produces mediocrity. This doesn't mean we can't develop skills in a wide variety of areas or cultivate interests in domains in which we are not inherently gifted. It does, however, suggest that being able to recognize the areas of competence in which we are especially gifted and that give us energy are key elements to creating a sense of meaning, vibrancy, and effectiveness in adults and children.

Let's ground this shift in thinking with a down-to-earth, here-and-now example. Come into my kitchen for a moment. My son, David, has come over for breakfast. One of his gifts is thinking in a focused way. One of mine is storytelling. He sits down at the table and asks me what we're going to eat. I respond by doing what comes naturally—I tell him about how I ran into Bud Gloucester, his elementary school soccer coach, in Safeway while shopping for breakfast and how his son Robert is building car washes in Arizona. David begins to pace and asks if he can help me prepare our breakfast and how long I think it will take to cook whatever I have planned.

At this point in the story, we can go positive or negative, depending on whether we have a deficit or asset focus. Let's go negative first and then do a makeover. After David asks how long breakfast is going to take to prepare, I tell myself that he's not interested in anything I have to say and that I'm losing my only son. I try to tell him a more interesting story to keep his attention. I describe the details of Louise's near bankruptcy and two divorces. David, his stomach growling, throws open the refrigerator door and pulls out four eggs, a loaf of bread, and orange juice. I tell myself that he has no patience for me anymore, and besides, he doesn't even need me to cook his breakfast and . . .

You can probably figure out where that scenario will go. Let's try the asset-focused makeover, understanding and respecting our different thinking talents. David asks how long breakfast will take to prepare. I tell myself how lucky I am to have a son who is so gifted in areas that I am not. I ask him to give me an estimated preparation time based on his appetite. He opens the refrigerator, takes out the eggs, bread, and juice and suggests I entertain him with more stories about Bud and Robert while cooking. I tell myself that I am so fortunate to have a son who appreciates me for who I am. He relaxes while organizing the magazines on the countertop. We need each other.

When I know I have specific gifts to offer, and recognize others that I am lacking, collaboration becomes an obvious necessity. I understand my part in the whole of things, and know as well that I need other people. Like fingers on a hand, our unique differences connected to a common goal are what make a human reach possible. Trying to hold to the illusion of "independence," and the assumption that each of us should be able to do and know everything, has resulted in a booming self-help industry, a therapist for every suburban household, and pharmacology that we depend on to deaden the pain of feeling inadequate to the task. During the last thirty years, billions of dollars and thousands of hours have been spent trying to raise children's self-esteem so they would not have to suffer feelings of inadequacy. But raising self-esteem didn't do it. Remember the *Saturday Night Live* skit where week after week Stuart Smiley looked in a mirror telling himself he was good enough and smart enough and "Gosh darn it, people like me!"? Current research indicates that children with high self-esteem score no better on tests and do no better in life than children with low self-esteem.

I would like to suggest that understanding one's inherent self-worth— knowing what *specific* value you bring to the larger community—is essential in today's complexity. You can praise Isabella from morning to night, tell her she is daddy's darling and a beautiful girl. But this in no way prepares her to feel as if she matters and can make a difference in a world teeming with six billion people. On the other hand, if Isabella knows her gifts and talents—for example, that she's quite talented at helping others resolve disputes; that her sense of humor can make a crying friend heal; that she can take herself from frustration to wonder by walking around; that playing the piano can melt her anger; that she is very talented in innovative thinking, which will help her design herself and others out of scary situations—then she feels as if she is unique and belongs to a community that needs her.

We live in an interconnected world that demands we accept our *inter*dependence. Consider your child's hand. Its DNA was passed on to him or her by all those who came before, yet those fingertips, at the very edge of his or her reach, carry the marks that prove, in all the history of humankind, there has never been another such as this one. Now, imagine raising your child with the understanding that he or she carries a unique gift that is needed by the rest of the world, a gift that must be uncovered and cultivated, a gift that he or she is responsible for caretaking and contributing to the rest of us so we can all move forward. If you can imagine that, you can create it.

The SMART Parenting Revolution

"Pay attention to the curiosities of a child; this is where the search for knowledge is freshest and most valuable."

—ALBERT EINSTEIN

Parents and teachers often complain to me that a particular child is resistant to learning. I find it comforting to remind them that learning comes hardwired into the equipment. Human beings are designed to learn. "The drive to learn," says anthropologist Edward T. Hall, "is more basic than the drive to reproduce." Children may be resistant to being taught, or, more to the point, to how and what they are being taught, but not to learning. No human child resists learning.

Nothing is as compelling to me as the light that is emitted from a person who is learning. It has always been my handhold in the darkness. For sixty-two years, I've followed that glow from playgrounds to corporate boardrooms, from Harlem to The Hague. I've pursued it through graduate degrees in psychology and education, through the professions of classroom teacher, psychotherapist, trainer of trainers, educational consultant, corporate consultant. It doesn't matter what labels were attached to me—what has always drawn me forward is my desire to be around that radiance, to foster it, to encourage it, and to study the conditions that generate and direct it.

Learning is so much more than a transfer of information. It can mean wholeness, empowerment, actualization, liberation. Observe any young child any place in the world and you will find a seeker of excellence. They embody this inherent impulse in their rampant curiosity about themselves and their world, the way they naturally follow their interests and rhythms, seek out and risk experimentation, honor their dreams and daydreams, consider mistakes as information rather than something wrong. Children have taught me that learning is discovering that something is possible.

Why do we respond by telling them what is not possible for them? Parker Palmer asks, "Why is it that in this country, with the most widespread educational system on the globe, so many people walk around feeling stupid?" It hurts me on a cellular level when I think about that. I ache when I remember seeing shining five-year-olds who thought in images or were clever with their hands or danced and sang and told brilliant stories and who, six years later, had become hungry ghosts or haunted pariahs because they didn't catch on to reading or multiplication.

What interferes with this natural impulse? What causes the lights to dim? What hinders our children's innate passion? Why do kids complain that they're bored, that they can't do it, that they don't know how to do it, that they don't need to know it? Why is it that Griffin charges in the door, kisses the air, and yells at his mother, "Don't bother me now, I've got to go to soccer practice. The coach says I need to work on kicking with my left foot," but when it's time for him to write a report on the Lewis and Clark expedition, he stubbornly collapses on the couch?

Does it have to be that way? Why do we as parents change from coaches to cops? Even more important, how can we transform the forces that limit the expression of our children's natural intelligence? What can we do to foster the love of learning that is the birthright of every child?

These questions lurked in the shadows of every session I did with families and individuals as a psychotherapist in private practice. They pursued me into the adult world of organizations—businesses, health care, social service agencies, teacher training programs—places where I thought I could make a difference. They followed me to the Organizational Learning Center of the Sloan School at

MIT and the Visions of a Better World Foundation. Everywhere I went, I found people who were obsessed with these same questions.

The most passionate people I found were parents, who are quietly leading the change in thinking about children and learning. What I hear from them is the desire to shift in perspective from judgment—"What's wrong with my kid and how can I fix her?"—to engagement—"No matter what anyone says, I want to help my child keep his love of learning," and "I want to do something more than be a homework cop for my kid. Where do I start?"

We don't like what is happening to children in this country. As a grandmother, a parent, a teacher, a psychologist, a human being, it hurts my heart. I am writing this book to and for other parents and guardians because we can profoundly change the way we have been taught to think about our children's abilities. We can start a revolution in which the full range of children's natural intelligence can flourish, where all who are different can belong, and where uniqueness is not a disability but the norm. We can shift our perspective from worrying about what is wrong with our children to wondering what could be possible for them.

Hardwired to Connect

> *"If a child is to keep alive his inborn sense of wonder, he needs the companionship of at least one adult who can share it, rediscovering with him the joy, excitement, and mystery of the world we live in."*
>
> —RACHEL CARSON, BIOLOGIST AND WRITER

There is very important news in the most recent research findings in neuroscience that parents and guardians need to know. Science is increasingly demonstrating that children are hardwired to connect in two specific ways: They need close, positive connections to other people and they need to form meaning from their experiences. Meeting the human child's need for this connectedness is essential to his or her health and development.

Thus, the various social environments that we create or fail to create for our children matter a great deal. They matter not only for their immediate futures, but the latest research tells us that the environments we create for our children can influence them at a genetic level. Whether a particular gene or combination of genes ends up helping or hurting depends largely on the social context. Researcher W. T. Boyce puts it this way in "Hardwired to Connect": "Both extreme vulnerability and uncommon resilience can be found in the same highly reactive children depending on the basic stressfulness or supportiveness of the surrounding social context." This research indicates that social environments can impact us at the cellular level to reduce genetically based risks and help to transform such risks into behavioral assets. They can also help substantially to raise intelligence. In essence, what these findings are saying is that good parenting or bad parenting can be passed on to future generations genetically.

In recent decades, groups that sustain our connectedness to others have gotten weaker. Fragmented families, deteriorating participation in community clubs, and a vast array of informal social networks from card-playing groups to family meals are all part of this thinning of community.

In addition, the deficit focus of our culture has fragmented us from ourselves and our own resources. Having been taught that the right answers are always outside of us, we frantically search for something or someone else to fix the various challenges we encounter: a new therapist, coach, counselor, car, love, house, and so on. But many of these challenges are too complex to have only one right answer, so we go from one specialist to another without having a sense of how to think about the whole.

Meeting these needs for connection is essential to health and fulfillment. For the past ten years, I have been forming alliances with people who are also deeply concerned about the fragmentation in American childhood. The SMART Parenting Revolution has developed from endless conversations about what could be done to help the world become worthy of its children. Passionate members of my family and committed colleagues from diverse backgrounds have joined together to create multimedia learning adventures that connect children of all ages and adults to themselves and others in meaningful ways. The book you now hold is one of the SmartWired processes. It is meant to be connective tissue—first, to help you connect your children to their unique ways of being smart. Second, to connect you to the experiences that will help them use those resources to move through challenges. Third, to connect you to others who can support your children in contributing their resources to the larger community so they learn they can make a difference.

Parenting, no matter what experts say, always seems to be like groping in the dark. We move through the unknown trying to do more of what works and less of what doesn't. It is a journey of discovery. This book is meant to be a guide to new ways of thinking about yourself and your children with compassion and respect.

The SMART Parenting Revolution, however, is not just a how-to book. Rather, it will take you from "how come" to "how now." It is as close as I can come to writing the user-friendly operating manual you wish you were given when your child first came into your life. It will help you to find "the grain" of both of your minds. It will show you how to communicate effectively with each of your unique patterns of processing information. It offers specific ways to study the path of a child's success and use what is learned in areas of challenge. In addition, there are suggestions for Smart Families—creating the conditions within a family where differences are fostered rather than excluded, where children of all ages learn to recognize the differences in others as a gift and work with them collaboratively. You'll also be given practical suggestions for creating alliances of support with teachers, mentors, and coaches. Interspersed throughout the book are inspirational stories of "ordinary" smart kids who have used their unique gifts and talents to make a difference in the world.

This book is written to help us remember that the child we are guarding is gifted as well as a gift—gifted with a desire to learn, grow, and make a difference. It is offered so you can give yourself and your children a sense of their own potency in shaping the future.

Inspiration

Ben Durskin, Greenbrae, California

Even at five, Ben was passionate about video games. Three and a half years ago, he was diagnosed with ALL—acute lymphoblastic leukemia. He had to go through long and punishing chemotherapy sessions, where he passed the time playing video games. That gave him an idea. He decided that he wanted to invent a video game for kids with cancer that would be fun and help them understand what was going on in their bodies. It's called Ben's Game and went on-line as a free site when he was nine (www.makewish.org/ben). It drew 200,000 hits in its first three months. The hero of the game is a boy who skateboards his way around the screen blasting cancer cells and shielding against the side effects of chemo. The best part is that a player can't lose. Ben was supported by his parents, who were supported in turn by the Make-A-Wish Foundation. Software engineer Eric Johnson donated six months of his time and talents helping Ben's game become a reality.

Chapter Two

Every Child Left Behind

"The mark of every Golden Age in history is when children are the most valued members of the society and teaching is the most valued profession."

—PETER SENGE, AUTHOR AND SENIOR LECTURER, MIT

Imagine a dim cave filled with prisoners who are chained in such a way that they can't move their heads. All day, they stare at a wall. Because of a small fire, the prisoners can see only the shadows of their captors projected on the wall. Having always been in the cave, they believe the shadows are real people; they also believe the echoed voices they hear are true voices.

One day, a prisoner is released. The secrets of the cave are disclosed to him and he is led up into the sunlight. At first, his eyes, unaccustomed to light, are blinded. When he has adjusted to the light of the sun, and contemplated all he sees, he returns excitedly to the cave to tell the others. Once again, his eyes have to readjust, this time to darkness. The other prisoners mock him when he explains they are only looking at shadows. Nonetheless, he perseveres.

I've always identified with this story from Plato's *Republic*. As we begin this journey, I feel a bit like the prisoner who was released from the cave. All too often, when I ask parents how their child is smart, they respond by telling me what experts have informed them about the child's deficits and disorders—the things that are wrong and need to be treated—the shadows. Even when I explain that this keeps them chained to diminished views of their child's capacities, they often are reluctant to risk turning away from what has become familiar.

At dinner several weeks after September 11, 2001, a group of adults were deeply engaged in conversation about why it all happened, and how the world would never be the same. Ana Li, my honorary granddaughter, aged four, pulled repeatedly on her mother's shirt to no avail. Mary Jane, my friend, told her to wait a minute, this conversation was really important. Exasperated, Ana Li crawled up on her mother's knees and whispered something into her left ear. Mary Jane's eyes lit up and she laughed her way through a very intense whispered conversation. It went something like this:

"Momma, this isn't interesting."

"What would be interesting, sweetheart?"

"Well . . . pay attention to something important."

"Like what, Ana Li?"

Ana Li put her hand over her mouth and giggled. "Pay attention to me!"

Mary Jane smiled and said, "Okay, I'm paying attention to you. Now what?"

"Tell them about me."

She looked quickly around the table at the rest of us.

"What should I tell them, Ana?"

"Tell them how cute I am." Again, her chubby fingers covered her mouth for just a second and then she said, "And don't forget to tell them how smart I am, too!" It was the first time in weeks many of us had laughed. Little did I realize at the time that Ana Li was also leading me to my own next step.

It is three years later. Mary Jane has just returned from a conference with Ana Li's first-grade teacher. Her shoulders hang. Her chest is caved in. Her voice is flat. I lean over the edge of the maple table toward her and ask softly, "What's going on, M.J.?"

She shrugs. "Well, when I asked Ana's teacher how she was doing in math—she's been so excited about it, you know—she told me that Ana's test scores were average for a child her age."

"Average?" I think of the thick book of multiplication problems Ana Li has been scribbling in for days, the tip of her tongue sticking out between her lips. After completing each page, she runs over holding the book out proudly for me to check. Page after page, all correct. Page after page of multiplication problems complicated enough for any ten-year-old. One smiley face after another. "Did you ask her to explain what was on the test?" I ask.

"Of course I did," Mary Jane answers, her jaw muscles tight as violin strings. "The teacher said that the test was the standardized one administered by the state, and that Ana Li couldn't do horizontal addition, or subtraction. I guess I shouldn't be making such a fuss, but Ana loves math so much and I thought she was so bright and excellent in it but . . ."

I am up on my feet. "Wait a minute! Ana Li's been doing vertical math problems. I don't think she's ever even seen a horizontal problem. What is a cotton-picking horizontal problem? And what does it have to do with how bright she is?" I glared at Mary Jane, my knuckles white on the table's edge.

She responds sheepishly, "Well, I told her that I don't even know how to do horizontal addition and it hasn't hindered my success in the world. The teacher told me that she needs to know how to do it for the test, not for the world. Maybe we should get her flash cards or something." The light in her eyes is gone. She is so quiet, it is as if she were staring at shadows.

"Mary Jane! I cannot believe you are saying these things! Einstein never used flash cards. Besides, I'll bet he couldn't do horizontal addition either! The next thing you'll be telling me is that she has an attention deficit disorder."

Hell hath no fury like this grandmother's outrage. There is not a compassionate cell left in my entire body. Mary Jane always looks as if her face is about to melt right before she cries. In this moment, she is about to become a puddle. Her words spill out. "Well, I know it's silly of me, but this teacher has been in the school for a long time and she said Ana Li didn't pay attention when everyone had to recite their multiplication tables, and I am just worried that I'm not helping her enough or the right way. Maybe I'm not seeing her accurately, although I always thought she was special, maybe she is just average and I'm not being fair to her and . . ."

My fire is washed away in her flood. I kneel next to her and tug on her sleeve. I lean over and whisper in her ear, "And don't forget to tell them how smart I am, Mommy." We cry the moment clean.

In order to risk breaking the chains of how we habitually perceive children, it is necessary to have a framework for understanding the whole: You have to understand how shadows are made, and you need to have a sense of how vast and bright the world outside your cave can be. You also have to prepare for readjusting your vision. The remainder of this chapter seeks to do just that by tracing how we have learned to focus on deficits, the effect on our culture of doing so, the forces that are pulling us apart, and the shift in direction we all need to be making if we want to bring about a revolution in how our children are seen.

Beyond the Cave of the Industrial Age

"It's not failure to fall short of realizing all that we might dream. The failure is to fall short of dreaming all that we might realize."
—DEE HOCK, FOUNDER AND FORMER CEO, VISA INTERNATIONAL

What really matters most about how our children are being educated? When I began teaching, I thought it was helping kids love learning. I assumed my job was to foster the unique brilliance of each child. Year after year, from classroom to classroom, I watched that shine turn dull by the very process that was supposed to enhance it. I was interested in the art of learning and encouraging ingenuity, but I was supposed to be training children to be obedient workers, to maintain the status quo. I taught in order to eradicate ignorance, but instead found myself in a massive battle with fear—the fear of being different, the fear of vulnerability, the fear of the unknown. I thought I was there to help children learn, but found that I was supposed to be part of an "expertocracy" whose main responsibility was to prepare children for standardized tests and keep accurate records.

In my frustration and pain, I searched for someone to blame. It was the other teachers' fault. It was the administrators' fault. It was the parents, the school board members, the public at large, the culture. But everywhere I turned, I found victims of the same misunderstandings about what a person is, what learning and intelligence are, what education itself can be. Everywhere, people spoke of the Golden Rule but passed on a Legacy of the Led. They did unto others as was done unto them. After fifteen years, I felt as if I were trying to teach children to breathe deeply in an oven with the gas turned on.

The day I left school in 1983 to become what Parker Palmer calls "an educator at large," a commission appointed by President Ronald Reagan issued its report: "A Nation at Risk." It accused the country's school systems of failing to keep up with international competition, threatening the very security of the nation. It called for reform and its remedies were to standardize curriculum, lessen choice, increase the amount of homework, and adopt "more rigorous and measurable standards." It was the fourth reform I had lived through. Each came with "new" testing strategies that ensured that large majorities of children would regularly "fail" in comparison with others. Inevitably, the reforms failed and so did half the children.

People have been trying to fix education for at least a hundred years. The task is impossible. Impossible, because it's not broken. Schools today haven't changed much from when you went to them because they don't need to. They are spectacularly successful doing just what they were originally designed to do: ensure a docile workforce for the twentieth century. The twentieth century, however, is over. There are new demands that cannot be met by those means any more than a typewriter can access the Internet.

All children are being left behind by today's educational system because we're preparing them for what will be by giving them skills for what was. We will be sending our children tomorrow to yesterday's schools. And as difficult as it is for us, unless you and I shift our focus, bells will continue to tell these children when they are supposed to start and stop learning. They will continue to relate to educators as bosses who will determine what they should learn by yesterday's standards, how and at what speed they should learn it, and how to prove it has been learned.

Schools as we know them today were designed to prepare children for the Industrial Age. One hundred years ago, problems were static—they stood still while we broke them into pieces and analyzed them. Education's job back then was to make children into workers who could perform in factories like parts of a well-oiled machine. People were hired for their hands. They learned to work at a fixed pace, as quickly as possible, so production on assembly lines would be increased. Their days were dictated by a bell, and motivated by a boss. If you produced more, you earned more. You did your job and left the rest up to the boss. All you had to do was please him. The system worked fairly well—in its time.

Welcome to the Information Age and the twenty-first century. Where we used to hire hands to produce the same thing over and over, we now hire minds to think about situations that are dynamic, interconnected, interrelated. There is no issue in today's world that can be solved by understanding a single, fixed, compartmentalized subject. What is required is integrating science and political science, economics and physics. In the Industrial Age, our expertise was in the creation and control of constants, uniformity, and efficiency. In the Information Age, the need has become the understanding and coordination of variability, complexity, and effectiveness. Motivation and evaluation have to be intrinsic. If we wait for the boss to decide whether we've done a good job or not and reward/approve of us, we lose our sense of purpose and intention. Life becomes the same damn thing over and over. Instead, we need to develop a specific sense of the value we bring to a given task, and discover what genuinely motivates us to contribute. We have met the boss and it is us! W. Edwards Deming, the guru of the quality movement in business, used to say that you can never pay someone to be kind. It needs to come from their intrinsic nature, and if you've got to pay someone for it, you are sending the signal that you don't value who they really are.

The current failure of many of our institutions is also related to the compression of time and events. It took centuries for information about the smelting of ore to cross a single continent and bring about the Iron Age. When the first human stepped on the moon, it took less than 1.4 seconds for the whole of humanity to know. Even that is hopelessly slow by today's standards. Some of you may remember "float time"—the time between writing a check and when it cleared the bank. Just like there is no more monetary float, in today's world there is virtually no float time anywhere; the time between what was and what will be has almost disappeared. The present barely exists. Everything is change and ambiguity. Yet what most of us have been trained for is constancy and certainty.

Today's workers need to not only analyze but synthesize—to be able to think about an issue from several angles in combination. We need to think of the individual leaf, but we also need to step back and be able to ponder the whole forest.

One of the most frequently diagnosed "deficits" in our country is ADD—what is commonly called "attention deficit disorder." Yet what we commonly think of as "attention," concentration, is in fact only one of the many ways our brains are capable of "paying attention," the most useful for succeeding at what was, but perhaps not for what will be. Attention can be likened to adjusting the focal range of a camera. We need to know how to shift to states of attention that help us understand the relationships between things, and states that increase our generativity and imagination. Like high-performance athletes, we need to learn to trigger our own "flow" state of attention, where we are at the energized edge of our competence. We also need to learn how to engage the "wider" states of attention that we now know increase our health and capacity to see things from many perspectives.

Each of us was born with the capacity to give our attention in many ways to both the internal and external world. Dee Hock, the author of *Birth of the Chaordic Age* and founder of Visa International, describes how thought changes as it is metabolized, if you will, by attention. Imagine a pyramid. At the base is data. As you move upward, data is processed into information that is digested into knowledge. Distilling knowledge leads us to understanding that is ultimately transformed into wisdom.

When I heard Dee talk about this, I thought of a high school trip I took to a museum in New York City. I saw a pointillist painting for the first time. I stood up very close to this canvas by Georges Seurat, fascinated with each tiny dot and its unique color. Then ever so slowly, I stepped back and the dots began to drift and float in space, then coalesce until they were shapes, then forms blending together into a scene of people gathered on the shore of an island. Then, in some mysterious way, I joined those people on that Sunday afternoon, and I knew exactly what the breeze felt like on my cheek.

Data and dots become information, then knowledge, understanding, and if we step back far enough, wisdom. Dee says that many indigenous cultures of the world spend as much time stepping back to cultivate wisdom as they do in processing data. In current Western cultures, we are so flooded with data that we spend most of our time just processing it into information. We give little of the kind of attention needed for the rest of the process to occur: pondering, discussing, wondering, contemplating, musing, reflecting, all of which make it possible to notice patterns, stories, relationships, and interactions. These are the modes of attention that Dee says can help us move from machine crafting to what he calls "mindcrafting."

A Nation of Standardized Thinkers

> "The U.S., for generations known around the world as the land of opportunity and innovation—is on the verge of losing its competitive edge. It is facing perhaps its greatest economic challenge since the dawn of the industrial revolution. . . . America's growth miracle turns on one key factor—its openness to new ideas, which has allowed it to mobilize and harness the creative energies of its people."
> —RICHARD FLORIDA, AUTHOR

Imagination and its offspring, creativity and innovation, may not be tangible assets like oil or gold. They cannot be bought or sold. They belong to everyone and are essential to what it is to be human. They can be nourished or depleted. They can be renewed or dissipated. The most abundant, least expensive, most underutilized, and frequently abused resource in the world today is human ingenuity.

In the years that I served as a thinking partner to corporate leaders, I was stunned to see how all our educational reforms have resulted in the diminishment of that resource.

The CEO of one of the largest global companies in the world, while pacing back and forth on the burgundy carpeting behind the desk of his New York office, complained to me, "Dawna, what is wrong with my leadership team? There's not an original thinker in the bunch. We have to think globally and innovatively and they can't think past their own noses. I hired each of them because they were supposed to be the best and the brightest. All engineers with M.B.A.s. They can't think together and they can't think on behalf of the whole. . . ."

"Where did they go to school?" I asked quietly.

He glared at me. "To the best, of course! The top ten business schools in the country. And they were each in the top ten percent of their class!"

I answered immediately. "Ah, well, that's your problem, then."

He stopped pacing. "What are you talking about?"

"How in the world do you think they got to be at the top of their class in those schools?" I waited while he shook his head in confusion and shrugged. Then I responded, "My friend, to get to the top of their class, they had to learn to take tests, not to think originally or innovatively. And they had to learn to compete with the other ninety percent of students and beat them. No one ever *taught* them to think collaboratively."

His complaints and my predictions played out in every leadership team meeting I observed for a year. Together, the twelve men and one woman controlled the lives of over 200,000 people and $50 billion worth of business. Never once did I hear one of them ask another an open question about a business-related issue. They never used metaphors or images—an indication that the part of their brain that thinks about the whole system wasn't functioning.

I never heard one of them say "I don't know" or "I wonder." They seemed to have lost their capacity to step back and perceive the whole of things. They seemed lost in any kind of ambiguity. They were almost always jet-lagged, and neglected their bodies, families, and souls. They were, of course, highly skilled at jockeying for political position. They sat in chairs for hours, arms folded tight across their black suits and pale yellow ties, heads nodding whenever the CEO spoke. They flipped surreptitiously through five hundred pages of preread material, or looked furtively at hundreds of e-mail messages on small, handheld computers in their laps as if they were preparing at the last minute for the inevitable standardized test. Any decision that could be postponed was, any action that could be prevented was. When it came time to discuss shared vision for the company, they brought in teams of consultants who offered them endless colorful PowerPoint presentations to which they would react. This was something they could do—react. Each of them leaned forward, eagerly pointing out what was wrong with the vision.

If you keep doing what you've always done, you'll keep getting what you've always gotten. The corporate leaders I worked with were functioning like officers trained to run a battleship. The only problem is that in this global economy, aptly named by author and management guru Peter Vaill "permanent whitewater," battleships are useless. What is needed are the skills to navigate quickly in small, sleek, fast-moving crafts, kayaks perhaps, capable of changing direction at a moment's notice. You can't navigate a kayak by focusing in a fixed way on one point in the river. You have to be able to shift back and forth between noticing your current position and the constantly changing river. You also have to be able to hold an image of where you want to go, even as you struggle over rocks and rapids.

This requires you to use all the capacity of your brain. You have to be able to think in a linear, logical, left-brained mode and shift easily to intuitive, innovative, imaginative, right-brained mode. You have to be able to integrate these different ways of thinking with great facility. Neuroscientist Daniel Siegel calls this integration "coherence," and it is thought of by some as an essential indicator of mental health. Most of the business leaders I worked with had been trained into thinking incoherently—that is, with only half of their brain. They described themselves proudly as "rational, linear thinkers." Their schooling "deskilled" them as surely as if they had to sacrifice one of their hands to get good grades and salary raises. People who asked open questions were thought of as weak. People who used images and metaphors and were concerned about relationships were thought of as "soft" and "out of touch with the realities of the bottom line." Even the field of what is called "human resources" was focused on the linear data of flow charts, insurance rates, and statistical projections of the maximum grade level a person would be able to rise to in his or her career. There was a standardized coding system used to determine this grade level. I listened to hundreds of people being discussed for the most senior level promotions, and all the leadership team talked about was their rank and length of time in their previous position. I never heard anyone discuss their talent or try to match it to the task required. Over and over, the leaders chose people who thought just the way they did: logically, linearly, and "rationally." But everything I have learned in neuroscience as well as my life experience tells me there is no such thing as a rational person. Einstein, the paragon of brilliance, first "intuited" the way the universe ought to be. He then spent decades trying to prove it.

America's greatness was derived from our capacity to think imaginatively. Until recently, we have drawn extensively on our capacity for ingenuity and innovation. Our growth has turned on one key factor—an openness to new ideas—which allows us to engage the creativity of our people. Every new product or convenience, university or corporation, masterpiece of technology or entertainment, comes from creative thinking.

Standardization does not, however, produce ingenuity or innovation. If you think about it, in fact, it can only result in an atrophy of the imagination. I am remembering LEGOs, the small red and white plastic blocks that David used to play with for hours on end, creating creatures and crafts, large and small. There were no diagrams or instruction for LEGOs back then. All that was needed was an endless supply of those blocks and a child's imagination. A friend told me recently that LEGOs hadn't been selling too well, because children were used to kits that told them what to create and gave them specific directions on how to make it. The company decided that to keep up with the competition, they'd have to follow the trend. Now a child can buy a different kit for each craft he or she decides to build, complete with instructions for where to put each block. Same little red and white plastic LEGOs. All that's been left out is imagination.

A woman who has been an outstanding kindergarten teacher for twenty years in California said that a few years ago the best thing she could bring into school was a huge cardboard refrigerator box. The children of her class used to crawl all over it, making spaceships and a secret universe. She says that these days "the kids just sit and stare at the box, then ask, 'What are we supposed to do with that, Ms. Adams?' If I tell them to do whatever they want with it, they sit passively waiting for directions." She pauses for one long moment, then says quietly, "Everything else in their lives tells them what to do and how to do it." What's being left out is imagination.

Today's global economy centers on competition for talent rather than goods and services. Can the United States continue to be a beacon of openness for creativity? It built the world's most powerful economy by producing and attracting human capital. It has a long history of resourcefulness and creativity to draw on. It has transformed itself many times. Wherever creativity goes—and by extension, wherever talent goes—innovation and economic growth are sure to follow.

They are currently draining out of the United States at an alarming rate. Richard Florida, author of *The Flight of the Creative Class*, has analyzed the percentage of what he calls the "creative class" of twenty-five nations: At its core are the scientists, architects, designers, artists, engineers, musicians, and entertainers whose function is to create new ideas, new technology, new content. When compared with other countries, the United States is not even in the top ten. With 23.6 percent, it ranks eleventh in the world. While the percentage of the "creative class" in countries such as New Zealand, Ireland, and Canada is rapidly increasing, 45 percent of Americans fall into the service class, and *this* number is steadily increasing.

I read recently that the job held by the largest number of individuals in the United States, as well as the fastest-growing occupation over the past thirty years, is that of Wal-Mart clerk. Second is McDonald's burger flipper. Close behind? Elementary school teacher. The number of people employed by Wal-Mart plus their families is greater than the population of Alabama. Or Connecticut. Or Hawaii. Or South Dakota.

Given the recent economic cutbacks in education and how they have been applied, one can assume that the future has no real need for artists, poets, dancers, musicians, self-sufficient farmers, philosophers, diplomats, or stay-at-home parents. What is needed are Wal-Mart clerks and burger flippers and low-paid teachers who keep the natives from getting restless. At least those jobs can't be outsourced. But is this really what is needed for America to remain the land of opportunity and innovation? Is this the future you want your child to inhabit?

Creativity and competition go hand in hand. Florida asserts that employing so many citizens in noncreative jobs is a terrible waste of talent and potential. The global talent pool and the high-end, high-margin creative industries that used to be the sole province of the United States and a crucial source of its prosperity have begun to disperse around the globe. These trends are a direct result of the increased drive toward standardization in education. We are rapidly losing our ability to think innovatively.

Where are we fostering innovation in this culture? State governments have slashed funding for arts and culture while pumping millions into stadiums, convention centers, brick-and-mortar projects. These choices signal a profound failure to understand what's required if we are to maintain an atmosphere of innovation. Americans revel in the stories of young creators like Michael Dell, building new businesses in their spare time or in garages. Why are they doing these things in their *spare* time? Isn't this the real stuff of education? Imagination thrives in openness, as it did in the time of the social movements of the 1960s. To be different then did not mean being an outcast, but rather it became a quality to be admired. Freedom of expression allowed new technologies and cultural reforms to flourish.

The data create an unsettling picture of a nation that is allowing its creative infrastructure to decay. For the first time in its history, the United States is confronting the possibility of a reverse brain drain. Today, foreign-owned companies and foreign-born inventors account for nearly half of all patents issued in the United States. In terms of publications, the National Science Board reports that the U.S. lead in publications fell from 61 to 29 percent in the past twenty years.

Today's global economy centers on competition for talented people rather than goods and services. We have to build what Richard Florida calls a creative infrastructure for the future of our children, our country, and the world. And your home plays an essential role in that infrastructure.

Preparing Today's Children for Tomorrow's World

> *"Our current system, telling kids to study, study, study for their tests has been a failure. Endless study worked in the past, when . . . Japan was rebuilding. . . . But that is no longer the case. Telling them to study more will no longer work. . . . We want to give them time to think. . . . There is concern that an orderly and unimaginative school system excels at producing pliant disciplined workers . . . but is failing to produce the problem solvers and innovators of the future."*
>
> —KEN TERAWAKI, JAPANESE MINISTRY OF EDUCATION

Twenty-seven years ago, my son and I lived in a small New England Ivy League town. After school, he and his pack of eleven-year-old friends would go on campus to play around at the computer center. I wasn't really sure what computers were at the time, but David seemed to enjoy doing something called "writing programs." It seemed a creative thing to do—perhaps someday he would write for television. At the very least, I imagined it would help with his schoolwork.

David's teachers evidently knew as little as I did about computers or writing programs. When his math teacher presented him with a multiplication problem and asked for the right answer, David replied, "Well, that depends on what number system you're talking about, doesn't it?" They were thinking about right and wrong, he was thinking in hypertext. Unbeknownst to me, Kiewitt Computer Center and the local ski slopes became more and more relevant to him as school became less. Even if I had known, how could I have blamed him? By and large, classroom practice was a boring routine, led by teachers who had been deskilled and had to spend at least one third of their time drilling students so they would perform well on standardized tests. David never dropped out of school exactly. He just went someplace more interesting. Though the value of what was being taught was irrelevant to his world, it was measurable. He always managed to slip in for tests.

His friends knew what he was doing, and eventually his teachers did as well. (His mother was clueless. He seemed so happy!) For an entire semester, David attended less than 10 percent of his classes, but ranked in the ninety-eighth percentile of all of his standardized tests. The assistant principal pointed out what a bad example he was setting for the other students, and how he couldn't expect to get away with this forever, not if he wanted to go to a good college. I was not as concerned with his getting into a good college as I was with helping him stay out of reform school and porn shops. We went to the bowling alley that evening. It had been the scene of some of our best conversations. As he was about to slide the ball down the polished wooden lane, I asked him, in what I thought was a reasonable tone of voice, "David, you've always loved to learn. Why are you trying to drive me crazy like this?"

After the pins exploded, and he shouted an obscenity in delight, he turned to me and said, "Ma, what does learning have to do with school? I'm learning how to write computer programs and I'm learning how to ski black diamond slopes. I already know how to take tests."

We are preparing children for what was, not for what will be. Learning the three R's was adequate one hundred years ago. In today's world, the three R's have become reorganizing, reengineering, and reinventing. But the innovation that is needed today is not a rehash of what was.

Computers can now do rote thinking faster than any human brain and access virtually any information that could be needed. In a global economy, however, without cultural perceptiveness—the ability to enter another's model of the world—and conflict transformation skills, we will literally be dead in the water. No one can afford to not understand how they learn. In addition, whatever they learn today will be outmoded tomorrow, so they also need to know how to *unlearn* what is no longer relevant.

Since our children will inherit our chaos, we need to make sure we are giving them the skills and capacities to think their way through and beyond it. Since they are inheriting a fragmented world, we need to ensure they will know how to think coherently—beyond either/or, good and bad. Since we are leaving them so many questions that cannot be answered, we must ensure that they can be comfortable in ambiguity. We must ensure they can both analyze and synthesize: to think of a leaf, think of a forest, as well as think of how the drought in the Sudan affects that forest.

Research has shown that standardized tests and intelligence tests cannot predict who will excel in life. The kind of intelligence our children will need in the twenty-first-century workplace is not about knowing more facts, but about being able to cope with new situations and challenges. Creativity, independent thinking, as well as the capacity to think with others who think differently are the skills they will need. In the martial art of aikido, which is dedicated to bringing forces that seem to be in opposition with each other into harmony, there are three aspects to training: personal mastery, mastery of change, and mastery with others. These are domains that today's children will most certainly need if they are to succeed in their own future.

In *And the Skylark Sings with Me: Adventures in Homeschooling and Community-Based Education*, Dan Greenberg, the founder of the successful Sudbury Valley Learning community, is quoted summarizing the points of consensus that leading educators, business leaders, and government officials believe are the essential features of an education that would meet the needs of society in the twenty-first century. Among them are:

- People will be faced with greater individual responsibility to direct their own lives. Children must grow up in an environment that stresses self-motivation and self-assessment. Focusing on external motivation, rewards, and punishments for meeting goals set by others is denying children the tools they most need to survive.

- The ability to communicate with others, to share experiences, to collaborate, and to exchange information is critical. Conversation must be a central part of a sound education as well as understanding those who are different.

- Technology now makes it possible for individuals to learn when they wish, whatever they wish, and in the manner they wish. Students must be empowered with both the technology and the responsibility for their own learning and educational timetable.

• Children have an immense inborn capacity for concentration and hard work when they are passionate about what they are doing, and the skills they acquire in any area of interest are readily transferable to other fields. Schools must become far more tolerant of individual variation and far more reliant on self-initiated activities. They must be given the conditions where they can self-initiate and help to be more effective doing it.

Developmental psychologists Roberta Golinkoff and Kathy Hirsch-Pasek, authors of *Einstein Never Used Flash Cards*, summarize what they see as necessary for today's children to be ready for tomorrow's world: "We don't need children who can spit back facts. We've got Google. What children need from their education are opportunities to explore, invent and discuss. They learn best when they experience, not when they sit numbly. Factors such as self-awareness, self-discipline, empathy and understanding others are all part of being truly smart and successful."

We cannot prepare children to live satisfying lives in this fast-changing, highly technical, and exciting culture by developing more out-of-date standards and dedicating immense amounts of time and money forcing students to meet them. Rather, we must support them in recognizing, developing, and contributing their natural strengths, assets, and talents to the larger community. It will take all of us, and all the ingenuity we are capable of fostering, to ensure that our children can think collaboratively. They have to learn to recognize difference as a gift. They have to learn how to maximize that difference so the future will be born of their design instead of from our limitations.

The Differences That Make a Difference

> "*Understanding the human mind will be the greatest scientific adventure of the twenty-first century. There's no more profound or worthy study than how we learn, remember, think and communicate.*"
> —CHARLES VEST, PRESIDENT, MIT

How do we *all*—parents, educators, the larger community of citizens—transform the environment in which children are growing up and the way they are perceived? Our children are not only our future, we are *theirs* as well.

The latest research in neuroscience indicates that there are certain specific conditions that foster the environment we create in our homes and schools. Daniel Siegel, M.D., co-author of *Parenting from the Inside Out*, describes them as stability, adaptability, flexibility, and energy (S.A.F.E.). As he explained it to me:

Stability is created through connecting all the differentiated parts into a coherent and integrated whole. It gives the feeling of belonging. "We are the Brown family and we live in Cleveland. We always have a large Thanksgiving dinner with turkey and sweet potatoes."

Adaptability is the ability to ride the waves of change, to be comfortable with reality as it presents itself, and to be influenced by internal and external forces. "We used to pick out our children's clothes. Now that they are teenagers, we give them each a yearly clothing allowance and let them select their own wardrobe."

Flexibility is the ability to open one's mind and be influenced by external and internal forces. "I thought I wanted to major in architecture, the way my father did, but I notice it drains me. I find myself most engaged when I'm studying psychology."

Energy might be described as the sense of aliveness and spontaneity that exists within the environment. "My favorite times are Sunday evenings when we're all just hanging out doing our own thing. Then someone starts to sing a favorite song we all know and each one of us joins in and harmonizes."

At first, these conditions might seem to be contradictory—how can an environment be stable *and* adaptable? These are words we usually think of in opposition to each other. But emerging research indicates that not only is it possible to balance these forces, we are designed to do so.

I have been told by those who understand complexity theory that a complex system such as a family or a country is always changing. It moves between two extremes: integration at one end, differentiation at the other. Imagine a pendulum swinging back and forth. As it moves toward one pole things differentiate and become more flexible—a cell defines itself for a specific function, a particular child is the only one in the family who likes chocolate ice cream, an executive specializes in business development because he has the unique skill of being able to see multiple scenarios for the future, a company seeks a culture of innovation to set it apart from the rest of its competitors. When it is moving toward the other pole, things start connecting and integrating. A family defines itself as "We're the Browns and we never frown." A person thinks of herself as being "one of the gang," whether a Red Sox fan or a civil servant. Employees of a company talk about it as if it were an entity that could be put in a box, smelled, photographed: "I'm just your run-of-the-mill Wal-Mart (substitute any company name) person. I keep my head down and try to do what's best for the company."

A pendulum is a balancing structure. It's supposed to be moving back and forth. Likewise, a healthy complex system balances itself by moving between the poles of integration and differentiation. We all need connection and a sense of belonging to a greater whole. And we all need autonomy and a sense of our own uniqueness. Thus, a healthy system (person, family, organization, country) can be defined as one that is capable of integrating differentiated parts. If the pendulum gets stuck on one side, rigidity and rigor mortis set in. If it gets stuck on the other, psychosis reigns supreme.

We live in a time when many of our institutions seem to be stuck in rigidity, standardization, and sameness. They seem to have lost the capacity for differentiation. Politicians have different parties but they all seem to be saying the same thing. One suburb seems to be pretty much the same as another. In health care, professionals are required to become as proficient at filling out standardized forms as they are at healing illness. In corporations, we are merging into larger and larger entities, while trying to instill "team spirit." In education, we are measuring learning by standardized tests, administering them to three- and four-year-olds, and labeling/medicating/isolating any who are different, as if they were diseased.

We live in a wounded time when fear is the prevalent emotional undercurrent. We are afraid our children will be left behind, afraid they won't succeed. Becoming rigid is how we habitually respond to fear. Think vividly of something you are afraid of, terrorists or tarantulas, and you'll notice rigidity in your muscles as you "freeze up," trying to pull away from the source of your fear. It is no surprise, then, that we chain ourselves to standardization searching for safety. I am reminded of how some of the concentration camp inmates at the end of World War II tried to cower deeper in the shadows of their prisons. They were more afraid of the insecurity of moving into the unknown than the misery of their known confinement.

In spite of what seems to be a habitual response, rigidity and clinging to the known does not make us safer. Our periphery narrows and we only notice that which we find terrifying. We only notice where we are stuck. If, on the other hand, we widen our periphery, as martial artists do, we begin to perceive more options. We notice where we are free. We differentiate. We begin to recognize our uniqueness, which inevitably leads us to question what our unique dream and purpose is. This inquiry engages our imagination. And ultimately, it is our imagination that makes it possible for us to design our way out of trouble.

In accepting our differences, we begin to realize we have inherent self-worth, unique gifts that only we can bring to the rest of the community. This realization leads us to the understanding that we are needed and significant. With this understanding comes the deep sense of belonging we all search for, and the realization that we hold one another's destiny.

When I worked with corporate leadership teams, I was frequently asked to do "team building" with them, which really meant help them think as one. That seemed like the last thing they needed. When given an assessment of thinking talents, for example, one team insisted that the assessment was incorrect, because it indicated that some members were highly innovative or relational in their thinking talents. "Nonsense! We are all analytic thinkers. We're engineers," they insisted. They could not believe that any one of them thought differently from the rest. Their assumption was that all "normal" male engineers thought the same way. Trying to "get them all on the same team" was the last thing they needed.

What was most effective was encouraging them to differentiate (without telling them that that was what we were doing) by sharing stories of how each person's unique background and upbringing had prepared them for their current position. By asking them to include stories of the land and people that had shaped their lives, I was, in fact, asking them to differentiate. By the time we had finished, there was more "team spirit" in the room than there had ever been. Each person had touched the different background, experiences, and talents that make contribution possible. Instead of each one fighting for his own territory and proving his own point, he knew there was something specific only he could contribute to the thinking. What characterizes any great team is when individuality becomes harmonized instead of homogenized.

Standardization is all about "average." No one wants their child to be "average," like everyone else's child. Imagine a scale that goes from −10 to 0 to +10. In a standardized world, 0 = average, the ultimate absence of difference. Why would anyone want that for their child? Yet over and over, I hear parents saying, "My child has been diagnosed with a learning disability" (minus 4). "They say he needs to be (medicated, treated, remediated) so he'll be at the same level as the other kids and can fit in" (0, "average," "normal").

Because each parent perceives a child's uniqueness, we know that they are special—a miracle, if you will. The prints at the very ends of their fingertips prove that never before has there been one such as this. Differentiation. Yet those differentiated cells have integrated together to form the fingers and hands that are pretty much standard equipment for human beings.

We all have aspects of ourselves that are different from the norm. It is what makes us human. We all struggle with trying to be normal, in whatever way "normal" was defined for us. Without help in understanding how to integrate these differences, we either exile them or try to make them fit the standard mold.

When we can't accept and integrate our differences, we also can't accept them in others—be they our mates, friends, children, or enemies. We try to norm all difference, as if it were something to be improved, fixed, isolated, and ultimately destroyed. What results is a loss of vibrancy, vitality, and life energy. When we lose a sense of our uniqueness and difference, we become another cog in the wheel, and lose any sense of life purpose. We then search outside of ourselves in the hope that something out there will complete us.

A mother called yesterday asking me to speak to her beloved fifteen-year-old son, Mason. He had just been kicked out of the third school in six months for smoking and selling marijuana. I asked him to tell me about what really mattered to him about smoking pot. As I listened quietly, he told me how he just wanted to be like everyone else. I asked when was the last time he felt as if he belonged. He replied immediately, "When I was ten."

"What was it about being ten that helped you feel as if you belonged?"

Again, without pausing, he said, "Because I wasn't shorter than everyone else then. I didn't feel different, you know, 'weird.' " He told me about the ruthless teasing he experienced in school as the short boy. I asked him what it was about his ten-year-old self that had made him so popular.

"Oh, I was really funny. I had a great sense of humor then."

I was silent for several breaths and asked, "Where is that humor now?"

"It only comes out when I'm stoned. And if the other kids are stoned with me, we're all the same somehow. They laugh at all my jokes, and I laugh at all of theirs."

Is there anyone reading this, I wonder, who wasn't teased or humiliated for some way in which you were different? Each of us has some differentiated aspect of ourselves, whether it be the short one or the shy one, the sensitive one or the slow one, the geek, weirdo, or nerd who was never integrated into the family, the gang, the team. They still hang out in the cave of our mind, waiting to be welcomed and connected into the light of the whole system of who we are. They are our own private prisoners, chained exiles waiting to finally be freed and welcomed home. The more standardized the time, school, or family that you grew up in, the tighter the chains in that cave. We assume that the shadows we see on the walls of our mind are all there is. We have been trained to think we can be unique in the same way as everyone else.

A woman called me when I was speaking on a radio show. She was fiercely defending having put her daughter on medication so the daughter wouldn't have to suffer the way she did in school. When I asked her to tell me how she had suffered, she choked up and said that she had ADD, and her daughter was just like she was. I asked her to pretend that I didn't know what ADD was and describe to me what behavior caused her to suffer. She said, "Well, I guess it was that I was always daydreaming, just like my daughter. I couldn't pay attention in class. I kept thinking about what clothes I wanted to wear, stuff like that."

I asked her what she does for a living now. She replied she is a fashion designer for television. "Successful?" I asked.

"Oh, yes. I've always been good at thinking up ways to make people look good. Interior designs, too. My daughter's the same way. We're both really creative."

"So, you're saying that both you and your daughter had problems in school paying attention because your imagination kept getting in the way?"

There was a long pause and then a click.

Imagination, ingenuity, and innovation all occur when the brain takes the same old data and makes new and different patterns with it. Differentiation means thinking different, looking different, acting different. Yet in classrooms and corporate boardrooms, the single thing that intimidates most of us is speaking up, standing out, "being different." Difference is currently isolated as if it were a disease. What would it be like if, instead, we were to integrate it, welcome it, recognize it for what it truly is?

Every parent and guardian is pulled on a daily basis between the two forces of integration—"I want my child to fit in, to belong"—and differentiation—"I want my child to know he or she is a unique miracle who can make a difference in the world." This book is meant as a companion, a hand to hold as you search to find balance, to create an environment for your children that is stable, adaptable, flexible, and energizing. The first stage of the process—recognizing your child's gifts and talents—is a differentiation strategy. The next stage—utilizing those strengths to overcome challenges—is also a differentiation strategy, calling for adaptability and flexibility. The third stage—development—in which you create an environment of support that can help your child develop his or her resources—is an integration strategy.

In order to bring this concept home, I'd like to invite you to do just that. Spend some time noticing the forces within your home, family, and within yourself that are trying to connect the system. Who is the strongest advocate of integration? What are the customs and traditions that create this kind of connection? What do you do to make yourself feel safe? How do you attempt to create a sense of belonging in your family? Notice the moments when you feel rigid or tense. What are you trying to stabilize?

Notice the forces of differentiation at play in your home. How do they manifest? Who is the strongest advocate of adaptability and flexibility? Are defiance and temper tantrums ever requests for differentiation? What are the times or situations where it is possible for each person to be completely his or her own self and yet still be part of the family?

What are the moments when energy just flows through your home spontaneously, when it feels vibrant and alive? What are the conditions that make that possible? What do you do that contributes to that?

What would be going on if you were to create as S.A.F.E. an environment as possible in your home? What could you contribute to making that happen?

Inspiration

Michael Munds, Denver, Colorado

Michael was born with Treacher Collins syndrome: He was born without a chin, cheekbones, or ears, and was hard of hearing. He had seven surgeries before the age of twelve. He has not always fit in, but he does stand up for what's right. When he saw the Oklahoma bombing on TV in 1995, he postponed surgery to raise money to help the victims. He sponsored a bowl-a-thon in his home state of Colorado. He flew to Oklahoma with $37,000. He also started the 168 Pennies Campaign in Denver, which became a nationwide effort in which schoolchildren donate pennies to help pay for the building of the children's section of a national memorial for the victims and survivors of the bombing. He has done fund-raisers for the AIDS walk-a-thon, Arapahoe Advocates for Children,

Loving Hands "unlimited," and the Sewall Child Development Center. He raised money and donated it to Kosovo in honor of the Columbine students. Overall, he raised $87,000 by the time he was twelve and a half. He says, "I believe everyone can make a difference, and it doesn't matter how old you are, or who you are, or if you feel different, because everyone is different in one way or another. Some differences are on the outside and other people can see them, but some differences are on the inside."

(For more information or to make a donation, write to 168 Pennies Campaign, Oklahoma City National Memorial Foundation, Oklahoma City, OK 73101.)

Chapter Three

The Art of the Possible

"If a child is to keep alive his inborn sense of wonder, he needs the companionship of at least one adult who can share it, rediscovering with him the joy, excitement, and mystery of the world we live in."
— RACHEL CARSON, BIOLOGIST AND WRITER

The Navajo tell a story of Spider Woman, who emerges from the center of the earth in times of powerful transition. She pulls apart the threads that formed the old world and spins stories that will bring new forms into existence. She joins all nations, tribes, and worlds in her web. It is this that helps us get a larger perspective on what we cannot understand.

Some say Spider Woman is a part of each of us. It is the aspect that cares deeply about what really matters and insists that we live from our values rather than just talk about them. These values string together experiences, events, and people into a life of meaning. Spider Woman reminds us that since we are connected in this way, what happens at one part of our web touches all.

When I became a grandmother, I realized that my granddaughter's future was connected to all children's. What makes me a good grandmother is what made me a good teacher: I am a possiblist. Please do not confuse this with being an optimist. Optimism can be like putting whipped cream over garbage and pretending it's a cupcake. Possiblism, on the other hand, recognizes garbage for what it is, and then explores how it could be composted into fertilizer for growing wheat that could be made into cupcakes. Possiblism requires that you pull apart the threads of every limiting story you've been given about a child, and explore how to spin new stories that expand the fabric of that child's future. Possiblism challenges us to ask ourselves four questions:

- What really matters about a given situation?
- What has been possible in the past and what did it take to do it?

- What else could be possible in the future?
- What are the steps we can take now to make that possibility a reality?

In the last chapter we explored the threads of the past that have been pulled apart in these fragmenting times, leaving a family's survival dependent upon a parent's ability to reweave and strengthen its connectedness. This chapter uses stories, examples, and principles to explore how you can begin to do just that.

The threads of this new weave that I call the Smart Revolution begin with what really matters: strengthening the connection between you and your child, and between your child and his or her inner resources. It is this process that will help you become a possiblist who brings out the best of your child.

All of us reading this have had at least one person in our life who believed there was something special inside of us. We wouldn't be here if that weren't true. Who was your "Spider Woman"? Whether you know it or not, that person wove a matrix of possibility at your core, enabling you to do the same thing for others, especially those you care deeply about. Jerome was a young man for whom I was fortunate enough to weave possibilities several decades ago. He was described as "retarded" and "resistant" instead of, well, let me tell you a story about Jerome.

He was a six-foot-tall, bittersweet-chocolate, fourteen-year-old sixth grader living in a migrant labor camp in a small Florida town with his mother and two sisters. The elementary school was built on the edge of the camp. It had won a prize for its innovative design: It consisted of one immense open room for all five hundred students, an enclosed teacher's room, and the principal's office.

I was the "learning specialist." My office was the former utility closet where they kept the mops and buckets. Each morning at 7:45, the kids from the camp (all black) would arrive in their yellow buses on one side of the building and the town kids (all white) would arrive in their yellow buses on the other side. While the teachers drank their coffee out of cardboard cups and smoked their cigarettes in the "faculty lounge," the students entered the building and "integrated." Jerome headed a gang of the camp kids across that big empty room. He worked his way through the "Townie" lunch boxes, distributing milk money, sandwiches, and pencils to the kids who stood behind him.

At 8:00 the bell rang and the teachers dragged themselves to their section of the open space. At 8:05, Jerome was escorted into principal Freida Varney's office. Above her desk was a large wooden paddle that she referred to as "The Convincer." At 8:30, after applying said paddle to Jerome's backside, she delivered him to my "office," with the instructions "Just keep him out of trouble. He'll never be able to learn to read; he's trainable, not educable. Train him to behave in my school."

Jerome's cumulative folder was full of labels listing all of his deficits and disorders. His deep eyes held both mischief and misery. He told me the first day not to bother trying to teach him, because he wasn't ever going to read. That made it almost unanimous—and a challenge. I love challenges.

I learned from Jerome's mother that he was the chess champion of the migrant camp. I went to watch him play one night, evidently an unusual event. No white teacher had ever done such a thing. I found Jerome surrounded by a small crowd, sitting on boxes or squatting. As he paced, no one made a sound. His eyes scanned the board, and then suddenly, like a lion, Jerome pounced. "Checkmate!"

You and I know you can't play chess well if you're stupid. I was fascinated. I spent days trying to make my mind work like his. Why did he have to move? What would it feel like to need silence to learn? Why did he need to do a visual scan to think of his next move?

Finally, I had an idea. I brought a large book to my office; its title, *A Black History of America*, was spelled out in gold letters across the cover. Jerome, who had never seen a book with photographs of African Americans, did everything he could to try to get me to read it to him. I stubbornly refused. Finally, though, I offered to play a game of chess with him, but only on these conditions: If he won, I'd read the book to him. If I won, he'd have to learn to read it, even if it took all year.

Jerome agreed. He was so sure he would win. I was a beginning chess player and he was an expert. It must have been divine intervention: I won that game— the *only* game of chess I have ever won. It took us the rest of the school year, but Jerome did learn to read that book. We explored the pattern his mind used when he played chess, and figured out how to use that pattern to help him read.

"I need to be standing and moving. It's gotta be real quiet so I can think. Then I have to look steady with my eyes at the whole board until I can see it in my mind. After that, a voice way inside tells me what to do."

I told him Einstein said he learned "muscularly and in images," just like Jerome. To learn to read, therefore, we needed to follow the Einstein pattern that Jerome's brain used so successfully in playing chess. Phonics were out. While he moved, I traced words on his back. Then he'd find them in the book, write them on paper while saying them. It was laborious, but Jerome wasn't afraid of hard work. He learned very quickly. In the process, he taught me as much as I taught him.

On his last day of school, Jerome disappeared, leaving the book behind, even though I had given it to him as a celebration present. His mother told me he was afraid it would get stolen, and that would hurt too much. She handed me a poem he had written for me:

> *I don't know*
> *how to show*
> *the delight of feeling right*
> *about what was wrong*
> *or so they said*
> *with my head.*
> *Thanks.*

I mourn when I think of Jerome, caught in a battle for control of his spirit, whose only power was refusal. He helped me to understand that learning, truly, is discovering what can be possible for each child. The statistical chances of Jerome being alive today are very slight. African-American men who begin life the way he did are an endangered species. He does live, however, in everything I teach and touch.

What Really Matters: Minimizing Interference

> *"Learning emerges from our individual and collective abilities to tap existing human capabilities and transform the forces that interfere with their expression."*
>
> —MAYA ANGELOU, POET

I never used to be a good chemistry student, because I had trouble remembering all the formulas. But one formula I have remembered and used since the day I learned it several years ago.

It was taught to me by author and high-performance trainer Timothy Gallwey in a large conference. He was giving a keynote address, but instead of the usual sixty-minute PowerPoint presentation, he wrote the following on a simple flip-chart page: $p = P-i$. I remember thinking, "Uh-oh, here's comes boredom!" But when he turned around to face the audience, I noticed that he had a bright fluorescent yellow tennis ball that he was throwing back and forth from one hand to the other as he spoke. While this captured my attention, it was the words he spoke to explain his formula that completely changed the way I think about what really matters in learning:

"The first small 'p' stands for 'performance,' so performance equals . . . the capital 'P' stand for 'Potential,' so performance equals our inherent Potential minus . . . the 'i' stands for 'interference' . . . so performance equals our inherent potential minus the interference created. Anyone willing to explore this formula with me?"

I have no idea why I raised my hand. I would rather wash every window in the Empire State Building than volunteer to demonstrate anything in front of a thousand people. Besides, he was still tossing that tennis ball back and forth. Tennis balls had been instruments of torture for me during much of my early childhood. Perhaps it's more accurate to say, therefore, that my hand raised me. I found myself walking to the front of the auditorium. In the ten minutes that followed, he demonstrated how I, a woman historically humiliated by any kind of ball, could learn to minimize the internal interference I created for myself and perform up to my full potential whenever I played with a tennis ball. He did it by asking me to shift my attention to the arc the ball took in the air, calling out "Now!" whenever it reached the peak. I was so fascinated by that task that I forgot all about camp counselors, humiliation, and failure. In other words, I was so interested in the experience itself that I couldn't interfere with my body's natural potential to throw and catch.

There is not a day that has gone by since then that I have not remembered the p = P–i formula and thanked Mr. Gallwey. For the purpose of this book I have taken the liberty of changing the formula somewhat while still holding true to its original message: p = P–i—possibility (as in what can be possible for a child or parent) equals that person's inherent Potential minus interference. It should be noted that interference can be created both internally, by the person herself, or externally, which in my case was camp counselors who only pointed out what I did wrong. Or both.

When I share this formula with parents in workshops, I ask them to spend the next day or so mumbling it to themselves, just getting curious about when they observe interference, both internally and externally, and when they don't.

The Principles of Smart Parenting

"It is easier to act your way into a new mode of thinking than it is to think your way into a new mode of acting."
—RICK LITTLE, FOUNDER, INTERNATIONAL YOUTH FOUNDATION

How do we even begin to minimize and transform the interferences that keep our children from being all they were meant to be? We have to first become aware of the ways of thinking that have contributed to them. The following four principles can help us uncover our awareness of our children's possibilities.

Think of Differences as Resources Rather Than Disorders

The desire to learn is one of the strongest human drives. Without it, we would not survive. Delight and success in learning, however, have been interfered with by the assumption that all children learn in the same way. This leads to labeling and medicating those who don't fit the norm.

Until the twentieth century most children were schooled at home, where they learned whole processes—tilling, planting, harvesting the fields. From sunrise to sunset they absorbed and observed the unending lessons of the world around them, their growth in balance with the laws of nature. The totality of the child was engaged. They gained a sense of competence from mastering basic life-sustaining tasks. The advent of compulsory education brought with it a focus on just one aspect of intelligence—the acquisition and expression of linear and linguistic information. For those who excel in thinking like this, there is no problem, except for the pressure to conform and compete that limits social imagination, compassion, and artistic creativity.

For others, the problem exists in the fact that they have a different kind of intelligence than the person who is teaching them. Our misconception has been that because all children learn, they all learn in the same way. I have come to the conclusion that a significant portion of "learning disabilities" are actually misunderstandings of how children's minds work. We don't all think and learn in the same way. In order to properly educate our children, we must come to understand the nature of the different ways they use their minds. When we assess talent without considering the entire spectrum of intelligences, we mismatch education, careers, and jobs. The tragedy is that they—our children—and we—society at large—forfeit the benefits of their achieving truly remarkable levels of performance, satisfaction, and competence in areas they love.

We know that musical instruments all produce music, but we understand that you play a guitar in a different way from a violin. Children's minds are like musical instruments. Each has a unique way of being smart, a particular style and pattern of conditions that are natural to follow when learning. It is far more effective to teach children how to play the specific instrument of their minds than it is to encourage them to struggle to play a guitar with a bow.

Most of us sense that children learn in different ways. If you hold Sally and rock her while reading, she can pay attention for hours. But if you were to hold her brother Sam and try the same thing, you'd be black and blue. Yet it is standard to judge children as if they all learn in the same way. When a child doesn't measure up, we label their difference as a disorder.

We know that computers use different operating systems. If I place a disc in my PC and it does not work, I don't assume it is disabled. I assume it is from a Macintosh, a computer that uses a different operating system. Research and my experience over the last four decades has brought me to the realization that different children use different operating systems to receive, integrate, and express information. These have nothing to do with temperament or personality. Each child has a different way of being smart—a particular style and pattern of conditions that are natural to follow when learning.

Nature loves diversity. Intellectual diversity is a natural condition of and gift to our species. As when working with wood, it is most effective to follow the grain. Going against it squanders human resources, while a willingness to wonder and be curious with a child increases our effectiveness. Because we are all wired differently, understanding how we and our children *are* wired is one of the most important keys to being able to learn how we learn. If we accept that all who are different belong, then children will stop judging, isolating, and bullying those who do not conform to the standardized norm.

Anyone who's ever had a child labeled with a disorder feels some reassurance when reading the following list of famous failures. Think of it as a handhold in the dark moments, when keeping faith is most difficult.

- French philosopher Jean-Paul Sartre had to pretend to read.
- Famous American orator and attorney Clarence Darrow was told by his teachers and parents that he'd never be able to speak or write.
- French writer Marcel Proust couldn't write a composition in school.
- British mystery author Agatha Christie refused to learn to write.
- Ludwig van Beethoven's music tutor said he was hopeless as a composer. He also never learned to multiply or divide.

- Louisa May Alcott, the American author of *Little Women*, had teachers who complained that she wasted her time drawing instead of doing addition.
- Pablo Picasso hated school and seemed unable to learn to read or write when other children his age were proficient.
- Impressionist painter Paul Cézanne was rejected by an art school in Paris.
- American writers Stephen Crane, Eugene O'Neill, William Faulkner, and F. Scott Fitzgerald all failed courses in college.
- French writer Émile Zola scored zero in his final literature examination.
- Author Honoré de Balzac was given up on by his teachers, who described him as a failure.
- Norwegian composer Edvard Grieg once said, "School developed in me nothing but what was evil and left the good untouched."
- U.S. president Woodrow Wilson didn't read until he was eleven.
- Physicist Albert Einstein did not speak until he was seven. Of middle school he remarked, "I prefer to endure all sorts of punishments rather than to learn gabble by rote."
- American inventor Thomas Edison, who went on to invent the lightbulb, the phonograph, fluorescent lights, and many other innovations of the twentieth century, ran away from school because his teacher beat him with a cane for not paying attention and for jiggling in his seat. "I was always at the foot of the class," he noted later in life.
- Winston Churchill was seen as dumb.
- General George Patton was left back.
- Bernard Baruch, presidential adviser in the field of international economics, failed math.

These individuals all struggled with standardized approaches in school. But somehow, they each held on to their uniqueness and developed their individual gifts. Most of them would be labeled as having a deficit or disorder today. In the United States, many would be medicated.

According to John Breeding, Ph.D., author of *The Wildest Colts Make the Best Horses*, in 2003 over eight million school-aged children in the United States were on some kind of stimulant medication. We are the only nation in the world to be drugging so many of our children. "These drugs work by turning curiosity, exploration, and socialization (expansive attention) into isolated, repetitive, stereotypical behavior (narrowing of attention)," writes Breeding. He goes on to state, emphatically, "The human brain is awesome, its intricacy and complexity beyond our ability to fathom. No drug improves its function; all of these drugs work by producing brain malfunction."

A few more facts to help you understand how powerful are the forces that support the deficit and disorder focus:

Dr. Lawrence Diller, author of *Running on Ritalin*, states that:

> No one knows precisely how many children in the U.S. have AD/HD. There's no definitive test for it—no blood test or brain scan or even standardized psychological assessment that can unequivocally determine whether a child is or isn't affected. In its milder forms, the symptoms of inattention, distractibility, impulsivity can look very much like the normal behavior of an active child. Currently it is estimated that nearly 1 in 10 eleven-year-old American boys takes some kind of stimulant medication—a classification that includes Dexedrine or amphetamine and now includes drugs like Ritalin, Adderall, and Concerta. The United States uses 80% of the world's stimulants. No other country addresses the behavior and school performance of children with such strong emphasis on psychiatric diagnosis and drug treatment.
>
> In fact, Ritalin and other stimulants improve *anybody's* ability to focus and pay attention to boring and difficult tasks. Studies from the National Institute of Mental Health in the 1970's proved that low-dose stimulants have the same effect on all children and adults as well, whether or not they have been diagnosed with AD/HD. Because the drug works so well to calm children down, the assumption is that the child must have AD/HD. But given Ritalin's universal effects on all children, by this logic it would follow that all children have AD/HD.

Why isn't there more research revealing this? The answer has much to do with the politics of American psychiatry and the influence of the multibillion-dollar psychopharmacology industry. The field has shifted from looking for causes of children's difficulties in their family and environment to the child's presumably malfunctioning brain. Taking stimulants does improve behavior. Aspirin also improves a headache, but no one says that a headache is caused by an aspirin deficiency. This belief in biological causality earns more than a billion dollars a year for the pharmaceutical industry. The runaway popularity of stimulants depends in turn upon the benediction they receive from leading academic experts who receive major research funding from more than half a dozen of the world's largest pharmaceutical companies. Virtually all leading psychiatry researchers are biologically oriented scientists who accept funding from these companies.

In 2001, Marcia Angell, then editor of the *New England Journal of Medicine*, wrote, "There is now considerable evidence that researchers with ties to drug companies are indeed more likely to report results that are favorable to the products of these companies than researchers without such ties."

It isn't just the power and money of psychopharmacology setting the agenda; it's also our deficit-focused culture that seems more and more captured by the notion that there is something wrong with our children.

This labeling and medicating can deprive children of the help they need in understanding and utilizing their particular ways of thinking. An asset focus encourages you to consider that your child—and you—may be different from the "norm," but if you learn how to use it well, that difference is a gift.

A teenaged friend, Kate, expressed this first principle as follows: "Finally I am being noticed for who I am, not for who I am supposed to be."

Track Assets Rather Than Deficits

Observe natural learning in a simple and powerful moment: Watch an infant learn to reach for a cup, a developmental task that is essential if the child is to learn to feed herself. First the baby reaches and gets Mommy's hair. Then air. Then Mommy's hand. Then air. Then cup. Then cup, cup, cup. What is natural for the infant's brain is *to track success and discard failure*. Like a heat-seeking device, the brain records each successful encounter with the cup and re-aims after each miss.

When a child gets to school, however, this natural process is often interfered with or reversed. We track failures. We pay attention to where the deficits are. As a consequence, we tend to deskill our children, train them in their incompetence, and interfere with their natural passion to learn.

In a very real way, children are brighter when they begin their education than when they complete it. Brighter, as in more alert, more willing to experiment, to be wrong and laugh about it, more willing to risk and reach. Very young children walk as if they belong on the earth, as if they trust their own minds. There is no gap between their true nature and their ability to express it. What happens to that hum and hunger? How do those same eyes become shadowed, suspicious, just a few years later? How do those bodies get rigid and closed? How do all those dreams become crushed under arms that fold tight over chests?

Unintentionally, we interfere with a child's curiosity and willingness to explore by focusing his or her attention on what does not work. We teach them to become aware of all the things that are wrong with them. We evaluate that "wrongness" in bloodred ink. The teacher marks how many words they get wrong on the spelling test, not how many they get right. They are told they are "weak in math." We groove an awareness of their mistakes into them. Thus, they take what they can do well for granted and come to distrust their mind's natural ability to learn.

Ask a group of older children to name their abilities, and they usually begin to splutter and give responses such as, "I'm pretty good at, um, well, I like to read the newspaper, and I know something about . . . sports, that's it, I know something about sports."

Now, ask those same children to talk about their shortcomings. They will gush forth: "I'm very shy and just not good at speaking in front of groups. I've always been terrible at reading, and I can't dance at all. I'm working on improving, but . . ."

This deficit focus is everywhere. It is so commonplace in our world that we think it's natural, but in reality, it's a very ineffective way for the human brain to work. Imagine for a moment that you keep depositing money in a savings account, but when it comes time to pay your bills you ignore that balance and only pay attention to what you don't have. You'd work even harder to make more money, which you'd put in the bank, then forget that you could withdraw it. You would always feel you were poor. Someday you might even want to take resources from someone else who seemed to have more, or perhaps you'd get so frustrated, you'd just give up altogether.

An asset focus doesn't mean ignoring limitations and difficulties. It means that instead of just worrying about what isn't enough about your children (not smart enough, not articulate enough, not creative enough), you help them learn to use their natural strengths to overcome the limitations they face. Obstacles become hurdles that their long legs can leap over. What if, for instance, you asked your child how she learned to spell those four words that *were* correct on the test, and then taught her to use that same method on the sixteen others she still had not mastered? What if the first response we gave to our frustrated child was "I understand you don't know how to do this. What part of the problem *do* you understand? How did you work out yesterday's math problem?" That's what happened with Fred, who had been labeled ADHD (attention deficit hyperactive disorder) by a learning specialist and a psychologist. One day Fred's parents put aside the thick file detailing all his deficits. They sat down together and tracked his assets, as described later in this book. Then they began to speak about how all those strengths could be used to help him with the problems he was having at school. Fred began to blossom.

We parents also tend to focus on our own deficits and "not enoughs." We remind ourselves about the mistakes we've made and fear our children will suffer as a result. Try an experiment yourself. At the end of reading this section, tell yourself everything you've done today that could have been done better. Point out everything that is "wrong" with how you've lived the day. Notice the effect within. Then think of the things you've done that have worked and been effective, the things that have been enjoyable, the things you've learned. Which one of these two ways would create less interference with what could be possible for you?

What if, instead of ending your days with a mental to-do list of what you could have done better as a parent, you were to make a Ta-Dah! list of the parenting moments you are proud of, studying how you achieved your own version of "cup, cup, cup"?

Learning is in the nature of things. It is a personal drive of abandon and trust. Watch a baby learn to walk toward a parent's outstretched hands. This play of energies is between each of us and life itself. Intelligence is a result not a cause. The cause lies in the life force that cracks a shell open and pushes the seed toward the light. We as parents can support that cracking open with our curiosity and belief.

Think of Mistakes as Experiments Rather Than Failures

The latest research in the study of the human brain indicates that experience can actually help the brain wire itself. It is for this reason that every child needs to be encouraged to explore his or her world through experiences and experiments. In the attempt to standardize the way we measure children's learning, however, we give them the message that the right answer is more important than having these important experiences.

We use far less of our mind's capacity than could be possible. It is as if we own an Italian racing car and only use it to go back and forth in the driveway. Although it is very difficult to measure our potential mental capacity accurately, it is very easy to evaluate a learning environment. All you have to do is ask the question "How safe is it here to make a mistake?" Since learning is increased through experimentation, and experimentation requires making mistakes, an environment that humiliates, judges, corrects, embarrasses, or labels a child for making mistakes is one that interferes with natural capacity.

A safe learning environment is one that starts where a child is competent and challenges him or her to stretch, not strain or stress. It is natural for children to quest, to pit themselves against outer obstacles and inner demons. To help them, you have only to work *with* that quest in a way that minimizes the habits of doubt and judgment that prevent performing at full capacity.

An effective learning environment should be fun, because play is the very essence of learning, whether it is the play of ideas and concepts or imagination and dreams. Without it, children lose their sense of wonder and the feeling of belonging to the world.

Armand, for instance, age five, is making something out of paper and masking tape in the kitchen as his mother cooks dinner. He has been at work quietly for at least twenty minutes. Now comes the moment when he sees if it can stand on its own. Down it crashes in record speed. "That was not a success," he says, and then runs to the cabinet for cardboard to reinforce his structure. In ten more minutes, he has created a standing house.

When children think of mistakes as failures, they become afraid to try new things. When they see mistakes as experiments, they are able to persist at something in order to reach their goal, as Armand did. They engage all their thinking in how it could be done differently. Inventor Thomas Edison is often used as an example of this principle. When he was criticized for failing seven hundred times to invent a lightbulb, he said, "I have not failed seven hundred times. I have not failed once. I have succeeded in proving that those seven hundred ways will not work. When I have eliminated all the ways that will not work, I will find the way that will." It took him a thousand tries.

The more we encourage our children to see mistakes as experiments, the less they will interfere with their natural potential to learn successfully. When we treat ourselves the same way, we enjoy helping them do that. What is at stake here is how a child will develop a sense of his or her inherent self-worth, the raw and wild gift of life that waits to open and be shared with the rest of us.

Learn from the Inside Out as Well as from the Outside In

The word *educate* comes either from the Latin *educare*, which means to instruct, as in training horses, or from *educere*, which means to lead forth that which is within. For the past one hundred years, most schools (and consequently many parents) have been instructing from the outside in. We decide what children should learn and how they should learn it; we determine how long it should take, and how to evaluate how well it has been learned. We interfere with children's own self-awareness of what works best and what is most important to them. We have long debates about what should be taught, but rarely ponder how to foster the art of learning from the source (inside the child) out. In addition, our children are not supported in developing the capacity to discern what *is* right for them. They become adults who don't trust their own judgment, and need someone on the outside to determine the direction their life should take. No wonder young adults can so easily get caught up in peer pressure. We have trained them to look outside themselves for answers.

If we always do what we always did, we'll always get what we always got. Let's explore this principle by thinking about the same situation in two different ways: from the outside in and from the inside out.

Think about helping a teenaged boy learn how to drive a car. Habitually, with the outside-in approach, the person teaching would sound something like this: (student is behind the wheel) "Okay, now remember the speed limit. Don't go over it or you'll get a ticket. In fact, you better drive even slower, so you have plenty of time to stop in case the car in front of you . . . *slow down!* Weren't you listening to me? I told you . . . you are too close to that green car on the left and . . . pull over this minute before you kill both of us!" (Any resemblance to characters living or similarities to actual events is not coincidental. This is exactly how I, a supposedly expert educator, taught my son to drive!)

The major difficulty with this way of teaching is that when the outside source of command and control is gone, the student is on his own in the car. All too often, it is only *then* that real learning occurs.

Now let's listen in on the same student being helped to learn how to drive from the inside out: (student is in the passenger seat) Mythical parent: "Okay, now we both have agreed that the purpose of learning to drive is to get from point A to point B, safely and legally, correct?" (The student nods and pats the piece of paper where this is written as a commitment and signed by both of them. They shake hands.) The parent starts the car, and begins to drive down the street into an empty parking lot. There is a piece of cardboard covering the speedometer. The parent says, "Okay, now I want you to guess how fast I am going." The student calls out, "Thirty-five." She removes the cardboard and he sees the car is actually going forty-five. She says nothing except, "Let's just keep trying, and you notice what different speeds feel like, and how the engine sounds."

After fifteen minutes of this, the student can guess accurately every time. The parent then says, "Okay, now I'd like you to guess how long it would take for me to bring the car to a full stop from forty-five miles per hour. Tell me when to put on the brakes, then count." After a short time, the student can estimate accurately when she should put on the brakes. They proceed in a similar manner until he can also estimate how close the car is to objects on the right and left.

Each succeeding lesson begins with a reminder of the commitment and a handshake. When the student is ready to take the wheel, the parent continues asking him to guess the speed, distance from objects in front and around, and time to stop. They begin to explore many different landscapes using this same approach of increasing his awareness through discovery in a safe environment, without judgment or accusation, where he can make mistakes but never fail.

This way of learning requires something new from parents. Timothy Gallwey explains, "Most of us are more committed to teaching than to seeing someone else learn. Our ideas of teaching may come from the past and involve instilling judgment, doubt, and fear. Learning happens in an atmosphere of experimentation and self-correction, where the relationship between the student and his or her potential is protected."

Instead of dictating and directing from the outside in, learning from the inside out means helping children jump over the hurdles that interfere with their doing quality work. The child has to be guided to take responsibility for solving his own problems. For example, a parent might say (in an even and curious tone of voice), "What were you doing when this problem started? Was it against the rules? How can you work it out so it doesn't happen again? What can I do to help you? What will you do? What if you don't? What consequence do you choose?" Most of us were not guided this way, and it may feel as awkward as eating with your non-dominant hand. But each time we help children learn from the inside out, we are sending them the message that we respect their natural intelligence and capacity to master challenges. Those messages will build children's inherent self-worth and self-respect.

Parenting is hard work. It requires a lot of *doing*. Bringing out what is best in your child, however, often requires simply *being with*, letting go of all roles, all techniques. It encourages "growing toward" what is desired. You already know how to do this. Think of what you did when your child was an infant and took the first faltering steps toward your outstretched arms. Passive observation wasn't enough. You had to get down. You had to pay attention. You had to be in touch. You had to wonder *when* your child would walk, not *if*. Your encouragement is what drew him or her forward. The desire and the capacity to learn were inherent to your child. What you provided was the open arms to fall into and the belief that those inherent abilities would emerge.

What Has Been Possible and How?

> *"If you can create ways in which people can have* constructive *imaginations, you will make a difference."*
>
> —BLISS BROWNE, FOUNDER OF IMAGINE CHICAGO,
> GRASS-ROOTS INITIATIVE

I'd like to tell you a few stories about environments that have minimized interference in order to help children connect to their own capacities and make a difference in the world. Hopefully, they'll inspire the Spider Woman within you to begin to wonder what could be possible in your world. One takes place within a family, one within a school, and the last within a country.

The family was referred to me by a colleague. He told me his son Paul and Paul's wife, Sylvia, had an eleven-year-old son, Jonathan, and a fourteen-year-old, Jason, who was having big-time difficulties in school and at home.

Paul shook my hand, but as soon as we sat down, it was Sylvia who began to speak. She described Jason as "sullen, aggressive, with anger control problems and ADHD." This description took thirty minutes. While she spoke, Jason stared at the floor, jiggled his feet, and punched his brother whenever possible.

I asked Paul to describe one moment they had shared as a family that brought him joy to think of. He smiled, but then shrugged. "I can't think of one," he said. Jason got up and began to pace around the perimeter of my office, touching every object and book within reach. I asked him if he could think of such a moment, and he, too, shrugged. Sylvia jumped in to describe all they had tried to do for Jason, the therapy, the tutoring, the medication. Jonathan interrupted and said, "That isn't what she asked you, Ma." Jason punched him in the shoulder.

I won't go into the arduous details of the rest of that session. Suffice it to say things were not going well in the Brown family, and talking things out was only going to produce more of the same. They had been studying the negative for several years and all it seemed to accomplish was to make them more proficient in explaining their suffering and lack of connection. I told them that if they wanted to come back for a second session, each person would have to be able to tell me about one experience they had shared with another member of the family that had made them really happy.

The second session was much easier to sit through. I asked Jason and Paul to tell each other their stories in one corner of the room, and Jonathan and Sylvia to do the same on the couch. Then I put a big pile of old magazines on the floor and asked them to tear out pictures silently that represented what quality it was inside them that made the story they had told possible. While they were ruffling and ripping through the magazines, I placed a large sheet of blank newsprint in the middle of the floor and asked them to silently arrange their pictures on it so it would represent a whole picture of the way they wanted their family to be six months from that day. I played some high-energy music while they rushed around arranging and rearranging their own pictures. At the end of fifteen minutes, they taped it all down.

I invited them to walk all around the collage while wondering in silence what surprised them about it, what touched them, what challenged them, and what they learned from it. Each circled the collage slowly, reverently, as if it was a work of art. Which it was.

We closed that session with Paul and Jason in the corner sharing with each other what they had learned and Jonathan and Sylvia doing the same on the couch. In the weeks and months that followed, we used the collage as a master map to plan alliances and activities that would make it a reality. Paul, a high school music teacher, discovered that Jason really wanted to learn to play the piano. Paul taught him the fundamentals of jazz three times a week. Jason and

Jonathan started taking martial arts lessons together, giving them a new structure to work out all the feelings that had no words. Sylvia began to write daily in a journal, realizing how much Jason reminded her of her own troubled high school years. She left him daily notes under his pillow describing specific positive things she noticed and respected about him. She and Paul began to have "best friend's time" every Saturday night, strengthening their own relationship and unifying their approach to the boys.

The story doesn't have an ending or a moral. We never did "therapy" together and no one got "fixed." In it, however, you will find Spider Woman weaving an environment that minimizes interference and maximizes possibility. It was obvious that talking wasn't working and equally obvious that Jason needed to move and look. I chose to shift my focus from the stories of his problems, differences, and deficits to a collective search for past successes. If we could mine these, we had a chance of finding the real jewels that were deeply buried when we began. Because they were evoked from inside each family member, rather than imposed from outside, we were building on solid ground that all could trust. They didn't have to become different people for the family to heal. Working with common magazine images leveled the playing field. They were all exploring and experimenting together, so no one could be wrong or fail.

Our next visit is to a fifth/sixth-grade classroom in downtown Toronto. We enter the laboratory school of the Institute of Child Study. Anne Cassidy's class has just begun a unit about urban studies, though the children don't know that. Last week, they were camping at a wilderness park in Ontario for three days, lugging their water from a pump and cooking in the great outdoors. Now they are on their feet, rushing to the board, and brainstorming about the elements that make a city. Ms. Cassidy asks what it would take to build a city in the place where they had camped. One boy is sitting up on the table, the better to make his points to the girl who is writing down his ideas on a poster-sized piece of paper. Another is drawing out his ideas because that is the way he explains best. A small cluster is in the closet debating wave-theory physics and how it relates to building a city.

There is no script here. No government mandated questions on a set topic. The children are constructing their own curriculum, the one no government can engineer. They are problem solving with spontaneity, creativity, and intellectual agility. As for the official curriculum, Ms. Cassidy confides that the children are actually digging into units on government, energy, community, and current affairs. For the creative writing unit, she's going to ask them to write a story that takes place in a water treatment plant like the one they'll see on a later field trip. The children seem to be having so much fun discovering and experimenting, it's even possible they don't realize they are learning.

This laboratory school is a decades-old experiment devoted to putting into practice theories of education, psychology, and neuroscience. Each child expresses what he or she is learning in the style and at the rhythm that is most natural for his or her brain. Since intellectual diversity is appreciated and harnessed instead of interfered with, every child contributes and has a sense of their inherent self-worth. There is no focus on tests, marks, no pressure on teachers that accountability is paramount, no imperative to rush through learning units. The end point is not a test or a product. It's learning. Nonetheless, on the Canadian Test of Basic Skills, the students of this school routinely score in the ninety-fourth to ninety-ninth percentile. Many of them go on to excel at the best universities in the world.

The last story of possibility helped children translate their values into action. It was initiated by Richard Ford, one of Canada's most distinguished teachers, and Vicki Saunders, one of the World Economic Forum's Global Leaders of Tomorrow. Together, they started Impactanation, a Canadian-based organization that designs youth engagement programs and initiatives around issues of social justice, health, and the environment. The question that compelled them was: "How can you give significant leadership opportunities to youth?" From it grew Earthcare, a youth-inspired environmental stewardship program that positively impacts individuals, classes, schools, and communities.

Saunders sums up the external interference they faced: "With a focus on public service over public purpose, we expect our institutions to treat us like customers, reacting to our every need. We forget that we are all part of the problem *and* the solution. The problems get more complex, leading to more disengagement. Youth are streamed toward activism over action. Most young activists have never been asked to come up with creative solutions to some of the challenges they see in front of them. Society denies youth any productive role until they are in their twenties."

Earthcare is an activity-based, curriculum-aligned program designed in 2003 to develop students and staff as environmental stewards. The unique student engagement process involves youth from kindergarten through twelfth grade as action-oriented leaders who not only develop their own awareness but act as catalysts for increasing their school, community, and region's awareness to encourage energy savings and conservation. The program, led by students and facilitated by key teachers, inspires behavioral change through the completion of water, waste, and energy audits four times a year. By measuring results, mapping successes, and sharing positive stories, the program develops new partnerships between facility managers and classrooms, students and community leaders, senior and junior students, teachers and superintendents.

At a time when educational programs are being cut from the budget because of insufficient funds, Earthcare developed a unique business model, requiring no new dollars from participating school districts. In the first year, in a school district (Ottawa-Carleton DSB) with 76,000 students, 90 percent of schools were involved. One million dollars in savings were attributed to the program's activities. This money could then be used to fund the rollout of other youth engagement or innovational educational programs.

Richard Ford explains what he considers to be the foundation of the program's success: "The philosophy of youth as resources is simple. If youth know that their community needs them, they realize that they can be partners in solving some of society's most vexing problems. They see that their actions improve the community's and their own situation."

Practicing the Possible in Your Home

"We die on the day when our lives cease to be illuminated by the steady radiance, renewed daily, of wonder, the source of which is beyond all reason."
—Dag Hammarskjold, former U.N. secretary-general

The first night my husband, Andy, and I went to a class in the martial art of aikido, we watched dumbfounded as twelve large and burly young men simultaneously attacked the sensei (teacher). He was a small, wiry man in his seventies. Within minutes, he whirled and swirled as if dancing, and the twelve attackers went flying here, there, everywhere.

After class was over, I approached him rather sheepishly, keeping a respectful distance. When he turned to face me, I felt every molecule of his attention surround me. I was only going to thank him, but my curiosity took over. I had to ask one question. "Excuse me, Sensei, but how long did it take you to learn to do that—what you did with those men, I mean?"

His eyes momentarily shifted to the right and the corners of his mouth lifted ever so slightly before he answered. "You mean the *rondori*? The multiple attack?"

"Sure, if that's what you call it. You made it look so simple!"

"I have been practicing *rondori* for forty years, but I am sorry, I have not learned it yet. Still, I practice. That's all there is. Simple. Practice. Like life, yes?"

He bowed, turned, and was simply and completely gone.

I'd like to invite you to practice what you've been learning in this chapter by returning to the four possiblist's questions introduced at the beginning. Take a moment to gaze out the window, or grab your journal and reflect on these questions:

- What really matters to you about how your child develops?
- What was one time in the past when you felt fully alive and engaged and were having a positive influence on your child's development? What quality or gift of yours made that moment possible?
- What would you like to make possible for your child in the future?
- What could you learn from reading this book that might help you take a step toward making that possibility a reality?

The next time your children approach you for help with a social problem, ask them what really matters to them about it, and then ask about a time in the past when they've been successful in a similar situation. Find out what it was about them that made that possible. In this way, you will be reminding them of a capacity they have used successfully in the past, and thus they can trust it with confidence in the present. Then be curious together about how they could use that quality in this situation.

The sensei didn't master the *rondori* by memorizing a predetermined series of steps. But he did have to practice. Similarly, there aren't specific words you need to learn in order to become a possiblist. The more you seek out what has worked in the past and create positive images of where you want to go, the better able you'll be to keep up with the complexity of change all around you. Begin in your own imagination, perhaps *after* the fact, wondering how else you could have helped your child in that given situation. Then, like the baby reaching for the cup, you'll find yourself realizing *during* the fact that there could be a different way to approach a problem. Eventually, you'll begin to realize *before* you go down the old route of interference that there could be another way possible, and you'll implement it. That's practice. And that's all there really is. Practice. Like life. Simple.

Inspiration

Charlie Simmons, Littleton, Colorado

Charlie was at choir practice at Columbine High School on April 20, 1999, when two students went on the infamous shooting spree. He barely made it out of the front doors of the school and four of his close friends were killed. "It was a living nightmare, a bad day multiplied by the biggest number you can think of." Days later, the students gathered in a community church. While waiting for the faculty, Charlie volunteered to conduct the choir singing "Ave Maria." About a week later Charlie joined with a woman from a local community group to create a safe place for kids to be with one another and not have to worry about not being accepted. He believed that if there had been such a place for the two shooters, there would have been a very different outcome. He wanted to create an environment that promoted outreach, counseling, and healing for Littleton teens.

They decided to name it S.H.O.U.T.S., which stands for Students Helping Others Unite Together Socially. The local mental health center found them space on the top floor of the local theater. They hired two "cool adults" to serve as mentors and make sure everyone there was treated with respect.

Charlie says, "Creating S.H.O.U.T.S. has helped me move forward. Having a positive focus took my mind off the tragedy. I could deal with it more easily knowing I was doing something to help others. . . . I recently heard an awesome quote: 'You can build walls and you can build bridges with the same material.' We're tearing down the walls and building strong bridges."

(For information and help to form a S.H.O.U.T.S. in your area, contact: S.H.O.U.T.S., Ascot Theater, 9136 West Bowles Ave., Littleton, CO 80123.)

Chapter Four

Conversations of Discovery

"We will come to regard our children not as creatures to manipulate or to change, but rather as messengers from a world we once deeply knew, which we have long since forgotten, who can reveal to us more about the secrets of life, and also our own lives, than our parents were ever able to do for us."

—ALICE MILLER, PSYCHOTHERAPIST AND RESEARCHER

The Heart of an Eagle (adapted from an African folktale)

Once upon a time, while traveling from Here to There, a woman and her young son came upon a poultry farm. The boy was very curious and pressed his face into the rusty wire fence that penned in hundreds of chickens.

"Mommy, there is a very weird-looking chicken in this cage. He's not anything like the others."

As the woman peered at the bird her son was pointing to, a scraggly man in dirty clothing approached them.

"What are you doing to my chickens?" he snarled.

"Just looking. But would you mind telling me, sir, about that odd bird who is huddled in the far corner there? It seems to me he is quite different from the other chickens. In fact, I was thinking he might be a young eagle."

"Nonsense," the farmer replied. "I've had him since he was barely a hatchling. He acts like a chicken, he eats like a chicken, therefore he *is* a chicken."

"Do you mind if we go in the cage to get a better look?"

"Do what you please," he grumbled.

The woman and her son had to bend over to fit through the makeshift door. She went down on her knees and scooped up the bird.

"You are an eagle, not a chicken. You can fly. You can fly free!"

She held him above her head and tossed him in the air.

The bird flapped its wings once, twice, but fell flat on its beak as it collapsed to the ground, then began to scratch in the dirt. The farmer, watching from the other side of the fence, snickered. "I told you so. The bird is a chicken, just an ordinary chicken. You're wasting your time!"

As the man turned his back, the boy shouted, "Excuse me, mister, but would you sell him to us? Since he's just an ordinary chicken, I'm sure you wouldn't miss him."

"That's fine with me. Five dollars is my price."

The woman knew it was an exorbitant amount to pay, but her son's eyes were pleading. She gave the old man the money. The boy scooped the bird to his chest, ran out of the cage and down the dusty dirt road. His mother followed him to the top of a small hill.

"What are you going to do?"

The boy didn't answer. Instead, he lifted the young bird as high as his arms would stretch and implored, "You have the heart of an eagle. I know you do. You're a fine and wonderful creature. You're meant to be free. Spread your wings, follow your heart, and fly. Please eagle, fly!"

A gentle current of air ruffled the feathers of the bird. The woman held her breath as her son tossed it into the wind. The creature stretched out its wings, trembled, and then, as if carried by their silent prayers, lifted. The eagle glided smoothly in a wide circle high above the two of them, above the farm, above the entire valley.

The woman and her son never saw the eagle again. They never discovered where its heart directed it to go. They only knew it would never return to live the life of a chicken.

Each child comes into the world with a unique spark. We, their parents, are caretakers of that flame. Even if it is reduced to a tiny ember buried in a charred timber, it is our responsibility to provide the wind that will help it rekindle. Like the eagle in the folktale, all children need to be recognized, to be noticed for their uniqueness, to know that they matter. They don't just like it, they *need* it.

We send our children off to school hoping they will find their hearts, their minds, their courage, their magic, and their way back home. Too often, they become convinced that they must change the very nature of who they are. Their belief in their own abilities shrivels as they are taught to doubt their own minds. Unfortunately, we ourselves have been deskilled and wounded. We do not trust what we know about our children's abilities.

This is a tragedy, for the most essential ingredient of success is an inherent sense of self-worth, which is built by trusting your own mind to accomplish what is relevant in your life. Schooling should be about learning how to access the intelligence you have, as well as how to widen and deepen it. You should come out of school more confident in knowing how to use your mind, not less.

It's time to stop following the old standardized yellow brick road. Your children are learning self-abuse as they travel on it instead of self-worth; their minds are being stunted, not expanded deeper and wider with the desire to learn. It's time for us to build the road in a new way, a way that takes our children's individual differences into account and teaches them how best to use the minds they have.

Enormous problems demand new ways of thinking that challenge us to consider what is really important. The Smart Revolution is based on the belief that the uniqueness and diversity of young people, our greatest natural resource, must be recognized, valued, and empowered.

The most common mistake we make as parents is thinking one person can't make a difference. As the young boy did in the African folktale, I would like to help you find the eagle inside your children. I would like to convince you that they are not chickens, and don't need to live their lives as if they were. I would like to support your saving their minds by learning to understand the unique intellectual assets they use to think, learn, and communicate. I would like to help you find ways to support their flying beyond their belief that they can't fly.

The word *recognize* means to know again as if for the first time. Much of the process of recognition that is suggested in this book takes the form of having "conversations of discovery" with your child. In order to do this, you will need to unlearn everything you've learned about your children that has led you to think of them as "chickens."

Here's a brief practice that demonstrates the challenge of this kind of unlearning:

- Fold your hands with your fingers interlaced the way you always did when you were being "good" in school.
- Bring awareness to your hands—that is, notice whether your right thumb is on top of the left or the reverse.
- Slowly, unlace them from this habitual position and relace them in the nonhabitual way—that is, if right was on top of left, reverse it so now left is on top of right.
- Go back and forth several times, noticing which one feels more comfortable. Which one feels safer?

Most people find the habitual way more comfortable and say it feels safer.

- As you repeat the lacing and unlacing, ask yourself: "Which way do my hands seem more alive? Which way can I feel the spaces between my fingers? If there were danger, which way could I move my hands the quickest?"

Most people find the nonhabitual way brings the most aliveness and awareness to their hands, and results in the quickest reaction time. (Which implies that the nonhabitual way might actually be safer, because you can move more quickly to avoid danger.)

- Slow down a little and notice what happens the moment you shift from the habitual to the nonhabitual way—when your fingers are unlaced and trying to find the new way.

The awkwardness of this placement is exactly what it is like to "unlearn" a way of thinking, to open your mind and shift your perception from a deficit focus to one of noticing assets or strengths. You may have had a particular way of thinking for years, decades. Changing your mind requires patience and compassion.

There are three basic practices that will enable you to recognize your child's gifts and talents: clearing your mind, opening your mind, and establishing an empathetic connection with him or her. This chapter describes these practices as well as what we mean when we talk about a child's assets.

Taming Your Rational Mind

"You cannot solve a problem with the same consciousness that created it."

—ALBERT EINSTEIN

Several years ago, there was a fiftieth birthday party for the Golden Gate Bridge in San Francisco. Traffic was stopped and hundreds of people stood in the center of the bridge, silently waiting for the mayor's speech. Before he could begin, a strange humming sound filled the air. "What's that?" someone shouted. "Listen," someone else said, "the bridge is singing. It's singing itself 'Happy Birthday!'" Everyone laughed, of course, but in the hush that followed, it was apparent that the bridge *was* singing. One old man who had been present at the opening of the bridge a half century before called out, "The same thing happened back then. When we opened the bridge." People turned to face him. "It's true. The bridge is like a harp. The wind plays it all the time, but you can only hear the music when all the traffic is stopped."

As humans, we have a highly developed capacity at our disposal: the ability to be aware. But awareness is no more available to us than the bridge's song was audible to the partygoers if we don't stop the traffic of our own minds. In order to find the song in the souls of our children, we must develop ways to silence the static of blame, judgment, and fear.

When the water of a lake is very still, it is possible to see the bottom very clearly. If the wind ruffles the surface, our vision becomes obscured. Recognizing our children's gifts is an essential and challenging responsibility. The thoughts of what has happened in the past, what might happen in the future, the labels you and others use to describe your child are like the wind. To perceive our children's potential, we must create an internal mental stillness, where interferences to our clarity dissolve.

Before dealing with these interferences, however, it is important to understand how lack of clarity might serve us. It gives us an immediate sense of security. A quick explanation is simpler than a complex exploration through the unknown. Put in a box, the unknown can appear to be contained. "Oh, so that's what's wrong with my child. It's not my fault he's having trouble. He doesn't have to struggle until I figure out how to make things easier for him. I don't have to feel helpless." This box becomes the place in which we can lock away all of our anxieties.

It may lock away our worries, but it also blinds and limits our awareness of what is possible. Our perceptions were similarly boxed in when we were taught to color inside the black lines of a predrawn tree. This freed us from any worries about how to deal with the blank page. It also made it impossible for us to represent the unique ways we perceived the glorious form of a tree.

What is the way, then, to calm the interfering thoughts and labels that arise in your mind when you face the unknown of how to guide your child? Fighting with these thoughts, or reasoning with them, only creates more ripples. What is most effective is to just become neutrally aware of them, in the same way you were when you laced and unlaced your fingers. "Oh, there's a story I'm telling myself that Sally will never get into an advanced placement math class if she doesn't memorize the multiplication tables tonight. Isn't that interesting? Now let me notice what she *is* doing well in this moment." Simply observe what your mind is telling you—"Isn't that interesting?"—and bring your own attention back to the present.

The human mind, like the surface of a lake, is never still. Winds come and go; thoughts and feelings, stories and explanations come and go. It's not possible to *stay* calm or *stay* clear. All that's necessary is to simply notice the interferences that are present, one by one, notice your breath, and within a minute or two, your mind will settle down. The storm will pass.

Taming your mind like this for a few minutes before you engage in the recognition practices suggested in this book produces clarity, and helps you approach your child with an open mind. Remember, it's just practice. Simple.

Aiming Your Curiosity, Opening Your Mind

"It is, in fact, nothing short of a miracle that the modern methods of instruction have not entirely strangled the holy curiosity of inquiry."
—ALBERT EINSTEIN

Two more conditions were necessary in order for the people standing on the bridge to hear it sing once the traffic had stopped: Someone had to ask a question that aimed everyone's attention to the sound, and all had to listen with the kind of "holy curiosity of inquiry" that Einstein refers to.

When he was fifteen, Einstein asked, "What do you suppose it would be like if you could sit on the front end of a beam of light and travel with it through the night?" This is called an open question, because it evokes the human mind to open and listen in fascination. Einstein wasn't the only one to ask open questions. It is, in fact, a natural way for the human mind to open itself and wonder. It has been used through the ages by poets, artists, scientists, philosophers, musicians, mystics, and people falling in love! It evokes relational thinking at its best. We have been trained out of it by standardized thinking that insists every question must not only have an answer, but the *right* answer.

What are the characteristics of an open question? First of all, there is no "right answer." Second, there are no hidden agendas behind it, just true curiosity and wonder. Third, open questions make others want to open up instead of shut up.

Here are several "closed" questions I heard this morning while walking Shaka, our golden retriever, in a local playground. A group of children were roughhousing on the swing set. Their parents shouted to them from a bench.

"Johnny, are you sure you want to do that?"

"Rebecca, what *are* you doing?"

"Hunter, don't you think you should stop now?"

"Tiffany, why did you hit Logan?"

None of these are open questions. Many of us have difficulty framing questions that are not advice in disguise. An open question is one you ask without possibly being able to say to yourself, "I know the answer to this question and I sure hope this child gives it to me." An open question expands rather than limits thinking. It doesn't try to urge the child in any particular direction. Open questions are grounded in respect because they imply that inside the child there is a source of developing wisdom and curiosity.

One father firmly escorted a sheepish-looking six-year-old to a nearby oak tree and sat down next to him. Placing his hand on his son's back, he sat quietly for a moment. Then he asked, "What are you feeling right now, Mark?"

Mark shrugged. His father waited quietly. Finally, the boy said, "I'm really mad because Johnny took the swing away from me. Just 'cause he's bigger he thinks he can have my swing."

His father nodded and then asked, "Have you ever had something like this happen to you before?"

Mark replied, "Well, yeah, in school during recess."

His father nodded again and asked, "What did you learn then that could help you now?"

Mark answered quickly, "I socked that kid right in the stomach and he started to cry and then the teacher came over and then I got in trouble and had to have a time out."

His father asked, "How did you feel then?"

"At first I felt good because I showed that kid he couldn't take away my swing, but when I got punished, the good feeling turned bad."

His father rubbed Mark's back and asked, "So what did you learn then that could help you now?"

Mark looked up at his dad and grinned before answering, "If I'm gonna hit another kid, I'd better do it when no grown-ups are around!"

The incident touched me. It wasn't the perfect way to resolve the fight. I'm not really sure what the perfect way to do that would be. Solving one problem for a child only means you will have a thousand more to resolve in the next week. But unless we help our children learn to solve their own problems from the inside out through asking open questions, they'll continue to rely on outside sources for answers the rest of their lives.

Open questions focus more on the child than on the problem. Because the way Mark's father asked questions implied that the answers were inside his son, the boy felt respected enough to begin to think his own way through the problem. Since Mark's initial affront was someone bigger taking away something that was his, he now had an experience of someone bigger, his father, returning something that was his, self-respect.

Open questions need to be accompanied by open listening. Neither are passive. Both are receptive and engaged. Barbara was trying to ask her daughter Stephanie some questions about what her successes have been. Barbara's natural rhythm of speaking and thinking was upbeat. She was revved high most of the time, like the rapids of a river in the spring. Stephanie's natural rhythm of speaking, on the other hand, was like the Mississippi in August, wide rolling and easy. There were long pauses between her sentences.

Barbara asked a question, Stephanie twirled her hair around her finger, looked out the window, inhaled . . . and Barbara jumped in. "You know, honey, you won all those swim races . . . don't you think that's a success? What about those poems you wrote last month . . . and you've learned how to knit and play soccer really well. . . ." Stephanie nodded, and like a deer spooked in the forest, retreated further into herself.

When Barbara and I talked about it later, she was not happy with how she had listened to Stephanie. "How would you have preferred to be?" I asked. She told me she just didn't have the patience to wait for her "slowpoke" daughter. I asked her if she had ever been patient in that way. Without hesitation, she said, "Not since I was a kid. My father was in the military and he demanded I answer him as quickly as any soldier would. I never had to salute or anything, but I'd get whacked if I didn't answer up immediately."

I asked her if anyone had ever been patient with her in the way she'd like to be with Stephanie. Her fingers unconsciously began to twirl her long black hair before she answered. The corners of her mouth tilted up as she said, "Now that you mention it, what first attracted me to Phil, my husband, was his slow and easy way of speaking and listening to me."

Like Barbara, few of us have experienced this kind of open inquiry, except, perhaps, when we fall in love. Conversations of discovery demand that we put our love into practice, unencumbered by the limitations of our history.

The most effective way to begin is within your own mind. Notice the kinds of questions you ask yourself, and the kind of listening you do when your mind responds. If you'd like to begin now, here's an open question to yeast the practice: "What do you hope your love will create?"

Now, as if approaching a deer in the woods, just listen patiently for whatever emerges.

Claiming Your Relational Mind

"When surveyed, the majority of students who were having problems believed that their teachers didn't like them, that no one cared, that their work was irrelevant and had no value. The majority of parents said they knew there were problems, they wanted to do things differently, but they didn't know how. What they ranked as most important was learning how to understand their children and be understood by them."

—WILLIAM GLASSER, EDUCATOR

In the research labs, neuroscientists are discovering that a particular cluster of neurons is specifically designed to mirror another's bodily intentions and emotions. We're hardwired, it appears, to feel one another's happiness and pain more deeply than we ever knew. This news is both exciting and humbling. It means we are truly born to connect. Facial expressions, for example, are contagious. When baby smiles, Mom does as well. Such mirroring affects the nervous system and conveys emotions. People commonly, if unconsciously, copy one another's breathing patterns and body posture.

Neuroscientists now think they can locate the site of empathy in the brain, a network of what are called "mirror neurons," first discovered in monkeys. They appear to actually reflect the activity of another's brain cells. Subsequent research suggests that humans, too, may have a similar mirror neuron system that allows us to deeply "get" the experience of others. When you watch another person jiggle his foot, reach for a glass, or bite into an apple, the sectors of your brain that turn on are the same sectors that activate when you perform these behaviors yourself. It is thought that emotions displayed by others are also felt inside you and therefore implicitly understood through a mirror-matching mechanism in the brain. Soon, scientists will discover this network, which establishes, beyond a doubt, that we're born to resonate with one another at the deepest emotional levels.

As a psychologist, I am excited by this finding. As a mother and grandmother, my reaction is more "Oh, that old thing?" I could feel what my son was feeling in my body from the moment he was born. He could frequently "scan" me and know what I was feeling long before I did myself. Empathy is the connective tissue of parenting. It's what enables us to establish a bond of trust with our children and to meet them with our hearts as well as our minds. Empathy enhances our insights, sharpens our hunches, and at times even allows us to "read" one another's minds.

While neuroscientists continue the work of confirming these promising findings and theories, parents can begin now to apply them so they can empathize more effectively and strategically with their children.

If we are truly designed to mirror one another's feelings, we parents may be particularly vulnerable to "catching" our child's rage, anxiety, sadness, and fear. And our children may be hardwired to catch ours! Given this nature of empathy, how do we say yes or no to its effects on us? What steps might we take to harness and channel this natural-born capacity for the good of our children—and ourselves?

Empathy is experienced in the body. Therefore, the more mindful a parent can be of his or her own bodily responses and sensations, the more skillfully the parent can choose to engage mirror neurons to gain valuable information about a child's emotional state. Equally important, a parent can choose to slow down or even halt his or her brain's rush to empathize when it might overwhelm the child or the parent.

Notwithstanding the river of words that flow through your family home, it's the sight of your child looking unhappy or tense or relieved or enraged that really gets your mirror neurons firing. And this is equally true the other way around, as we shall see.

Empathy can be a bit of a tightrope act. You can easily lose your balance and crash to earth. When my son would come home from school "down" after having had a fight with his best friend John, I would listen empathetically and offer milk and cookies. He'd go outside and ride his bike, feeling better for the love and attention, but often I had a case of "emotional infection." It was as if a mysterious dark cloud had crossed my own sky for the rest of the day. My mirror neurons had done their job too well. I believe this kind of brain-to-brain communication occurs at an unconscious level between parents and their children all the time.

There's liberation here as well as limitation, because once you are aware of what is going on, you can "come back" to yourself in a matter of moments. Martial artists call this "centering." What's involved can be as simple as doing any one or a combination of the following: Take a few deep breaths, feel the sensations in your own body, feel your own center of gravity in your pelvis, doodle, look at the details of your own hand, listen to a favorite piece of music, hum a song to yourself, touch your heart tenderly, or think of a time when you felt truly connected and spacious inside. Once you choose to become actively aware of your own sensations and feelings, you will come out of sync with your child, as if you are employing an empathy "shut-off" valve. Rather than short-circuiting empathy altogether or seeing it as a handicap, knowing how to turn it on and off can enable you to get to a place of clarity and presence when you want.

This river of empathy runs two ways. Our children unconsciously mimic our posture and body movements and take on our corresponding emotional states. When you slow your breathing down, for example, your child, by engaging his mirror neurons, may calm down. Your serenity, therefore, is contagious and so is your anxiety.

I have a friend, Dora, who has always been told that she is "too sensitive." (What artist or poet or mother hasn't been told the same thing?) One day, I watched her silently calm her own fear while embracing her young frightened son, Jacob. The effect was mutual. Dora's breathing slowed and then Jacob's breathing slowed. Dora's voice got deeper, Jacob's cries became murmurs. She rocked him rhythmically and her shoulders relaxed as his did. This resonance born of voice, smile, tears, and touch is encoded in us far more deeply than we ever knew. Perhaps discovering these tiny vessels of empathy, mirror neurons, will help us to name, claim, and aim one of the most exciting challenges of parenthood—attuning two brains and two hearts so they vibrate together without merging into each other.

Please note that sympathy is not the same as empathy. Merging into each other is what is commonly called "sympathy," where the essence of two becomes one. When the individual essence of each is maintained, the connection is called "empathy."

Objectivity balances our rational mind and helps it to focus on the details of a given situation. Empathy, when centered like two wings on a bird's back, helps our relational mind balance and lift above a situation to see it from the widest perspective possible. If I hadn't been able to establish an empathetic connection with Jerome, I never would have been able to walk in his shoes, see the world through his eyes, recognize his gift, and help him utilize it to learn to read. It was his empathetic connection with the bird that helped the boy in the African folktale recognize its potential and believe it could fly beyond the cage in which it was imprisoned. It was the father's empathetic connection with his son that gave him the patience and faith to return Mark's self-respect.

Asset-Focused Conversations of Discovery

> *"Our lives begin to end the day we become silent about things that matter."*
>
> —MARTIN LUTHER KING JR.

When we think of assets, we usually think about money in the bank or property, and natural resources such as oil or gold. But every human being also has personal assets—gifts of the heart, mind, and body that are an individual's true wealth. The more a person understands what these are and develops them, the richer his or her life will be.

Every child has a unique way of being smart: particular talents, strengths, and conditions that are natural to follow when he or she learns. Being ineffective and going against a child's grain is what squanders human resources. A willingness to wonder and be curious with a child about how to use his or her assets to overcome challenges increases effectiveness.

Every child has potential that, when used effectively, can become a fulfilling, purposeful, and joyful contribution to the world. A child's assets are transportable gifts—internal resources that can be drawn upon wherever he or she is in the world, whatever he or she chooses to do in life.

In the chapter that follows, by using open questions and empathy you'll be able to have conversations of discovery with your child about these assets. I have arranged them into five categories for ease of remembering.

- **S**uccesses and Skills: your child's accomplishments
- **M**ind Patterns: what helps your child concentrate, make decisions, and imagine new possibilities
- **A**ttractions and Interests: the ongoing things that interest your child
- **R**esources: the people, places, and things outside your child that are available as support to him or her, as well as the inner resources developed from facing challenges and overcoming obstacles
- **T**hinking Talents: innate ways of thinking that your child excels at and is energized by

Children whose assets have been recognized and supported are strong learners who trust their own abilities; they know and can explain how they learn and recognize what they need in any given situation. They can maximize both internal and external resources to satisfy those needs. They have ready access to their inventiveness, courage, intuition, and concentration. They know how to solve problems creatively, to care for themselves, to think well with others, to motivate themselves, and to evaluate their own performance. They know they matter, they know they are important, they know they can make a difference in the world. This is the birthright of every child.

For many of us, recognizing assets requires unlearning previous training. My grandparents believed that if you spoke about these positive things, the dark spirits would come and take away your wonderful child. In some cultures, it is thought that noticing a child's talents means they will be "too full of themselves" or think they are superior to others. But knowing how much money you have in the bank doesn't mean someone will steal it or that you'll go around bragging about how rich you are. It just helps you to know what's available for you to spend.

Recognizing your child's assets does not require that you become a different or better parent; merely that you shift what you are paying attention to. Rather than worrying that your child won't measure up to other children, won't get into a good college, won't do well on the test, you can "worry well," by thinking about what he or she *does* do well and wondering how to grow that. You and your child will be having conversations that will help you both investigate the pattern of what works and apply it to situations where something doesn't work.

It is important to understand that recognizing assets is not the same as giving praise or compliments. As I'm using it in this book, to praise is to give generalized compliments about a child in order to make him or her feel good. "You're so cute." "What a handsome young man." "Oh, your picture is beautiful." I think of praise like candy. It may taste good, but it doesn't nourish. Consuming too much can spoil a child's appetite. Recognizing assets, on the other hand, is noticing what *specifically* is true about a child's abilities, what he or she has accomplished, learned, and achieved, his or her patterns of success. A father, when shown his five-year-old daughter's drawing says, "Oh, that's beautiful; it should go in a museum." He is giving praise. On the other hand, if he were to ask her questions about what made it fun, what part she liked the best, what she learned while she was drawing it, he would be holding a conversation of discovery that would help her recognize her own assets. Unlike praise, this type of true recognition nourishes a child's inherent sense of self-worth, the understanding that he or she possesses certain gifts, and it is his or her responsibility to share them with the rest of the world.

It's also important to note here that choosing this positive focus does not mean you are positive all the time. Rather, it implies that your ultimate goal is to relate in a way that has the most positive effect possible on both you and your child. It also means that you are willing to assume that there is what researcher/author David Cooperrider calls a "positive change core" inside of both of you. Like a plant turning toward the light, when given the right conditions growth springs from this core.

Recognizing children's assets is a practice that you learn by unlearning. Most of us have spent decades being trained to think about what's wrong, until it seems "natural" and habitual. We are skilled in focusing on problems and what needs to be changed. You don't have to stop doing that. In the same way we have both a right and a left hand that complement each other, we can practice the habit of tracking what is working to balance our expertise in tracking what isn't. This takes patience, as it would if you tried to write or brush your teeth with your non-dominant hand.

The next section of this book focuses on specific conversations that will help you and your child discover the pattern of his or her natural intelligence and passion to learn. Rather than being a passenger in a bus driven by someone else to a predetermined destination, you will drive your own vehicle, at your own rhythm. Each chapter will invite you to pull off the highway at a rest stop to get a wider perspective on the whole landscape of your children's capacities. Some will be brief, some more extended, but in each you will find new and fruitful terrain for conversations of discovery. It will not be stressful. What will happen is that your focus will gradually expand from one of only noticing insufficient results to one of seeing the ways you can help your children use their gifts to enjoy the total experience of learning.

Inspiration

Jacob Komar, Hartford, Connecticut

At two years of age, Jacob typed DOS commands on a computer. At six, he could take a computer apart and put it back together. At nine, when a school custodian showed him a garage full of desktop computers bound for recycling, Jacob started a program to refurbish broken computers and give them away to needy families. By twelve years of age, he was a sophomore in college and he had donated two hundred computers. He took the idea to local community-service organizations, which have provided a running list of applicants. Now he teaches other kids to follow in his footsteps. "You cannot imagine," Jacob says, "how good it makes you feel to help other people."

Contact: www.computers4communities.org

You Can't Learn to Swim on a Piano Bench: Smart Family Practices

For the human mind to integrate new learning, it must be multidimensional—that is, it must be seen, heard, and experienced (although not necessarily in that order, as we shall discover in the next chapter). Dr. Milton Erickson, a brilliant clinician and masterful teacher of medical hypnotherapy, used to say, "You may think you can swim if you're sprawled across a piano bench, but if you really want to learn, you've got to get in the water." From this chapter on, the practices offered will invite you to get wet in your own home, practicing with your own family. Though it might be exquisitely awkward at first, it is this experience that will integrate the learning and make it yours.

Clearing Your Mind

Choose one regular time that you commit to clear your mind and focus your attention on yourself and your child. It may be just three minutes every Wednesday morning when you take him to school, or two minutes while running her bathwater. Underwhelm yourself. What's important is making a commitment to practice.

Opening Your Mind

During one conflict or troubling situation, ask your child, in a curious tone of voice, the following open question: "What do you really need right now?" They will probably shrug or say they don't know. That's fine. Just patiently encourage them to think about it and then come to you when they *do* know. If they don't come back to you, ask the question again the next day. And the day after that. Persisting curiously lets them know you really mean it.

Variation: Pick a time when you feel angry about something. Take three minutes to breathe and sit back, watching your own mind as if it were a Punch and Judy puppet show (instead of being in the show and acting out your anger). *Have* the feeling instead of *being* the feeling. Rather than blaming or punishing, feel the sensations in your body and sit back as an audience member who is watching and listening to the show. You may need to pace in the back row. That's fine, just remember to ask yourself compassionately, "What do I need right now?" Wait patiently for the response to emerge.

Establishing an Empathetic Connection

Think of one time you felt deeply connected to your child in a wholesome and wonderful way. Allow that time and place to become very vivid in your mind, as if you stepped into the memory. This is the opposite of the above practice, where you stepped out of a negative feeling. Here you step into a positive feeling, because it is a desired state you want to feel.

Ask yourself what symbol would represent this feeling. It may be a visual image, a song, a phrase, or a particular place you touch on your body.

Find one time during the next week when you are with your child. Bring the symbol to mind, as if it were an icon for a software program, so you can evoke that feeling of connection.

Having an Asset-Focused Conversation

Sit next to your child as you tuck him or her into bed, each of you sharing three things that went right during the day.

SECTION TWO

Listening in the Place Where the Music Is Born

"In the millions of years that have passed, there has never been another like you. . . . You are a miracle because you are unique."

—Pablo Casals, cellist

It is said there is a tribe of artisans living on the east coast of Africa that is known all over the continent for its fine carvings, as well as the unusual way in which they craft them.

As the sun rises over the Indian Ocean, the people gather in small groups on the edge of a crescent-shaped golden beach. They cluster around a large chunk of dark native wood. As the waves slide in and out over the glistening sand, each member of the tribe gets quite still. One at a time, they place their hands on the wood, tilting their heads to one side, then the other. It is said they are listening for the song that is captured in the wood.

After many long minutes of this listening, someone picks up a carving tool, then another does the same. A third squats on her haunches and begins to rock back and forth slowly. When this happens, it is said that the song's whisper has been heard. One or two of the people begin to carve away everything that interferes with its release. Several sit very still, listening to the song emerge. Chips fly as others gouge deep into the wood. Some file rough spots smooth, eliminating whatever seems to cause static. All are supporting the work of the whole. All are guided by the growing clarity of what they hear. The carving is considered complete when the whole tribe can hear and sing the song.

It is said that these people do not think of themselves as wood-carvers, but as liberators of the song that waits in the wood.

The art of parenting lies in remembering that, like the African tribe, we don't have to create the song that waits within our child, we just have to recognize and liberate it. The artisans also remind us that we need one another to search for and release that song, to polish and enable the gifts children bring to the world so they can become the music of our collective future. Fortunately, you're not alone. There's a community of people around you who can help with the conversations of discovery in which you'll be engaged—neighbors, aunts/uncles, siblings, grandparents, cousins, friends, coaches, teachers, janitors—anyone who has had any experience with your child might have some valuable input and perspective on his or her assets. You merely have to ask them and then listen.

I'd like to ask you to consider partnering with your child in this recognition process by searching for your own assets as well. In this way, you are not doing something "to" your child but "with" him or her. Chances are, you may discover your child has assets that are similar to your own, but also ones that are very different. One mother told me how surprised she was to discover that the child she thought was "so much like her" did actually have a similar way of processing information, but a very different way of approaching problems. She realized that these similarities and differences had been at the root of both the connection and conflict between them.

My son, David, as I mentioned earlier, is a procedural genius. He organizes everything, is always on time, and is neat as a pin. To say those are not my talents is a gross understatement. I am creatively chaotic, incurably defiant. My sister Joan, however, has many of the same assets as David does. Since she is seven years older than me, our differences frequently created a great deal of tension between us as we grew up. Each time David asserted his natural procedural brilliance, therefore, I would unconsciously be reminded of my "superior" sister and want to wring his neatly pressed neck. In coming to realize how our differences could complement each other, I now can frequently call on his logical mind and benefit immensely from it, and he has learned to appreciate how I can be of use when he wants to experience flights of fancy.

When you and your child are engaged in the conversations of discovery in the following five chapters, you'll be leading with inquiry and influence. Jazz musician Stephen Nachmanovitch offers a potent description of the feel of such an improvisational collaboration: "I play with my partner. We listen to each other. We mirror each other; we connect with what we hear. We anticipate, sense, follow, and lead each other. We open each other's minds like an infinite series of Chinese boxes. . . . What comes is a revelation to both of us."

You may not think of yourself as a musician, but nature is on your side, encouraging you to liberate the song that waits within you. The latest research in neuroscience indicates that any time we engage in an experience that develops our capacity or helps another human being in some meaningful way, there is a release of endorphins as well as the possibility of "neurogenesis"—new cell growth. Because both of these experiences promote the development of our species, nature reinforces them by giving us a rush of good feeling as well as making new neurons, which increase our capacity to reduce our own pain. Recognizing your own assets and collaborating with your child to do the same thing will feel good to you and is good for the world.

Each of the next five chapters is an inquiry into one particular domain of personal assets. There are reflective questions and examples. Some of you will want to read through the whole section first to get an overall perspective and then go back and begin the step-by-step process. Others will want to dig right in, reflecting on each chapter, and letting your reflections prompt conversations of discovery with your child.

To facilitate your joint involvement I suggest you begin by making a commitment with your child to become thinking partners so you can learn about learning together. This commitment puts you both on the same side. The basic message to deliver, *in your own words,* is: "I want to help each of us find out what our special talents and gifts are and how we learn best. I think that we can discover a lot about how we're alike and how each of us is unique. We can do this by investigating some questions that will help us notice what works and what doesn't work. We can do it for (*fill in how long and how often—for example, fifteen minutes every Saturday*). Are you willing to do this with me for (*fill in a set time—for example, a month*)?"

Create a one-sentence commitment in simple language that states why you are doing this together. It can be as simple as: "We agree to spend the next three months finding out more about the special ways each of us learns and thinks." Once you've developed the sentence and put it in writing, make sure you both sign it and shake on it.

Experience tells me that this will be easier than you might think. All human beings like learning and developing themselves. Most of us welcome the chance to reflect and compare notes about what we do well and how we do it. Our differences and our similarities fascinate us.

After you've made this commitment together, begin to work your way through this section, chapter by chapter. You don't need to go in sequence. I've chosen to place first the one most people find easiest to think of. It is meant to be a short and easy beginning step to give you confidence in the rest of the journey. Depending upon age and experience, your child may be more or less aware of how she or he does what he does. At various points in our development, we have more ability to step back from what we are doing and observe it, name it, or talk about it. If he or she seems completely unaware of assets in a particular area, begin with your own assets and then you can name specifically what you have noticed or what others have told you about your child. At some point, he or she will be able to add more observations. This awareness of one's successes, strengths, and talents is a muscle to be exercised, one that will develop over time. It may be very general at first: "I got a good mark on my spelling test." Later, it may get more sophisticated: "I make pictures in my mind that help me remember the words. I know it's right when I hear it. Movement helps me concentrate."

Decide together what would be the most fun way to track what you are learning. You may want to set up a journal. Your child may wish to create a scrapbook or make a collage. One family I know tape recorded their observations each week and when they were finished, they transferred what they had learned to a "Smart Guide" folder they kept on their computer. Another made a simple video that they added to each year on the child's birthday. It became a family ritual that celebrated how much growth had taken place from one year to the next.

Follow your own rhythm and that of your child through this process. Sometimes your excitement will propel you forward quickly, as if you're traveling on a superhighway. At other times, you'll need to slow down, as if you're lazily meandering on a country road. Remember that it is the simple attention we give to each other that helps us grow. One open question with that kind of attention can yield a great deal of awareness. "Remember that thing we were talking about last week about what helps me concentrate? Well, I've been noticing that I do think better if I'm walking around and letting my eyes look at whatever they want to."

Most important of all, remember there is no way either of you can fail in this adventure. There are no wrong answers. The process itself doesn't "take time." It creates space from the daily rush and fearful frenzy. It will help both of you breathe easier, as if you have more room inside to think, to connect with yourselves and each other.

Chapter Five

Recognizing Skills and Successes

"As you wander on through life, sister/brother, whatever be your goal, keep your eye upon the doughnut, not upon the hole."
—THE MAYFLOWER DOUGHNUT SHOP, CHICAGO, ILLINOIS

We begin the recognition process with a short and easy chapter in the most familiar parenting domain, the skills and successes of our children. Most of us recognize skills—those learned capacities that enable us to do something we could not previously do—although we may not track them in a systematized way. We might put our children's spelling tests on our refrigerator, their trophies on the mantel. We might do the kinds of things most proud parents do—brag about our kids' successes, put stickers saying "My child is an honor student at Hillside Elementary School" on the bumpers of our cars. For instance, Mel the carpenter, who is helping us build a new kitchen, introduced me to his son Jayontay, and immediately told me how good he is in wrestling and how, even at eight years old, he excels in everything he learns through his body.

We may brag and be proud of our children's successes, but this chapter is about keeping an ongoing track record that can be drawn upon for his or her entire life, in the same way that we might keep track of their first lost tooth, first steps taken, or first words spoken. This is not just to make him or her feel good or let the world know you have a great child. It is meant to be part of an ongoing inventory of your child's assets, as you would do with your stocks or the contents of a safe-deposit box in a bank. I'll be asking you to think not only about customary skills and successes, but also to search in areas you might not think of. Noting how your child learned to ride a bike without training wheels, for example, can later be a valuable reference when he or she is trying to figure out how to learn to play soccer or the most natural way for him or her to overcome frustration or master traveling alone to school for the first time.

Consider having the first conversation about what skills each of you have in a nonhabitual way. Perhaps go for a walk together or do it while driving to the supermarket. Expand your field of inquiry beyond the obvious. You might be an accountant, so having learned to keep a balance sheet is something you'd mention first. Your child may also be good in math, but consider other domains, such as the performing arts, handicrafts, carpentry, auto mechanics, nature photography, debate, reading, sports, bicycle and motorcycle riding, pet care.

Think together about areas of emotional skill, such as learning how to direct your anger, being able to express what you're feeling. Jeremy, age four, was having lunch with his father in the neighborhood delicatessen. Mark realized his son had gained unexpected social skills when he followed the waiter behind the counter asking him what the kitchen looked like. Simone went on an Outward Bound trip and came back relating all the survival skills she had acquired. "I spent twenty days straight with no cell phone, no computer, and no TV!"

The second conversation focuses on successes. This may be a bit more challenging than the one about skills. We all know what failures are, because we have been trained so meticulously to avoid them, but we rarely stop to think about what a success really means to us. James, the owner of a sports equipment store, had never discussed with his fourteen-year-old daughter, Lia, what success meant to him. He assumed she knew. When he began this particular conversation as they were preparing dinner one evening, he told her that success to him meant being able to send his kids to college and live in a comfortable home. She was totally surprised. She said that she thought he would consider himself a success only if he had the biggest store in town. Further talk revealed that Lia considered something a success only if she was the best in it—the best field hockey player on her team or if she got the best score on a math test. Rather than try to change her mind, James came to realize they were each motivated differently, and reported that he had learned a new way to demonstrate his respect for her hard work.

Margaret had been directed by the school's learning specialist to focus on her twelve-year-old daughter Amy's deficits. She had taken her for an evaluation and the psychologist gave her a long report of her learning disabilities. "She's a sweet child, but don't set your hopes too high. With her auditory processing problems, and ADD, she'll probably always struggle with learning." This report became part of Amy's cumulative record and was engraved in Margaret's mind. All she could notice was each time Amy failed to listen or struggled to learn. When they began these conversations of discovery, therefore, both were awkward and groping. After ten or fifteen minutes, though, they began to get the hang of it. Margaret talked about her successes as a librarian and Amy followed with how she was the only student selected to help the veterinarian at the corner of their street care for the animals. Recognizing *how* she achieved that success will help Amy trust her capacity to learn and accomplish things that are now challenging to her.

Most of us keep a long and secret list in our minds of our children's failures that we're worried will develop into adult flaws: If Mariana doesn't stand up for herself, she'll get walked on her whole life; if Tommy continues to explode in frustration and doesn't learn to control his temper, he could end up in prison; if Tanya doesn't get out and make new friends, she could be a social outcast; if Max keeps on collecting baseball cards, he might end up with an obsessive-compulsive disorder. You might call each of these a parent's "worry list."

That's why tracking successes may be as simple as giving these worries a possible ending: Mariana settles an argument between her younger brother and sister. That's a success. Someday she might be a famous lawyer. Last week, Tommy was so mad he went outside to hit rocks with a plastic bat. He is learning to direct his frustration. That is a success. One day he could have the highest batting average on his Little League team. Tanya broke up with her boyfriend, but instead of dressing in black and moping for weeks on end, she had a good cry, then redecorated her room. She succeeded in healing her own heart. Max arranged all of his baseball cards in a suitcase. Then he exchanged them for a skateboard. He was successful at organizing and trading what he no longer wanted for something he did. Many stockbrokers would value such a success!

Think of keeping track of skills and successes as you would the bank statement of a savings account. Keep adding to it. We've been trained to make a case for everything that's wrong: "You never clean your room. You've been leaving your clothes on the floor for me to pick up since you could dress yourself. Remember last Christmas when we couldn't even open the door to your room?" Now it's time to look at the other side. "Hey! You picked up all your baseball cards today! Bravo! Last Thursday, I noticed you also picked up your socks. You're really learning to arrange your things so you know where everything is."

In addition, tracking one success will give both of you ideas for increasing success in other domains. "I just realized, Tiffany, that you haven't whined in three days. How did you do that? Let's figure it out. Maybe there's something we can discover that will help you grow those delicious fingernails you've been chewing."

It's worth mentioning that sharing some of your own personal successes, particularly in domains you've been struggling with, will encourage your child to do the same. "You know, Cliff, how I've been struggling with not being uptight when I play golf? Well, last Sunday, I discovered that if I sing to myself I don't get so frustrated. I played eighteen holes and didn't yell or throw my clubs once. I wonder how this could help me when I have to clean up the garage."

Recognizing successes in this way isn't bragging. It will teach your child that as a human, he or she will make mistakes and have challenges, but one of the most glorious things about being human is that we can learn both from those mistakes and from our successes.

Recognizing successes in the conversations of discovery that follow will help your child come to understand one of the most basic and important premises of self-worth: the difference between *being* and *doing*. As humans, any of us can and will make mistakes, sometimes ones that have a horrible effect. This does not mean we are horrible people. We also do things that have great effects. This does not mean we are great people. We are all just human beings, capable of doing horrible things and great things. Knowing this opens the way to risk ("I can risk doing something I've never done before without worrying that if I fail I'll *be* a failure"), forgiveness ("I can be forgiven if I do something that turns out to have a bad effect, because I can learn. I'm not a bad person"), and freedom to choose actions that will contribute to rather than detract from our lives.

Inspiration

Here are a few brief success stories to encourage you as you begin this exploration:

- Chilean poet Pablo Neruda began to write poetry at the age of ten, hiding it from his family, who did not approve of his literary ambitions. At twelve, he met poet Gabriela Mistral, who encouraged his efforts. This success encouraged him to keep going. As an adult, he was awarded the Nobel Prize for Literature.
- James Barrie, the author of *Peter Pan*, had a mother who was very depressed. He began telling stories to cheer her up. He was so successful that she encouraged him to tell his stories to the whole world.
- At two and a half years of age, singer and actress Judy Garland joined her older sisters onstage. She sang a solo of "Jingle Bells." The audience roared approval, and her family encouraged her to continue the success. That was all she needed to make the stage her home.
- When she was ten years old, Golda Meir, the former Israeli prime minister, organized a protest group against the required purchase of schoolbooks. They were too expensive for

the poorer children in her class, who were thus denied equal opportunity to learn. As a result of her efforts, the school reversed its policy. This success enabled her to continue her fight for justice for the rest of her life.

- Ella Fitzgerald, the queen of jazz, had her first success as a skinny sixteen-year-old. She had planned to dance at Amateur Night at the Harlem Opera House in New York, but she was so frightened that she sang instead. She won first prize and that success gave the rest of us one of the greatest performers of the twentieth century.

Conversations of Discovery

- Talk together about how each of you know when you have succeeded at something. Is it when you get a prize or reward? Are there other ways that might mean more to you? How are your definitions of success the same and how are they different?
- Here are some categories you might explore together in this treasure hunt for skills and successes:

School subjects

Sports

Games and crafts

Social skills (including making friends, being on time, being polite, etc.)

Music

The arts (including creative writing, photography)

Personal successes (including saving money, not biting nails, dealing with a bully, etc.)

Example: Nanci and her youngest daughter, Kendall, aged six, were discussing successes. Kendall was completely stumped. Her mother gave many examples from her own life, but Kendall couldn't think of a single one of her own. "I can't read real good like Jordan, and I can't do math good like Ashlie. I can't ski like Max or design clothes like Dana. So I guess I just don't have any successes."

Kendall's lower lip quivered and there was nothing Nanci could say to encourage her. She followed her daughter outside, where Kendall was leaning over a cage and feeding her pet rabbit carrots from their garden. Suddenly Nanci realized something and leaned over and whispered in Kendall's ear. Kendall began to giggle and then shouted, "I do have a success, Mom, you're right. Yay! My bunny is fat because I feed him carrots that I planted. My bunny is my success!" Sometimes we don't notice the successes right under our noses because they are different from everyone else's.

Inspiration

Jason Crowe, Newburgh, Indiana

Jason was always interested in things different from his peers. His grandmother was his best friend. She accepted him just as he was, listened to him talk about all his ideas, and encouraged all his interests, such as Greek mythology and fossils. She died of cancer when he was nine and a half. He couldn't control his crying. His parents finally suggested he help someone else so he could feel some control over something. Since his grandmother loved to read, he decided to start a neighborhood newspaper to pay tribute to her. He writes stories featuring kids who are making a difference in the world, and stories to convince other kids that they can make a difference. He writes about all the things he used to talk to his grandmother about: racial unity, science, geography, peace, and harmony. He sells the paper for three dollars, giving the proceeds to the American Cancer Society. The paper is now sold in twenty-eight states and fifteen foreign countries and is used by classroom teachers.

Jason wrote a story about Vedran Smailovic, a cellist in Bosnia, who played beautiful music for twenty-two days on the exact spot that twenty-two people were bombed waiting in line for bread. He then organized a cello concert at the University of Evansville with twenty-two cellists, a memorial service on the fifth anniversary of the massacre, and decided to commission a statue of Mr. Smailovic playing his cello, from the kids of the world for Bosnia. Authors, educators, musicians, and entertainers from all over the world are supporting the statue, and many other kids are fundraising with Jason. Jason says, "I thank Nanny for always believing in me and for understanding me, even when I was very young. It doesn't take an adult to make a difference, and it doesn't take a president to bring peace to the world. It all starts with us—kids—and it all starts right around us—in our homes, neighborhoods, schools, and communities. All we have to do is reach out to help somebody, and we become part of the solution instead of part of the problem."

(For more information, or to make a contribution, contact The Cello Cries On, Inc., 619 Rose Dr., Newburgh, IN 47630.)

Chapter Six

Recognizing Mind Patterns

Understanding How Your Child Understands

"Learning is experience. Everything else is just information."
—ALBERT EINSTEIN

I've struggled with this particular chapter more than any other in the book because I've been studying, writing, and teaching about individuals' different mind patterns for four decades. Each time I do, I'm grossly dissatisfied, because I know how important it is, and I feel the responsibility to find new ways to explain it that are more effective, powerful, simple, and clear. I've written three books and numerous articles about the subject and still I've been giving myself an unduly hard time for a week now.

This morning, the sky of my mind opened up, realizing that I can never share it perfectly, but my job is to just keep carving away, removing as much static as possible so the songs of even more children will be liberated. Your job, should you decide to accept, is to pick and choose what works best for you from what follows. Some of you will skip right to the game and charts at the end of the chapter, some will want a more technical explanation and the reasons behind these mind patterns. And others may just want to read the stories and save the rest until later. Knowing you will allow yourself to select what enhances your understanding and disregard the rest frees me up to include as much as possible for all readers.

The truth is that it may be a very long time before we are truly able to unravel the wondrous mysteries of the human mind. But there are new insights available now, thanks to the cascade of neuroscientific observations in recent years that help point the way to the fullest development of our capacities. What follows is my understanding of the different patterns the mind uses to learn, think, and communicate, based on those findings and the experiences of myself and my colleagues.

For forty years, I've been noticing how each child's mind is like a unique musical instrument and wondering how to help him or her play it most effectively.

We take it for granted that you play a guitar in a different way than you play the violin. But still, to this day, we assume that each human mind is played in the same fashion.

I remember being in the subway on my way to my student teaching job in Harlem and reading the book *Beyond Culture*, by anthropologist Edward Hall. As we clattered past 110th Street, Hall was describing how communicating with architects "who came alive in a world of paper" was so different from communicating with psychiatrists, who were lost in paper but "came alive in a world of words." "Aha!" I yelled, unaware that there were other people on the train. As the doors slid open at the next station, my mind was walking out into a whole new way of understanding individual differences in learning.

We may notice that some children love hands-on projects and others will always fill out worksheets when given a choice. We may realize that some kinds of information stay with us longer than others, but most of us have no idea why this is true. Why does Kendall love to hold on to something when she is reading and Jordan always want to listen to music while doing her homework? Why could Jerome learn to read when he was pacing back and forth and having words traced on his back but not when he was sitting still?

One of the biggest misconceptions we suffer from is the assumption that all human beings use the same process for understanding. Obviously, we all think different thoughts. Not so obviously, we all have unique ways of thinking those thoughts. In school, little attention is given to how children think. In the model I'd like to share with you, there are six possible patterns of accessing and processing information. Coming to recognize them can open a symphony of possibilities for you and your child.

It's important to say here that the human brain is, in fact, nothing like the personal computer it designed. It doesn't process information and construct images by manipulating strings of digits such as zeros and ones. Instead it is largely composed of maps of feelings, sights, conversations, etcetera. Most of what we call "understanding" or "thinking" involves the interaction of maps from many parts of the brain at once. It is much more like an ecosystem than a machine. We also know that rather than using the predictive logic of microchips, the brain is an analog processor, meaning that it works by analogy and metaphor, as well as anecdotes.

As we explore these different patterns of thinking and understanding, which I call "mind patterns," it's important that we don't confuse the map with the territory, or better yet, the signposts with the trail. I have identified six patterns, and that has served me in very good stead over the past forty years in helping people be more effective. In any case, they are only signposts. They have nothing to do with personalities. They are not meant to put people in boxes or in pigeonholes. They are not related to birth dates, planetary alignment, gender, religious affiliation, or cultural bias. This model focuses entirely on the way we think, learn, understand, and communicate. It is meant to be used to liberate and expand human capacity. As the adage says, "Never confuse the finger pointing to the moon with the moon." The human mind is a miracle and a mystery that one can only hope to wander with awe and reverence.

The accepted wisdom has always been that the key to success in life is to know yourself. This still remains one of the most basic truths. To know ourselves, we must become good self-observers. Since every brain is different, and since each of us has a unique way of perceiving the world, if we want to empower our children, we begin by asking questions that will help us understand how thought moves through each of our minds in different states of attention. We'll then explore the different modes of perception that trigger those states.

Giving Attention to Attention

> *"The mind fits the world and shapes it as a river fits and shapes its own banks."*
>
> —ANNIE DILLARD, NATURALIST AND AUTHOR

Most of us know that children need attention. We may even realize that different children need different kinds of attention: Winston circles his teacher, waiting for an arm around his shoulder. Sally holds out a paper to her grandmother, wanting her to look and see how well she has done. Andy whines until he hears a word of approval from his father.

We also know that children need to be "paying" attention in order to learn, but most of us don't know that there are different kinds of attention and all are important for learning. When we witness confusion and distraction, we have been taught to call it "inattention" or even "attention deficit," but what we are really witnessing is a mind turning attention inward. In order for new information to get fully digested, it must be chewed and swallowed, churned and sorted. This is what is happening, beneath the surface, when we feel confused and distracted.

In order to recognize the pattern your child's mind uses, it is first necessary to understand that there are three basic kinds of attention our minds use to think, learn, and communicate:

- *Focusing*, when we concentrate. Our brains produce more "beta waves" to do this. This is when we pay attention in an organized, external, detailed way and have the most mental stamina.
- *Sorting*, when we are wondering or are confused. Our brains produce more "alpha waves" to do this. This is when we pay attention externally as well as internally, and feel as if we're daydreaming, in two places at the same time, or thinking about things from two perspectives.
- *Imagining*, when we "space out." Our brains produce more "theta waves" when we do this. This is where we pay attention receptively and are highly sensitive, private, and most easily distracted. We are in our own world, and unconsciously thinking about the whole of things.

For a moment, consider a thought to be like a drop of water. It changes form, evaporating into clouds, pouring down on your umbrella, rushing down a mountainside into the stream that feeds the spring behind your house where you draw your water. Likewise, thought also changes form, moving from one attentional state to another. If I ask you to think of the beach you may get a distinct and precise thought, and then wonder which beach I mean and scan over several different ones you've visited, and then stare out the window as you remember that remarkable afternoon you spent at the shore several years ago, when the warm water was lapping at your toes and the breeze was caressing . . . minutes go by without your noticing as you melt into that moment. What has happened is that your "thought" was changing form, shifting from "beta attention," where it was condensed and distinct, concentrating on one thing, to "alpha attention," where it was sorting and going back and forth, to "theta attention," where it was dispersing and you had the experience of being somewhere else inside your mind.

"Changing your way of thinking" is in fact true. It happens remarkably quickly and we barely even notice when our mind shifts from one state of attention to another. Unfortunately, most of us have been led to believe that we are learning only when we are paying attention in the alert, outward-focused beta mode. We have been trained to assume that sorting alpha attention (when our minds "understand" something), as well as wandering theta attention (when new ideas are generated), is a waste of time. We refer to both alpha and theta attention negatively as being confused and distracted.

My research indicates that each attentional state is part of what I call "mental metabolism," where your mind is taking in information, organizing it, digesting it, evaluating it, arranging it into new patterns and ideas, storing it, and then sorting it again to decide how to express it.

For example, when Jeffrey's teacher asks him a question, he looks away, and says nothing. That does not mean that he isn't paying attention. It probably means that his mind is digesting what he's heard, and "thinking" about it in an alpha state. Kendall, when writing a story, may stare out the window. That doesn't mean there is anything wrong with her, merely that she is "imagining," in a theta state of attention.

Therefore, taking information in and spitting it out as quickly as possible does not necessarily mean someone is learning. Concentrating, exploring, wondering, imagining, reflecting, deciding, expressing are all different parts of learning. They are all natural and different aspects of what could be called "smart thinking."

Smart Practice

Before we go any further, the most effective way to integrate this new information is to experience it. I invite you to put the book down for a few moments and just observe your own states of mind as they shift. It may all happen very quickly, in a split second, the way a river can move from apparent stillness to running over a rapid. At first you might only notice the shifting states of attention in hindsight: "Oh, I was just spaced out driving my car. I must have been in a theta state." Then you might notice while it's happening: "Interesting, I'm trying to decide what to wear and I'm going back and forth between the red shirt and the blue one. I bet I'm in alpha now." Finally, you may begin to notice when you're about to switch states: "I can't just daydream here, I've got a lot to do, I'd better get a move on. I'm about to concentrate on my list of things to do. Here I go into a beta state."

It may feel a bit awkward at first, the way shifting gears on a car is when you are learning, but soon you'll be noticing your friends, work associates, and especially your child shift from one state of attention to another.

Perceiving How We Perceive

"To begin to understand the gorgeous fever that is consciousness, we must try to understand the senses and what they can tell us about the ravishing world we have the privilege to inhabit."
—DIANE ACKERMAN, SCIENCE WRITER

All thinking is in fact multisensory, which means it involves aspects drawn from all of the sensory information our brains receive. The current theory is that when you have an experience, let's say visiting Disney World, the sensory input is first stored for the short term in one section of your brain, where it is encoded in something called "engrams," and then various aspects of that experience are stored in different places all over the brain: the visual in one, the words and their meanings in another, the things you did in another, etcetera. In this way, perhaps, evolution is assured that even if you injure one part of your brain, the whole experience will not be lost. Most of us just think that we are thinking, noticing the content of our thoughts but unaware of the multisensory quality of each thought.

Your Disney World engram includes linkages connecting each of these. Even if you and I have exactly the same experience, our recollections will be different because of the different ways in which our brains create representations and retrieve them. We "re-collect" the pieces differently. Three months later, I may first recollect what we saw, and then the things we said, and, lastly, what we did. You, on the other hand, may remember the things we did first and then the things we saw. You may not even remember the conversations we had or the name of the hotel we stayed at. This sequence is an essential component of what I am calling "mind patterns."

These Mind Patterns, or ways of knowing, have three different perceptual modes: visual (sight), auditory (sound), and kinesthetic (including movement, touch, smell, and taste). Each of us is more aware of some of these than others. What opens the door to recognizing the Mind Patterns you and your child use is observing how each of these stimuli *affect your states of mind* and in what *sequence* your brain becomes aware of them.

The following charts describe each perceptual mode in detail.

VISUAL THINKING

Looking · Watching · Reading · Showing
Observing · Writing · Drawing

What Visual Thinking Means

Visual thinking means using your eyes and "insight" as the windows of your mind. Experience is processed through sight and visual images. When your mind is thinking this way, it is observing and seeing colors, visions, lines, maps, lists, views, perspectives, visualizations, drawings, the written word, diagrams, movies, charts, television, and photographs. Visual creativity involves setting ideas to paper, canvas, computer, or film.

The active and receptive modes of visual

Receptive:
Watching
Reading
Seeing
Being shown

Active:
Writing
Editing
Drawing
Photographing

AUDITORY THINKING

Listening • Telling • Discussing
Singing • Talking

What Auditory Thinking Means

Auditory thinking means using your ears as the telephone of your mind.
Experience is processed through words and sounds. When your mind is thinking this way, it is listening
to and participating in conversations, tones of voice, jokes, sounds, music, meanings and messages,
poems, stories, debates, speeches, lectures, and arguments. Auditory creativity involves
expressing consciousness with sound and/or words.

The active and receptive modes of auditory

 Receptive:
Listening
Hearing

 Active:
Storytelling   Telling jokes
Lecturing   Speaking
Singing

KINESTHETIC THINKING

Doing • Moving • Feeling
Hands-On • Sports • Making Things

What Kinesthetic Thinking Means

Kinesthetic thinking means functioning through hands, body, and movement. Experiences are collected in feelings, taste, actions, touch, texture, temperature, pressure, spatial awareness, sensitivity to energy, and smell. Kinesthetic creativity involves using hands and bodies to sculpt, garden, dance, carve, cook, build, etcetera.

The active and receptive modes of kinesthetic

Receptive:

Smelling   Experiencing
Tasting   physical
Feeling   environment
Sensing

Active:

Playing sports   Doing
Hands-on   Moving
Building   Making

Smart Practice

• Think back to an experience in your education that has stayed with you, one that you will never forget. Which of your senses were involved? Which were left out, if any?

One such experience for me was a field trip to a planetarium. Fifty years later, I can still see the huge telescope, the studded night sky arcing above us (visual), hear the velvet silence (auditory), feel the goose bumps on my arms and the intake of breath (kinesthetic) as I saw the entire Milky Way unfurled above me (visual). We were told the story (auditory) of how picking out and naming the constellations enabled humans to notice the movement of the galaxies. We each received a plastic model of the telescope as a souvenir (kinesthetic). All of my senses were involved and I couldn't wait to share the experience with my family.

• Now think of an experience in your schooling from which you remember very little.

I think about a high school math class in which the teacher talked in a flat voice (auditory) about a series of algebraic equations that were written on the blackboard (visual). We had to copy them down in our notebooks (visual) and spent forty-five minutes silently solving them—or trying to. Very little of my senses were invited into this math class or into the homework assignments that related to it.

• Bring to mind an area in school where your child is vividly engaged. What patterns do you notice?

Jeremy's mom told me that he related to the world by asking endless, juicy questions, even as a toddler. It's no surprise, then, that he got excited anytime he was in class discussions, or small-group work where he really had time to express his views and inquire. It's also no surprise that he feels totally stifled in classes where he is required to be quiet most of the time.

On the other hand, Winston gets totally spaced out in classes where there's mostly talk. He loves art, especially sculpture and photography, where he can make beautiful things with his hands. Too much talking seems to get in the way of his learning and creating. David responded really well to his kindergarten teacher, who played the guitar and taught many concepts through songs. Her teaching style was a good match for his love of music.

Thinking About Thinking

"Each mind has its own method."
—RALPH WALDO EMERSON, ESSAYIST

Everyone uses all three perceptual modes. What distinguishes the different Mind Patterns is what kinds of information you are most aware of, and the effect each has on your state of attention. It may be that some representations are stored in the right hemisphere, some stored in the left, some in both. Why is this important? We know that left hemispheric functioning is more detailed, linear, logical—there are more beta waves being produced. Conversely, right hemispheric functioning is intuitive, holistic, imagistic. Thus it triggers more theta waves. Therefore, if your visual representations were wired to be stored in the right hemisphere, it could mean that visual input would trigger you into a theta state of attention. You would "remember" Disney World in the way Picasso would. On the other hand, if these visual fragments of experience are stored in the left hemisphere, producing more beta waves, you would recall the experience more like a documentary. If it is stored in both hemispheres, producing more alpha waves, you would be able to shift back and forth between seeing the whole and seeing the details.

My theory is that by the time we're adults, our brains have wired in a preferred sequence that we use to become aware of information and express it. Our brains pull bits of stored information from the right and left hemispheres that determines the characteristics of the thought. If we think of musical notes, you can play C, G, E, for example, but if you play them in one sequence, you'll hear reveille; in another, mess call, and in another, taps. Same notes, but the sequence determines whether we're called to wake up, to digest, or to go to sleep.

There are six possible sequences your brain can use to process information: three possibilities for beta, which leaves two for alpha and one for theta. These combine to create six Mind Patterns that describe the natural or habitual way your mind accesses and retrieves information. Each one of us uses one of these six.

By exploring the ways children do simple everyday things, you can begin to understand these different patterns. If three children walk into a new classroom, for instance, the first thing Jordan notices (her beta state) is what everyone is doing—kinesthetic information. Thomas, on the other hand, first pays attention to what everyone is talking about (his beta state is most aware of auditory information). Max initially scans the room to see what looks most interesting. His beta state is most aware of visual information.

Let's consider now how children get organized, a task best performed when their minds are producing mostly beta waves. In schools, it's discussed as if it were the same process for everyone. In fact, keeping track of details and prioritizing activities can be done in any number of ways: Jordan constructs piles of her books and papers to work through one at a time until everything's completed, organizing the world kinesthetically. Thomas, since his beta state is most aware of auditory information, finds it most natural to get himself organized for his evening's work by talking on the phone and telling his friends what he has to do and in what order he's going to do it. Max needs to write down every homework assignment and refer to his list in order to get everything done, since his mind organizes things visually.

Like a fish in water, it's very difficult to imagine that any creature can move around in an environment that is not wet. We assume that everyone processes information the way we do. If I, as a parent, organize things visually, I might assume Thomas is just wasting time talking on the telephone and not making a single list.

When I first met my husband, Andy, I couldn't understand why he would always seem to touch everyone he met. Since my most aware beta state of mind uses visual information, I thought that what was polite and "normal" was to look someone directly in the eye and smile when you first meet them. Andy's most "natural" way of connecting with someone in a beta state is kinesthetically. In his world, touching someone on the shoulder is the equivalent of my looking at them.

Since visual information triggers his brain into a theta state of mind, looking directly at someone seems too invasive and private. It causes his brain to get wide and absorbent. It spaces him out. In theta, one is very receptive, so looking at someone directly for a long time makes it difficult for him to filter the input in a "public," casual way. Kinesthetic information causes my mind to "go theta." It's only something I would do in the most private of situations because I become very receptive and spaced out, not a comfortable state in the fast-paced "regular" world. Obviously, if we didn't understand our own and each other's Mind Patterns, either Andy or I would always be "a fish out of water" with the other.

My friend Nanci just called, giving me a perfect opportunity to illustrate how the different Mind Patterns operate in a family. She, her two daughters, and her husband, Jim, are going away on a winter holiday. What Jim has decided to do is go to the mountains to ski. What Nanci and her older daughter, Jennifer, really would like is to read books (visual beta), talk to each other about what they are reading (auditory alpha), lie down on a beach and not move for seven days so they can soak up the sun (kinesthetic theta). Their minds both use the same pattern: V (visual) A (auditory) K (kinesthetic).

Jim and his younger daughter, Ashlie, on the other hand, use a different pattern. For them, vacation heaven is being in nature in constant movement (kinesthetic beta), being able to look anywhere they want (visual alpha), and being in silence (auditory theta). Their minds use the KVA (kinesthetic, visual, auditory) pattern.

Given the diversity of our Mind Patterns, it's amazing that we've made it as a species as far as we have! Remember Jerome, the chess champion? Movement (kinesthetic) triggered his brain into an alert, detailed beta state. It helped him concentrate and give his attention to something. This is why in school, having to sit still for long periods and not move was so difficult for him. If he had to play chess sitting down, he would not have been a champion. The absence of understanding about this caused him to be labeled as hyperactive, retarded, and so on. But that is like a fish labeling a bird as being flighty. Jerome moves to pay attention; he has to see things from many angles because visual information triggers his alpha state of mind. What was natural for his brain was to see both the whole picture and the visual details when given the freedom to do what is organic to him. Since auditory information triggered his brain into a theta state, hearing other people talk to him constantly distracted him and made it impossible for him to "think." This was labeled by others, whose minds did not work this way, as an attention deficit.

Let's think about three children. Jerome needs to move to organize the information coming into his mind. Writing it down helps Alicia. Talking about it first helps Suzanne. All three children are "beta thinking." All three are learning. They just each need something different to help them do that.

To sort through what he is learning, Jerome stares into space or doodles, making pictures in his mind. Alicia tells stories or says "Well, it's, um, kind of like sand going through your fingers." Suzanne jiggles her foot. All three children's brains are now producing more alpha waves, but each is using a different way to sort and make sense of information.

To make new patterns with this information and express it, Jerome will be quiet for quite some time and then ask a big wide question. Alicia will get absolutely still and feel herself floating off into space, and Suzanne will stare out the window and see movies in her mind. Different triggers are helping all three children's brains produce more theta waves so they can imagine.

It isn't clear at what age these Mind Patterns "groove in." Some children seem to use one pattern from birth. Others change from one to the other until they go through puberty and become neurologically mature. We do know that cells that fire together wire together, meaning that the brain creates neurological pathways according to use, habit, and conditioning. This creates order and helps us to function efficiently. This "grooving in" is the most likely way Mind Patterns are formed.

One word of caution before you go out in the world to discover the diverse Mind Patterns of your friends, family, and associates: We all struggle, and rightly so, with labeling and "pigeonholes." The mission of this book is liberation, not further limitation. Therefore, please understand that these patterns are only signposts to how your mind might process information. They are *not* identities. I grind my teeth every time I hear someone say "I'm a KVA." Or even worse, "My son is a KAV," as if that defines everything about who he is. We are, in fact, all human beings struggling to free ourselves from all confining stories that separate us from our full capacity, from one another, and from the present moment in which we live. This information is meant to help you in that liberation.

Another word of caution: There is no Mind Pattern that is better than any other. Nor does any Mind Pattern limit your capacity to accomplish anything you choose to do. All instruments make music, even though you strum a guitar and blow on a saxophone.

People often ask me how, in a classroom or a large family, with many children and as many as six different Mind Patterns, a teacher or a parent can manage to address all the diversity.

My response is always the same: Orchestra conductors have been doing it for centuries. When medical science discovered that infections were caused by bacteria, surgeons had to wash their hands before operating, something they did not previously do. Understanding that we perceive the world in different ways means that we need to stop blaming the victims—our children—and get creative about how to best meet their needs.

Inspiration

Just when I most needed it, the following arrived in today's e-mail. Perhaps it will inspire you to keep on learning, as it did for me.

Dear Dawna,

I hope that you remember me from the distant past. I came to a workshop in your home in Vermont almost twenty years ago, and I've read several of your books. I wanted to tell you about how I've used what I learned, to encourage you to keep sharing it.

I found out during that workshop that my daughter, a toddler at the time, learns first through her body, then her ears, then last through her eyes. I, on the other hand, learned that I start talking before I open my eyes in the morning. When I went to wake up Annie, I would start singing or talking softly even as I entered her room. When she was about seven, she said to me, "Mom, when I wake up in the morning, the first voice I want to hear is my own!" Knowing about our differences enabled me to love them and respect her.

I've shared an understanding of the differences in thinking patterns with friends and family. By the time Annie was in high school, she was introducing her boyfriends to us and asking for help figuring out their patterns. The first time she did, it totally cracked me up! Being an extremely bright and talented student who uses the KAV pattern, the information helped her (and us) think about her education. Her most exceptional ability is in math and she attended a Montessori classroom for most of her elementary education because the kids moved about the room freely and used math manipulatives regularly. She chose her college (Occidental College in L.A.—an incredible learning environment) based on her knowledge of herself as well. In high school, she learned that inquiry and dialogue (her auditory alpha state) were crucial to learning. Lectures just about killed her and so she chose a college that always had small classes with lots of teacher-student dialogue. She is delighted and excelling—she has always been a curious and quick learner. She is a natural at computer languages and recently was delighted to land the highest-paying work-study job at the school—being trained to build Web sites for faculty and providing training to students in this area as well. She loves her work.

Annie is a sophomore in college now and her major is cognitive science, which is a new combination of computers, math, neurobiology, psychology, and philosophy. She plans to apply to conduct original research at her school this summer and has discussed with me some ideas about applying her research opportunity to learning more about Mind Patterns, since it is something that she has grown up with and continues to fascinate her.

I've been teaching parent education classes for over fifteen years now, and I've found this information helps us all understand and accept our children so much more. Please keep telling the world about it!

Ruth Freeman, M.S.W.

Smart Practice

People have been asking me to create a test or assessment device that will define a child's Mind Pattern. For the past twenty years, I've refused. All tests, assessments, and inventories that I know of omit one crucial factor: the impact of the input itself on the person taking the test. If you gave Jerome a visual test of intelligence (which is what happened) and forced him to sit still and write down the answers, his brain would be triggered again and again into an alpha state. He would wonder, get confused, chew over a problem until the time was up. Thus the perceptual mode of the test itself is influencing Jerome in a different way than it would Alicia or Suzanne.

The simplest and most effective way to discover the pattern someone's mind uses is to have him or her teach you something you don't know. *Since we unconsciously teach the way we learn,* ask your child to teach you something and notice the order in which he or she does this. For example, Jerome would teach me by having me move the chess pieces on the board, then watch how he does it, and finally ask him questions. Alicia would draw me a picture of each piece and tell me a story about her own experience learning chess, and then lastly have me actually touch and move each piece. Suzanne would talk me through each move as I held on to each piece.

Now you find some small thing to teach your child. Notice the order in which it is most natural for you to do this.

Repeat this experiment both ways several times and with different people.

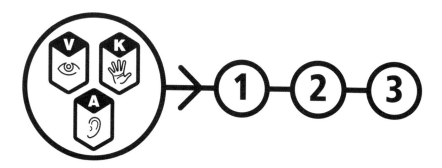

Stay curious. Avoid jumping to conclusions. Remember, you're searching for the grain of the wood, what is the most effective and natural way for you and your child to liberate the song that lies within.

The conversations of discovery, the charts and games that follow are all like sheet music that can help you find the unique music that waits within you and your child. The more you and your child understand the sequence of these modes of attention, the easier learning becomes. If you know that you need to strum a guitar and blow on a saxophone, making music simply becomes a lifetime practice. Please remember, however, that the sheet music is not the concert. Use whatever works for you and ignore that which doesn't. Explore with curiosity and wonder. The most important gift you bring to this is your own attentive heart.

Conversations of Discovery

Here are some questions that might help you discover more about what works best for you and your child:

Beta State

When you want this child to concentrate and focus, what is most helpful?
- ▶ Speaking directly to her
- ▶ Placing a hand on her shoulder
- ▶ Standing in front of her so she can look at you

What kinds of activities can your child most easily do for a long time?
- ▶ Physical activity, moving, doing, tinkering, building

- ▶ Watching, looking, drawing, writing, painting
- ▶ Listening and speaking, singing, making noises

How does your child learn most quickly? How does she think "fast"?

- ▶ By talking or asking questions
- ▶ By reading, watching, writing, or drawing
- ▶ By using her hands or her whole body

What's the easiest way for your child to greet someone he doesn't know?

- ▶ By shaking hands, by doing something together
- ▶ By saying hello, by having a conversation
- ▶ By making eye contact, by seeing their home, their things

What kinds of details does your child remember most easily?

- ▶ How things look
- ▶ How things are said
- ▶ How things are done, how things feel

Alpha State

How does your child naturally make decisions and think things over?

- ▶ Talking things out
- ▶ Seeing the options available
- ▶ Trying activities to notice how they feel

How does your child naturally like to explore?

- ▶ Saying the same thing in many different ways
- ▶ Experimenting with how things look—furniture arrangements, hairstyles, clothes, handwriting
- ▶ Making up new ways to play old games

Theta State

What seems to most trigger this child's daydreaming and spaciness? Where is he or she the most sensitive or shy?

- ▶ Watching or looking at something specific
- ▶ Listening to music
- ▶ Being touched or having to do something specific physically, like a dance pattern

What can most easily distract your child from the task at hand?

- ▶ Sounds, voices, noises, music
- ▶ Pictures, the view, faces, eye contact
- ▶ Touch, feelings, sensations, activity

What does your child have the hardest time remembering?

- ▶ How things looked, people's faces
- ▶ People's names, what people said
- ▶ Physical movements, what was done

Here's one mother's story of how this information has helped her and her sons. I offer it to invite you to keep on searching.

"Talking triggers beta waves in my son Liam's mind. He can talk and converse nonstop all day. Eventually, this causes me to put my hands over my ears because all this talking makes me space out and leaves me exhausted. To feel balanced, I can't have nonstop chatter. With this understanding, I am able to gently remind my very bright son that Mommy needs a few moments of quiet, and he understands why. Liam understands his strength is in his ability to verbally express himself in any situation. My other son, Aidan, is triggered into beta by visual information, like me, and waits to speak until after he has processed what he is seeing. Then his words are clear and important and full of heart.

"The greatest gift is to know their strengths and to actually support their differences. Aidan needs you to look at him. Liam just wants to be heard, often without eye contact. This has helped me be more appreciative of them and my ability to role-model this as a parent has had an amazing impact on their respect and understanding of each other, as well as their ability to do well in school."

Mind Pattern Walk-Through

The following game may help you and/or your children uncover more about your Mind Patterns. It is a quick process to help you narrow down your choices. Begin at the starting points and follow the footsteps, answering "yes" or "no" at each intersection until you get to one of the six patterns at the bottom of the page. Then turn to the corresponding page number to read the detailed description of your Mind Pattern.

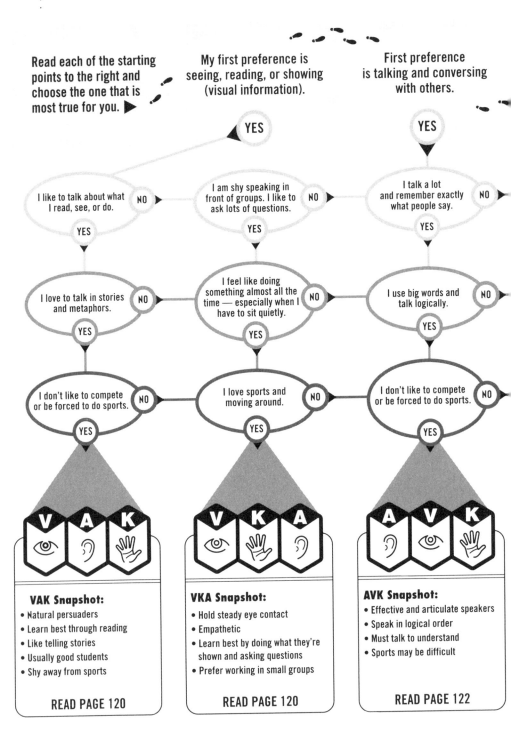

Read each of the starting points to the right and choose the one that is most true for you. ▶

My first preference is seeing, reading, or showing (visual information).

First preference is talking and conversing with others.

YES

YES

I like to talk about what I read, see, or do. — NO ▶

I am shy speaking in front of groups. I like to ask lots of questions. — NO ▶

I talk a lot and remember exactly what people say. — NO ▶

YES

YES

YES

I love to talk in stories and metaphors. — NO

I feel like doing something almost all the time — especially when I have to sit quietly. — NO

I use big words and talk logically. — NO

YES

YES

YES

I don't like to compete or be forced to do sports. — NO

I love sports and moving around. — NO

I don't like to compete or be forced to do sports. — NO

YES

YES

YES

V A K

V K A

A V K

VAK Snapshot:
- Natural persuaders
- Learn best through reading
- Like telling stories
- Usually good students
- Shy away from sports

READ PAGE 120

VKA Snapshot:
- Hold steady eye contact
- Empathetic
- Learn best by doing what they're shown and asking questions
- Prefer working in small groups

READ PAGE 120

AVK Snapshot:
- Effective and articulate speakers
- Speak in logical order
- Must talk to understand
- Sports may be difficult

READ PAGE 122

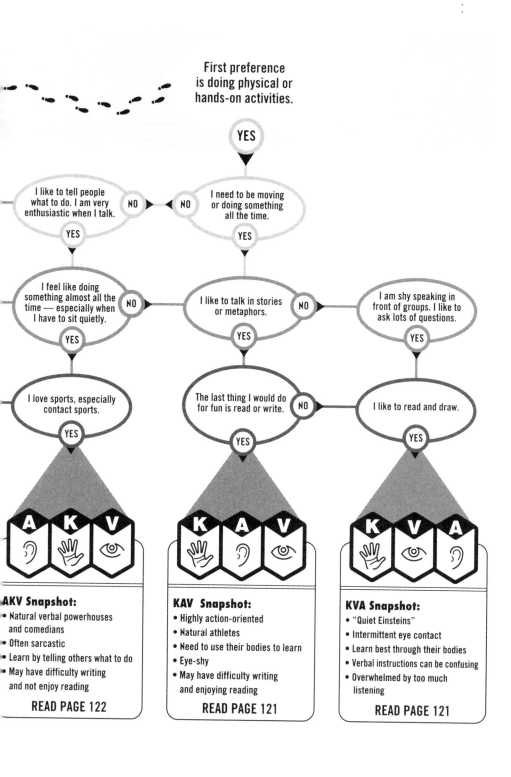

First preference is doing physical or hands-on activities.

YES

I like to tell people what to do. I am very enthusiastic when I talk. — NO — NO — I need to be moving or doing something all the time.

YES — YES

I feel like doing something almost all the time — especially when I have to sit quietly. — NO — I like to talk in stories or metaphors. — NO — I am shy speaking in front of groups. I like to ask lots of questions.

YES — YES — YES

I love sports, especially contact sports. — The last thing I would do for fun is read or write. — NO — I like to read and draw.

YES — YES — YES

A K V

K A V

K V A

AKV Snapshot:
- Natural verbal powerhouses and comedians
- Often sarcastic
- Learn by telling others what to do
- May have difficulty writing and not enjoy reading

READ PAGE 122

KAV Snapshot:
- Highly action-oriented
- Natural athletes
- Need to use their bodies to learn
- Eye-shy
- May have difficulty writing and enjoying reading

READ PAGE 121

KVA Snapshot:
- "Quiet Einsteins"
- Intermittent eye contact
- Learn best through their bodies
- Verbal instructions can be confusing
- Overwhelmed by too much listening

READ PAGE 121

Mind Pattern Chart

The chart and the overall pattern portraits that follow give all the essential characteristics of each of the six Mind Patterns. Use it as a reference and source of

	VAK-The Storyteller	**VKA- The Connector**
Detailed Thinking	Visual	Visual
Exploratory Thinking	Auditory	Kinesthetic
Innovative Thinking	Kinesthetic	Auditory
Easiest Way to Learn	1. See 2. Hear 3. Experience	1. See 2. Experience 3. Hear
Easiest to Express	1. Show 2. Say 3. Do	1. Show 2. Do 3. Say
Language Characteristics	• Speaks with feeling and emphasis. • Loves to tell stories; convince and teach others. • Talks out loud to sort ideas and make decisions. • Uses fillers such as "um," "like," or "you know."	• Speaks from personal experience in a circling, questioning way. • Must use hands or move while speaking. • May take a long time to find words, with pauses between them.
Visual Characteristics	• Easily connects with others through eye contact. • Shows what he/she feels on his/her face. • Keeps organized with lists and notes. • Likes visual order. • Has neat, legible handwriting.	• Easily connects with others through eye contact. • Feels what he/she sees. • Keeps organized with lists and notes. • Needs visual order to think clearly. • Has neat, legible handwriting.
Physical Characteristics	• Can sit still for long periods of time. • May be awkward or easily frustrated by physical activities. • Has sketchy sense of his/her body; needs to close eyes to feel sensation. • Is shy about touch and private about feelings. • Prefers free-form activities (running, swimming) to competitive sports.	• Has pent-up energy, right below the surface. • Learns sports easily and is a good athlete. • Can easily tell what he/she is feeling in body with eyes open. • Likes organized, competitive sports. • May confuse others' feelings and sensations with own feelings and sensations.
Learning Strengths and Challenges	• Is an avid reader. • Learns well by reading and talking or by teaching others. • Writes and spells well. • Has difficulty with hands-on learning activities or structured physical skill lessons.	• Can be a good reader, if taught to read words by s rather than phonics. • Easily learns by watching and then doing, without words or taking notes. • Writes, spells, and proofreads well. • Has difficulty with oral reports, concentrating in lec or participating in discussion classes.
Natural Gifts	Is a great teacher. Loves to show and tell. Wants to illuminate.	Is a great partner who works well with others. Wants create networks between people and make connectio
Typical Trouble	Shows off. Can't always do all he/she says.	Can whine and complain a lot. Can go along with th crowd too much.
Frustrations	May have difficulty making time estimates.	May have difficulty thinking for self and/or expressing desires.
"Spaces Out"	With touch, questions about how he/she feels.	With long verbal explanations, questions what he/she thinks or what he/she hears.
Helpful Hints	• Enter into dialogue with them. • Give them a metaphor to help them learn something physical. • Encourage them to go deeply enough so they can discover their feelings and vision.	• Know that they thrive through notes and cards. • Encourage them through touch. • Support regular physical exercise so they can feel themselves.
Famous People	**Oprah Winfrey:** Makes direct eye contact with guests and sits very still during interviews. Her face expresses whatever she's feeling. Always teaching and telling stories. **Martin Luther King Jr.:** Told stories to inspire others. He often spoke in colorful metaphors. Was a voracious reader and stood very still when he spoke.	**Dustin Hoffman:** Makes very direct eye contact and often speaks in questions rather than statements. Ha pent-up energy and is most comfortable speaking when he is moving. **Princess Diana:** Took in the world through her eyes Took action based on what she saw and experienced

comparison. Please remember that no one characteristic determines a pattern. It's finding the general cluster of characteristics that matters. These are only signposts, not the trail. Every violin makes a different sound and every person is unique in their ways of knowing.

	KAV-Mover and Shaker	KVA-The Investigator
Detailed Thinking	Kinesthetic	Kinesthetic
Exploratory Thinking	Auditory	Visual
Innovative Thinking	Visual	Auditory
Best Way to Learn	1. Experience 2. Hear 3. See	1. Experience 2. See 3. Hear
Best to Express	1. Do 2. Say 3. Show	1. Do 2. Show 3. Say
Language Characteristics	• Enjoys talking about personal experiences. • Is good at teaching activities and explaining movement. • Likes to tell stories. • Uses hand motions to help find his/her words.	• Is usually soft-spoken. • Uncomfortable speaking in large groups. • May take a long time to find words, with pauses between them. • Needs silence to find words. • Speaks in questions.
Visual Characteristics	• Is "eye-shy," uncomfortable maintaining steady eye contact. • Can take in the "whole" of something with a glance. • Organizes by making piles. • Is rarely aware of visual images. • May have messy handwriting with unique style.	• Maintains steady eye contact when listening, then looks away to find words. • Can pay attention to "big picture" and visual details at same time. • Can turn images around in his/her mind and see them from many angles with eyes open.
Physical Characteristics	• Easily interacts with others by doing something together or making physical contact. • Is constantly moving and doing. • Has a huge amount of physical energy. • Is usually a well-coordinated, natural athlete. • Likes competitive sports. • Likes to touch and be touched.	• Easily interacts with others by doing something together or making physical contact. • Loves to be active, and likes to move and do. • Has smooth, graceful energy. • Is usually a well-coordinated, natural athlete. • Likes competitive sports. • Learns physical skills easily.
Learning Strengths and Challenges	• Learns physical skills easily. • Easily learns with hands-on or experiential approaches. • Can learn well from discussions about relevant subjects. • Can have difficulty with reading, writing, and spelling.	• Learns easily with hands-on or experiential approaches. • Can be a good reader, if taught through experience and not phonics. • Has difficulty with oral reading. • Has difficulty concentrating in lecture classes or participating in large discussions.
Natural Gifts	Is a great "doer." Loves to take action and get things done. Wants what he/she does to be useful to others.	Is a great lover of nature, especially animals. Has many dissimilar interests (i.e., drawing and ice hockey). Wants to unite dissimilar elements.
Typical Trouble	Can get "hyperactive." Can have difficulty sitting still.	Can get sullen and withdrawn.
Frustrations	May have difficulty finding positive outlets for physical energy.	May have difficulty expressing feelings in words.
"Spaces Out"	With many things to look at, questions about what he/she sees.	With long verbal explanations, questions about what he/she thinks or what he/she hears.
Helpful Hints	• Give fun and practical outlets for their physical energy. • Touch them, or do things with them. • Give them freedom to look where they want and learn in concrete ways.	• Give them opportunities to actively explore their many interests. • Encourage them to write down what they're feeling instead of talking. • Allow them to have comfortable silences. • Walk in nature with them.
Famous People	**Michael Jordan:** Gestures and movements are steady and assertive. He's very competitive physically. He rarely makes steady eye contact. **Mother Teresa:** Constantly in action, she was hands-on helping people. Looked aside when speaking and was very energetic physically. Often said, "I want to die on my feet, serving people."	**Mia Hamm:** Leads by example rather than words. Physical presence is steady and solid. Ponders questions before answering; her replies are slow, thoughtful, and very deep. **Tiger Woods:** Practices and works out long hours and maintains a regimented schedule. Looks aside in interviews to ponder questions, then looks back to answer them.

	AVK–The Communicator	AKV–The Coach
Detailed Thinking	Auditory	Auditory
Exploratory Thinking	Visual	Kinesthetic
Innovative Thinking	Kinesthetic	Visual
Easiest Way to Learn	1. Hear 2. See 3. Experience	1. Hear 2. Experience 3. See
Easiest to Express	1. Say 2. Show 3. Do	1. Say 2. Do 3. Show
Language Characteristics	• Easily interacts with others by talking. • Has an extensive vocabulary. • Speaks logically about facts, ideas, and concepts. • Likes conversing with adults and older children.	• Easily interacts with others by talking to them. • Has an extensive vocabulary. • Speaks with lots of feeling and rhythm. • Likes to tell others what to do.
Visual Characteristics	• Maintains steady eye contact, then looks away to find words. • Can pay attention to the "big picture" and small details at same time. • Can turn images around in his/her mind and see them from many angles with eyes open. • Has hard-to-read handwriting.	• Is eye-shy. • Is uncomfortable maintaining eye contact. • Sees the whole picture. • Makes simple drawings. • Has messy handwriting with unique style.
Physical Characteristics	• May have sketchy sense of his/her body. • May be awkward or easily frustrated by physical activities. • Prefers free-form activities (running, swimming) to competitive sports. • Is shy about touch and private about feelings.	• Has pent-up energy, right below the surface. • Enjoys sports, are often good coaches and athletes. • Needs to talk or shout while doing sports.
Learning Strengths and Challenges	• Learns easily through discussion and lecture. • Learns well through reading. • Has difficulty learning hands-on activities and sports. • Can easily learn to speak languages by hearing and reading.	• Easily learns through discussion and lecture. • Learns well with a hands-on approach. • Can have difficulty with reading, writing, and spelling. • Can learn to speak languages by hearing.
Natural Gifts	Is a great communicator who loves to exchange ideas. Wants to help.	Is a visionary thinker who has many great ideas. Wants to inspire others.
Typical Trouble	Interrupts others. Monopolizes conversations and makes pointed, blunt statements.	Interrupts others. Can be sarcastic, makes wisecracks.
Frustrations	May have difficulty learning physical skills without words or visuals to follow.	May have difficulty feeling satisfied when trying to turn visions into reality.
"Spaces Out"	With touch, questions about what he/she wants to do or how he/she feels.	With too many things to look at, questions about what he/she sees.
Helpful Hints	• Whenever possible, respond verbally. • Ask questions that will encourage them to broaden their perspective and give voice to all that's inside them. • To slow down their words, get them to write down what they're saying.	• Walk and talk whenever possible. • Sit next to them and let them look wherever they want. • Give them chances to use their energy. • To slow their words, touch them or walk with them. • Respond verbally to them.
Famous People	**Larry King:** He's very direct with his words; his questions are almost statements. He speaks first then looks directly at his guests. Relatively still in his body. **Hillary Clinton:** Speaks directly and doesn't mince words. Voice is confident, crisp, and free of emotion. Very still as she speaks.	**Robin Williams:** Very energetic, first with his words, then his body. Can talk for hours without visual cues, and never stays still. Seldom makes direct eye contact. **Madonna:** Speaks and sings with a great deal of energy and movement. Makes a splash when she talks and is often sarcastic. Doesn't hold eye contact for very long.

Mind Pattern Overall Portraits

 ## THE COACH

- Is extremely articulate, often sarcastic, and has a high degree of physical energy right beneath the surface.
- Loves to take charge and tell everyone else what to do, and to discuss, argue, or debate anything, tell jokes, and make plays on words.
- Understands and makes verbal inferences easily and responds quickly to spoken questions.
- Has a distinctive, one-of-a-kind voice, and speaks with a lot of energy, feeling, and rhythm.
- It's easy to remember what is said, including poetry, song lyrics, rhymes, and jokes.
- Has an endless supply of physical energy that is not easily released.
- Well coordinated and can easily learn physical movement if given verbal instruction only.
- Very particular and sensitive about visual input, and most comfortable looking away rather than maintaining direct eye contact.

 ## THE COMMUNICATOR

- Often considered "smart" because he/she can easily verbalize thoughts and keep up with the pace of any conversation.
- Words pour out in logical order without hesitation in a straightforward manner. Tends to speak in statements rather than questions.
- The content of their words is largely conceptual, abstract, and detailed; may be fascinated with language and can often learn to speak other languages with ease.
- Most likely enjoys explaining, debating, discussing, and arguing about almost anything.
- May frequently use words and phrases like:
    "Hear, say, sounds like"
    "That rings a bell"
    "Let's play it by ear"
    "Talk to you soon"

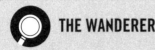 ## THE WANDERER

- Soft-spoken and private with a grounded physical presence.
- Seems to be surrounded by a deep silence.
- Interested in seemingly diverse things—football and art, for instance, or sewing and chemistry.
- Seems to have an intuitive sense of how everything all fits together. Generally very aware of the specific sensations in the body.
- Tends to choose clothes that are comfortable and allow freedom of movement.
- Prefers to be alone or with one or two others rather than be a part of a large social gathering.
- If in a group, will often look for a quiet place to sit back, watch, and listen.
- Often labeled shy, enjoys working or playing alone or with one close friend, or relating to animals or nature rather than to people.
- Eyes glaze over when listening to too many words, and facial expression usually goes flat when speaking.
- Frequently uses a lot of kinesthetic vocabulary, words that convey action or feelings, like:
    "grab, hold, soft, move,"
    and phrases like
    "That feels right"
    "I'll be in touch soon"

 ## THE MOVER AND SHAKER

- Very physically active, jiggly, with shy, sensitive eyes.
- When given a chance, prefers to be constantly in motion.
- Preference is to relate to the world first in some tangible way—by learning anything new experientially or tactilely.
- A well-coordinated, "natural" athlete who usually likes participatory sports and seems to have an endless supply of physical energy.
- Physical comfort is quite important.
- Clothes have to be comfortable with just the right weight and texture as opposed to how they look. In general, touch comes naturally and easily; a casual but important way to connect.
- Keenly aware of physical sensations, but doesn't show feelings on face: generally has flat facial expressions; body speaks in stance, movement, and gestures.
- Uses a lot of kinesthetic vocabulary—words and phrases that describe action or feeling, such as:
    "getting a feel for" or "How does that grab you?" or "I can't get a handle on it."
    Ends a conversation with:
    "Catch you later" or "Let's get together soon."
    Frequently uses kinesthetic metaphors: "Throw it fast and fierce like a bullet."

THE STORYTELLER

- Bright eyes, makes steady eye contact and makes a visual impression with the clothes worn, which are usually colorful, well-coordinated outfits.
- Loves visual details and looking at possibilities—flipping through catalogs, going window-shopping, or people-watching.
- Devours anything in print—cereal boxes, billboards, novels. Keeps lots of details stored visually, sometimes to the point of having a photographic memory.
- Face shows feelings while speaking.
- Could have invented "show and tell."
- Lots of energy in spoken words, and often very persuasive. Loves to tell stories and naturally teaches and sells, no matter what else is being done.
- Uses visual metaphors to paint pictures.
- Often uses visual vocabulary—words that present images, like:
      "see, look, colorful, show," or "bright,"
  and phrases like:
      "I can see your point" or "See you later."
- Often uses fillers, like "um, like," or "you know" between thoughts.

 THE EMPATH

- Visually meticulous, and appearance is very important.
- Can spot the one typo in a one-hundred-page report.
- Wants clothes, possessions, body, and surroundings to fit an inner image. Connects with others most easily by making eye contact, which is steadily maintained.
- May close eyes or move to listen in depth.
- Feels what is seen.
- Has pent-up energy right beneath the surface and so physical activity tends to be an important emotional and energetic outlet. May be a voracious reader, unless taught to read phonetically, in which case may have difficulty reading.
- Likes to take copious notes in meetings and classes.
- In large groups can be rather quiet, but with one or two peers or in small groups can be very talkative.
- May jump from topic to topic, and not seem to "get to the point," making connections in speaking that may not be understandable to the listener. Gesturing, moving, or touching are essential to speaking.
- Uses lots of visual vocabulary—words that paint images and phrases that include:
      "look, see, show, imagine," or "I can picture that" or "See you soon."
- Tends to ask a great number of questions.

Smart Family Practice

The following chart is meant to give you an overview of the different ways of knowing of each member of your family, a map of the whole family to help you find better and more effective ways to connect. It can also show you where you may have to shift and communicate in a different mode. As you and different family members discover your Mind Patterns, fill it out for everybody or ask each member to fill in their own column, and then place it somewhere prominent. You might also want to post one of the following questions nearby for people to think and talk about:

- What's the best way to support you when you're frustrated?
- What's the best way to let you know you're loved?
- Who's the best person to help you figure something out?
- What's the best way to give you feedback when someone is upset with you?
- What are the ways you know that we can treat you well?

Family Communications Center

As you and the different members of your family discover their Mind Patterns, put them on the following chart and hang it in an obvious place in your home.

	PARENT	PARENT	CHILD 1	CHILD 2
① BETA Detailed, Focused, External	Helps me focus, and what I need first			
② ALPHA Sort, Decide, Confuse	Helps me sort and explore			
③ THETA Distractable, Create, Sensitive	Where I am the most sensitive and distractable.			

Chapter Seven

Recognizing Attractions and Interests

Motivating from the Inside Out

"Pay attention to the curiosities of a child; this is where the search for knowledge is freshest and most valuable."
—ALBERT EINSTEIN

According to psychologist Jerome Bruner, learning is a constant process of discovery. He believes there are three questions any mind asks itself when it chooses to learn something: *What?*—as in "What about this attracts or is interesting to me?"; *So What?*—as in "So what is relevant about this to me?"; *Now What?*—as in "Now what will I be able to do or be as a result of learning this?"

If we think of each of these questions as gates that open and close in a child's mind, we can understand the importance of recognizing a child's attractions and interests.

When I hear parents and teachers talk about "motivating" a child to learn, I inevitably think about Bruner's three questions. You don't have to motivate a child to learn any more than you have to motivate a tree to grow. Learning is the deepest root of a child's passion. Children don't resist learning, though they might resist poor teaching. But you do have to provide light and water if you wish to cultivate what is green and growing. In order to do that you have to know how to open those three gates.

Since working with the "odd ones" has always been my favorite practice field, I often worked with pubescent boys. One fifteen-year-old boy, Danny Coulter, came from the back hills of Vermont. He lived with his father, a logger, and eight brothers. I was told he had an IQ of 40, which meant he could never learn to read. In our first conversation, I discovered there was only one thing that Danny was really interested in even looking at: *Mad* magazine. Each time I went to tutor him at his house, I found him flipping through the glossy pages. I tried to teach him using every standard reading text I could find, but he'd just shake his head and walk away. Finally, in total frustration, I grabbed the magazine from his hands and began to read the jokes to myself, chuckling. Danny wanted to know what I was laughing at. I just pointed to the lines of print and went on chuckling. I had his attention. He asked me to teach him to read them, but I refused. Then he begged me. Finally, I agreed to teach him to read just the jokes. I tore them from the magazine, and we began, word by word, line by line. We didn't consider it a success until he himself laughed at each joke. Within three months, he was reading at grade level—anything I handed to him!

Before you tsk-tsk at me, and tell me how politically incorrect I was, please understand that people had been trying to "motivate" Danny for eight years and failed miserably. Since he was already motivated by his magazines, what I did was grab on to the only handhold I could find and use it to help him pull himself up and learn to read something he found interesting. I am suggesting that finding what a child is already interested in can be a natural source of motivation. I'm sure Danny's interest in those magazines has waned over the years, but I'm also sure he can still read anything he wants to.

Here is a less controversial example of using children's interests and attractions. Four-year-old Yukio fought going to sleep at night. When he was two years old, his father gave him a xylophone. His eyes lit up as he used the mallets on those keys, totally amazed that he could be making such sounds. His mother finally had the idea to sit next to him at night and sing him a song, suggesting he imagine that his fingers are playing it on the xylophone. After a month or so, she played him songs on the tape recorder and had him do the same thing. His fingers played on his belly under the covers as he drifted off to sleep.

The venerable pioneer of quality management, Dr. W. Edwards Deming, describes the importance of motivation from the inside out. "People are born with intrinsic motivation, dignity, curiosity and joy in learning. The destruction begins with toddlers—a prize for the best Halloween costume, grades in school, gold stars—and on up through the university. On the job people, teams, divisions are ranked and given a reward for the one at the top, a punishment for the one at the bottom." He went on to say that we try to substitute rewards, a pat on the back, or approval or money, all of which matter, but at the deepest level, intrinsic motivation is the strongest force because you are doing something you genuinely want to do, which comes from what is deepest in your nature.

Opening the Gates: Loving What You Love

"Purpose is the place where your deep gladness meets the world's needs."
—FREDERICK BUECHNER, WRITER AND LECTURER

What attracts a child isn't always obvious, particularly in the rushed life of a busy family. I met a woman at a cocktail party who was the star of an award-winning television interview program. As we sipped white wine, she asked me an endless stream of fascinating questions, seducing me into telling her story after story about my life and love. After an hour or so, she asked if I'd come meet her eleven-year-old son, Joshua, who was struggling through fifth grade because he was "lazy and unmotivated."

The next week we sat in her kitchen sipping tea. This time I was asking her questions about Josh's passions and attractions. She stared blankly at me, shrugged, and replied, "He likes sports, I guess, and he spends hours playing video games. That's about it." When Josh came home, I asked him for a tour of his room. He showed me his football shirts and soccer balls. When I asked what he was really interested in, his reply was the same as his mother's, complete with the shrug. "Sports and video games." Then I noticed some intricate drawings he had made on the cover of his notebook. "Hey, Josh, what are these?" At first he said they were just scribbles, but when I persisted, wanting to know what he had been thinking about when he made them, and how he had done them in such detail, the gates of his mind flew wide open. "I've been drawing stuff like that since I was little. They're mostly planes and machines I make up in my mind. Wanna see some more?" Of course I did. He went to his closet and pulled out hundreds of drawings hidden behind all the sports equipment. We went through them, one by one, Josh talking animatedly about what he imagined each one would do, and how frustrated he became sometimes because he couldn't put them on paper the way they were in his mind. I asked him why they were stuffed in the closet. "My dad always tells me to stop wasting my time with this woosie stuff and get down to my homework."

There's nothing Josh couldn't learn if it were framed as helping him get better at imagining and drawing his machines. And if his mom used with her own son what she was an expert on with others—finding out about people by interviewing them—his natural interests would become apparent to her as well.

It's important to distinguish between what is entertainment—in Josh's case, that would be video games—and what is a passionate attraction. Geneen Roth, author of *When Food Is Love*, uses two words that are very helpful in discerning one from the other: searching for the "hums" rather than the "beckonings." Hums pull from the inside out—Josh's drawings, for example. They reflect a true hunger of the child's heart and mind, whereas beckonings are cravings or desires that pull from the outside in. Hums provide nourishment, beckonings are like candy that leave you wanting more.

A friend of mind adopted a little girl from Vietnam. When she went to the orphanage, the woman in charge, who could not speak English, pointed to the girl's hands and smiled. When I first saw this little year-old love lump, what I was most struck by were her long and agile fingers. She would put herself to sleep by lying on her back and staring at her hands. As she has grown, her hands have led the way. She can become passionately involved in making anything. She learned to use a scissors long before other children her age could. Similarly, she could sew, knit, weave, make birdhouses, dolls, costumes before any of her friends. But it is not just her skill level that is so outstanding. It is how involved and satisfied she is when following the hum of her hands.

David and his wife, Angie, used to do a practice in our workshops where they'd run a videotaped interview, asking the person many open questions about his or her passionate interests. Then they would sit and view the video together. People would be amazed at how they "lit up" when talking about this compared to other subjects. It is as if the life force starts to shine within the person or child when they talk about what they love.

If encouraged, attractions and interests can be the very things children end up pursuing their whole life, as well as clues to the potential inside them. But that does not mean a child needs to be directed into becoming what they are attracted to. A hum is not an identity, though it may be a light along the way. In the book *Einstein Never Used Flash Cards*, the authors point out that Einstein wasn't drilled in multiplication tables as a child. Rather, his parents paid attention to all of his interests and gave him opportunities to explore them. Another example is the early-twentieth-century American composer Cole Porter. His mother recognized her son's love of music when he was young and purposely moved to a new city and lied about his age so he could stay in public high school two years longer to get more free musical training. These guardians recognized and respected the interests of their children and found ways to help support them.

In recognizing your child's attractions and interests, you are discovering the compass points that he or she uses to navigate through daily life. When you know what these are, you can help them find their way in times when they get lost.

Inspiration

Stories abound of eminent people whose passions were evident in childhood. Many of them had great difficulty in school. In studies of people who have made great contributions, from Albert Einstein and Thomas Edison to Ella Fitzgerald and Eleanor Roosevelt, what has been found to be common to all is not intelligence, temperament, or personality type, not even inheritance, early environment, or inspiration. Rather, it is the motivation and opportunity to follow their passions.

- Elòn Graham is a fourteen-year-old boy who lives with his single mom in a rough part of Berkeley, California. Even when he was very young, he refused to eat the fast food his mother preferred. At two years old, he was asking for broccoli. By seven he was whipping up salads and entrées for his mother (who still prefers fast food). This year, he decided to create a cookbook for kids. He cooked and his grandmother wrote down what he did. He's now selling the book. The proceeds are going to a neighborhood rescue mission. About to enter high school, he dreams of becoming a professional chef. Neither his mother nor his grandmother can explain where his cooking passion comes from.

- When a significant English philosopher, R. G. Collingwood (1889–1943), was eight, he was searching through his father's library and curiously took down a black book by Immanuel Kant entitled *Theory of Ethics*. He began to read it and was indignant that he could not understand the words in the book. "I felt that the contents of this book, although I could not understand it, were somehow my business. . . . There came upon me by degrees after this a sense of being burdened with a task whose nature I could not define except by saying, 'I must think.' What I was to think about I did not know; and then, obeying this command, I fell silent and absent-minded." Collingwood went on to "think" out major works in metaphysics, aesthetics, religion, and history.

- The French writer Colette refused to write as a child. "I never made good marks in composition between the ages of twelve and fifteen. For I felt, and felt it every day more intensely, that I was made exactly for not writing. . . . I was the only one of my kind, the only creature sent into the world for the purpose of not writing." However, Colette was wildly attracted to all the materials of her calling: "A pad of virgin paper; an ebony ruler; one, two, four, six pencils, sharpened with a penknife and all of different colors; pens with medium nibs and fine pens with enormously broad nibs . . . reams of paper, cream-laid, ruled, watermarked."

- As a child, Pablo Picasso stubbornly refused to do anything but paint. He came to school with his pigeon and the paintbrush he always carried as if it were an extension of his body. His father, who was also a painter, used pigeons as models, but to Pablo, the pigeon was a friend.

- Albert Einstein is known to have made up his own religion as a child and "went about chanting to himself hymns he dedicated to his self-created deity."

- Cal Ripken Jr., the "Iron Man of Baseball," loved Ping-Pong as a kid. His mother recalls that her son, who holds the record for the most consecutive games played in baseball, would yell back to her from the Ping-Pong table after she called him for dinner, "Just one more game!"

- Barbara Shipman, a scholar in advanced mathematics, was fascinated with bees as a child. She studied their dances, even performed them herself. Barbara's adult work in math brought her back to her childhood passion, as she has discovered that the bees' dances can be comprehended at the level of math in the sixth dimension.

Conversations of Discovery

Think together with your child about what kinds of activities and subjects each of you is drawn to. Are there some that have been consistent attractors for a long time? What are the new ones? Does she love computers and all things electronic? Is he a stick and stone collector? Does she love insects? Does he love to play games? Does he draw and make things? Does she love messy things, or does she like to tidy up? What does he like to do with his hands?

In making a list of attractions, include everything you can both think of, even the things you might not be especially thrilled about, like an attraction to fire or speeding in cars. Make sure you consider both the activities that your child has selected on his own, the games he makes up, the things he does when alone and not prompted as well as the activities you have offered to him that received a positive response.

Hold the information you hear lightly. Try to let go of any judgments you might have about some of your child's choices or lack of choices. Recently, I met Nathan, an eight-year-old, who was described as "lazy." In probing deeper, what that meant about this child is that he would much rather play at the computer than do something physically active outdoors.

Get curious about what your child finds appealing in an activity you might never choose. Use the phrase "Isn't that interesting!" to keep your curiosity flowing. Be gentle with yourself. You may have to let go of some of your favorites that you want your child to love.

The following questions are meant only as guidelines to your child's passions. This is not about making the list as long as possible. It's about making it as true as you can get it, whether your child is deeply interested in two things or casually interested in twenty-five.

- What do each of you like to do alone, inside and outside?
- What do each of you like to do with other people?
- In what ways do each of you imagine or create?
- What kinds of vehicles and gadgets interest your child?
- What do each of you collect?
- What kinds of odd jobs do each of you like to do?
- What pets do you have or want to have? What living things interest you?
- What kinds of TV shows, movies, music do each of you enjoy?
- What musical instruments do each of you play or want to play?
- What parts of the world or times in history do you like to read about?
- Who are each of your favorite people?
- What are your favorite places?

Smart Family Practices

Whole family favorites: Pick ten of the following categories. Pick one family member to be the star and everyone has to guess what the favorites of that person would be in those categories. For example, if Jessica is the star, the whole family has to discuss Jessica's favorite color, cold food, summer sport, song, smell, art to do, card game, music group, shape, and sour food. Jessica is silent and just gets to enjoy people guessing about her favorites.

Variation for two: Make two copies of the whole list. Give yourselves a time limit, such as a week, to fill out what you think are your child's favorites, and he or she has to do the same for you. The one who gets the most correct answers gets to pick the activity for the next play day together.

1. Color	26. Board game
2. Flower	27. Video game
3. Bird	28. Computer game
4. Animal	29. Card game
5. Tree	30. Place in your house
6. Number	31. Place in nature
7. Time of day	32. Place you've visited
8. Day of the week	33. Place you've heard about
9. Month	34. Art to do
10. Season	35. Art to see
11. Weather	36. Movies
12. Holiday	37. TV show
13. Meal	38. Song
14. Hot food	39. Poem
15. Cold food	40. Music group
16. Hot drink	41. Musical instrument
17. Cold drink	42. Story
18. Sweet food	43. Book
19. Sour food	44. Play
20. Salty food	45. Shoes
21. Sport to watch	46. Article of clothing
22. Sport to play	47. Texture
23. Winter sport	48. Sound
24. Summer sport	49. Smell
25. Toy	50. Shape

Chapter Eight

Recognizing Resources

What Are You Given with Which to Give?

"The more sacred the object of your search, the nearer it is to you."
—SØREN KIERKEGAARD, PHILOSOPHER

Everyone knows the saying "It takes a village to raise a child." But who is in the village and where is it to be found? When my son was between the ages of four and fifteen, I carried the responsibility for raising him on my own. I carried it as if it were a heavy and secret weight. I was sick much of that time, which I also carried as if it were a heavy and secret weight. There was one night I will never forget when David was six years old. We had just moved into a tiny apartment above a garage on Poverty Lane in West Lebanon, New Hampshire. I didn't know a single person in the entire state. I remember being stunned by the realization that if anything were to happen to me, there would not be anyone familiar to whom David could turn.

One evening, while putting him to bed, I was in a great deal of physical pain. Of course, I did my best to hide it. You know how long it can take to put a six-year-old to bed when they want to stay up. Finally, *finally*, when he was snuffling under his quilt, I fled downstairs into the dark and cold night. All I wanted was to be held and scream. And yet I was afraid that, alone, if I made a sound, I would never stop screaming. I leaned back against a big old maple tree. It felt so strong when I felt so weak. It felt so solid when inside of me there was only a flood. I turned and wrapped my arms around that maple tree, pressed my cheek into its rough bark, and held on as tight as I could while the flood washed through me.

It washed me clean. It was enough. I was enough. I felt connected to something. In that moment, I felt connected to everything. I went upstairs and sat quietly by David's bed, memorizing the moment—the shadows of his eyelashes resting on his cheek, his toes wiggling inside his blue flannel pajama feet.

We all have moments as parents when the responsibility we carry seems like a heavy burden, when we forget that there are resources, external and internal, that can help us hold on and carry on. This chapter is meant to help you remember to widen your periphery and notice the wealth of resources, internal and external, that exist to help you bring out the greatness in your child . . . and in yourself.

In order to recognize the resources in your child's world, it's necessary for you to accept that even the most perfect guardian couldn't meet all of a child's needs—nor are we meant to.

One dictionary definition of *resources* is the source of aid, wealth, or support that may be drawn upon when needed. Another is the inner quality of being able to cope with a difficult situation. In this chapter we'll be turning our attention to the recognition of both aspects of resources.

Recognizing External Resources

> *"Love what is plentiful as well as what is scarce."*
> —ALICE WALKER, NOVELIST AND POET

When we are reminded (and reminding ourselves) of all we don't have, we feel disconnected, fragmented, and isolated. "If only I could afford a piano teacher for my daughter; if only I had more time to spend with my son." When, on the other hand, we shift and widen our attention to what is plentiful and available, we begin to think of possibilities and connections that are all around us. "Aunt Audrey plays the piano. I wonder if she'd be willing to teach Wendy," "What if I dropped Jonathan off at the Boys and Girls Club on Saturday morning so I could have some private time with Jason?"

These frenzied and tumultuous times carry with them a collective contagion of noticing what is scarce. Vietnamese teacher and poet Thich Nhat Hanh has said, "You say you want more peace, but perhaps it would be wasted on you if you don't even notice the peace that is available to you in this very moment. Stop, breathe, notice."

You can begin with the simplest of lists. In a situation when you just feel like giving up, sit down or pace back and forth, and breathe. Ask yourself what external resources would really be useful in this situation. Write down whatever you can think of. Perhaps beginning with the words *I wish.* . . . or *If only.* . . . It might loosen up your thinking a bit. For example, Marlene is a single mother with two children under the age of six. One late afternoon, when she was at her wit's end, she took a pen in her trembling hand and wrote the following: "I wish there were someone else here to help me, someone to hold one kid while I made dinner, someone to bathe the other while I got one ready for bed. I wish there were somebody who could just hold me for a change, and talk adult to me instead of preschool. I wish there were somebody who could say something funny so I could laugh at the end of this very long day." Marlene felt a little better when she put the pen down. She dragged both children and three bags of garbage into the elevator and pushed B. When the door opened in the basement, Mrs. Gorman was standing there, her eyes twinkling as she waved hello to the children. Marlene didn't talk much to her neighbors, but she knew Mrs. Gorman had lost her husband recently and lived alone on the fifth floor. Remembering her list, Marlene did something very nonhabitual—she invited Mrs. Gorman for dinner. Like a hand slipping into a glove, her overfull life and her neighbor's empty one were made for each other.

From basketball courts to libraries to favorite aunts, resources are all around us. They are the things, people, places, and environments that can help bring out our best. Dr. Milton Erickson used to tell the story of a lady who lived in the town where he grew up. She was very depressed and stayed in her house most of the time. One day, he noticed that there were African violets on every one of her windowsills. He started a conversation with her and she poured out her unhappiness to him, including her fantasies of suicide.

"But what would happen to all those African violets if you killed yourself?" he asked. When she shrugged, he told her that since she had brought all of them into the world, it was her responsibility to at least see that they had good homes before she killed herself. He suggested she read the newspaper and every time she found a cause for celebration, she send the person one of her African violets.

Over the months and then years that followed, she gave plants to many people. And they reciprocated by inviting her to weddings, birthday parties, and baseball games. Soon the windowsills of the town were filled with African violets and her life was filled with friends. When she died ten years later, three thousand people came to celebrate the life of their African violet queen.

I can't promise you that your life will be filled with flowers or sweet old ladies. But I do trust that increasing awareness of the external resources you and your child will need through the practice and conversation that follows will make it more possible for you to stop, breathe, and find them.

Conversations of Discovery

Resource	Example	Reflective Question
People	Miguel was going through a dark period until he spent time every day with his aunt Maria helping her rebuild her kitchen. She was the one person in the world who made him laugh no matter what.	**Who are the people that bring out the best in this child?**
Environments	Hans came home from school very wound up. A half hour in his room with music cranked up loud doing whatever he wanted calmed him down enough to focus on his homework.	**What is the environment that most helps this child concentrate? Sort things out? Come up with new ideas?**
Places	After his parents were divorced, Lawrence spent every afternoon in the Boys and Girls Club playing basketball with a coach who really believed in him.	**What is missing for this child and what kind of person or place would help him or her find it?**
Classes/workshops	Steffie had no friends in school and dressed in black clothes every day. After taking a pottery class at the local YWCA, she realized that she could create beautiful things and no longer felt worthless.	**What could this child learn that would increase his or her self-confidence and self-trust?**
Objects	Simon was small for his age and kept getting picked on in school. For his birthday he was given a drum. He spent hours using the drum to describe his frustration and anger. This release helped him feel as if the pain were outside of himself. He began to feel and act more confidently.	**What are the things that might assist this child in directing his or her energy in a positive way?**

Smart Practice

Think of a time when you were at your best. Whatever comes to mind will be fine. Tell your child a story about this time. Ask him or her to draw it or take notes as you speak. Be sure to include who you were with, what you were doing, what objects or tools you were using, where you were, and when this took place, including time of day, etcetera.

Reverse. Ask your child to tell you of a time when she was at her best, including all the specifics mentioned above. Take notes or sketch as you hear the story.

If it feels right, tell each other what you learned about the conditions and resources that help bring out your best.

Inspiration

This is the true story of a six-year-old boy who could never have done what he did alone. He inspires all of us to remember that if you are passionate enough about what you want to do on behalf of the rest of us, you will find the resources to do it.

In January 1998, six-year-old Ryan Hreljac of Ontario, Canada, listened intently when his first-grade teacher spoke about the plight of people in Africa who had to walk great distances every day just to fetch water, the most basic resource needed for human survival, and that hundreds of thousands of children die each year just from drinking contaminated water. Shocked, Ryan rushed home and told his parents he needed $70 to build a well for an African village. They explained distractedly that it was too much money. Ryan persisted until they finally agreed to give him extra chores to raise money. Within four months he was halfway to his goal. His mother helped him connect with an international development organization, WaterCan. They gratefully accepted his contribution, but explained that $70 would only cover the cost of a hand pump. It actually cost closer to $2,000 to drill a well. "I'll just have to do more chores, then," Ryan replied.

His parents sent out an e-mail to family and friends telling them about Ryan's project. The word spread. Newspaper articles appeared and donations for Ryan's well began to pour in. Ryan discovered that only 46 percent of Ugandans had access to safe water. He also learned that a small drill in the back of a truck would allow many more wells to be made. It cost $25,000. His mother called the local TV station, which sent out people to interview Ryan. Newspapers across the country carried the story of Ryan's well. Within two months, he had inspired $7,000 in donations and his teacher and class decided to help. They began a pen-pal relationship with the children at the school where the well would be built. Backed by his entire school, Ryan raised enough money to buy the new machinery. A neighbor gave him and his parents frequent-flyer miles to get them to Uganda. In July of 2000, Ryan, aged nine, and his parents were carried in a truck down a Ugandan dirt road. A line of five thousand children from nearby schools stood clapping and cheering for Ryan. Standing at the well, he was surrounded by healthy children.

As of last year, Ryan has helped raise over a million dollars and supported more than 120 water and sanitation projects in 8 developing countries.

(For more information, contact: www.ryanswell.ca.)

Recognizing Inner Resources

"In times of crisis, people reach for meaning. Meaning is strength. Our survival may depend on our seeking and finding it."
— VICTOR FRANKL, M.D., PH.D., PSYCHOLOGIST

Dr. Milton Erickson used to speak about what he called "terrible gifts." They were those challenges that life gives us, which appear at first to be terrible, but ultimately hide a gift or inner resource that carries us forward, making us stronger and more able to live fully and vitally. Cancer was a terrible gift for me. At first, I could only see it as an enemy to be feared and then destroyed before it destroyed me. Then, as the years passed, I remembered Milton's words, and realized it had, in fact, been a teacher to me. Through it I learned to travel the long road from my head to my heart. The entire axis of my life shifted and I began to develop inner resources that I had never really considered before: compassion, courage, and tenderness. The latest research findings indicate that children, when given the kind of support they need after a trauma, may develop inner strength and become more emotionally intelligent than children who went through the same trauma unsupported.

My grandmother used to say that your gift is the place where you will be most challenged when you are growing up so you can learn to develop it fiercely. I have found this to be true. The things that were the greatest challenges for me—storytelling and my wild imagination, my refusal to accept what authority figures told me at face value, my ardent loyalty to anything injured or maligned, my defense of how the glass could be half full—all were gifts that have become essential resources in finding and nurturing my purpose in life. These challenges can be the opening through which we can learn to trust ourselves and engage fully in the world.

One of my favorite ways to help children discover inner resources is to ask about their favorite scar. When I first began doing this, I'd set an example by telling about the time Stuie Stillman rode me on the handlebars of his bike when I was five and one of the spokes broke and tore a big hole in my leg that I couldn't feel until my mother pointed at it and screamed because blood was running in a stream down my leg. Then I'd show the three-inch scar on my right calf. Almost every time, the child would light up and unfold a tale of their own gory wounding while tenderly stroking their scar.

Scars are made of the strongest tissue in our bodies even though they are the result of deep injury. When I ask a child about a scar, I ask what message or lesson came through it. I tell them mine was to learn that my body has the capacity to heal itself, especially if I give it care. Oftentimes what I hear from children are stories of turning points—an event that they chose to turn toward in some way.

I worked with an eight-year-old girl, Mali, who had been adopted at six from Rwanda. Her entire family had been destroyed before her eyes in the war. Two years later, she still could not bear to watch a video or movie that involved loss and suffering of any kind without becoming terrified. I suggested that there was an inner resource she had already developed without even knowing it. She agreed to practice discovering what it could be. Once a week, her mother rented her a video such as *Bambi* that had an event of loss in the narrative. I taught her how to use the remote control to stop it, shut down the volume, reverse it, etcetera. Before watching, she got her room ready with comforting things: soft pillows, her favorite stuffed animals, pictures of herself in her moments of success, and so on. She began to watch the video and whenever she began to feel scared, she'd pause it, turn off the sound, and go in her room to comfort herself. Then, when she felt ready, she'd go back, choose the distance she wanted to be from the television set, and begin to watch again. I explained that she could do this as many times as necessary. After each video, I asked her to draw a picture of how she felt inside at the end of the movie. After doing this with five videos, she came back to my house for a conversation.

Mali was bubbling. She said she learned that she had developed a compassionate heart from her early experiences. She came to realize through her "practice" that she would never really be alone, because she felt such a strong connection for all the beings in the world who were wounded and suffering.

Inspiration

Rachel Naomi Remen, M.D., a beloved author, teacher, and healer, tells a remarkable story about how inner resources can grow us larger than the wounds that challenge us. She describes a patient of hers, a young man with juvenile diabetes, who, when he was first diagnosed, became self-destructive and full of rage. After six months in therapy with Rachel, he had a most amazing dream. He was sitting facing a small stone statue of the Buddha, young, serene, peaceful. Then, without warning, a dagger was thrown from behind the patient, and lodged itself deep in the Buddha's heart.

He felt betrayed, outraged, and in despair, but as he sat there crying, the statue, ever so slowly, began to grow. It was just as peaceful as before, but the Buddha grew and grew until it was enormous, filling the room. The knife remained, but it had become a tiny speck on the breast of the huge, smiling Buddha. Rachel ends the telling of this story by saying, "The life in us may be stronger than all that [challenges us] and free us even from that which we must endure. Sometimes someone dreams a dream for us all."

Conversation of Discovery

What is your favorite scar? Tell its story and ask your child to tell you the story of his or hers.

What wound or challenge in your life did you survive, even though you were not sure you would? What blow have you recovered from? How did you do it? What inner resources or strengths did you develop that helped you? How could its healing provide a connection to others. What would a symbol or image be of that resource?

If and when it feels right, tell this story to your child. Ask him or her to draw you a picture of that symbol or tell you a story about a similar time in his or her life.

Smart Family Practice

Begin a family storytelling time. It can be every Saturday morning, or it can be whenever you are in the car and have the time to tell stories without interruption.

You might tell Rachel's story of the boy and the Buddha and talk about the idea of growing bigger than your wounds. Ask them if they know of anyone who has done that or tell them of a time that you saw them do that. You might want to share some of the stories of children in this book or others you know who have experienced some difficulty that brought out the best in them, and then enriched the community.

This is an ongoing practice. When you find a movie, or read an article or book that carries the story of a character who developed inner resources as he or she met and moved through challenges in life, be sure to share it with your children and encourage them to do the same with you. There is often an implicit message buried in the media that can help children learn to frame their own hard times in a totally different way. They can begin to see themselves as the heroes and heroines of their own life story.

Chapter Nine

Recognizing Thinking Talents

Mapping the Mind's Sky

"I possess tremendous power to make life miserable or joyous. I can be a tool of torture or an instrument of inspiration. I can humiliate or humor, hurt or heal. In all situations, it is my response that decides whether a crisis is escalated or de-escalated, and a person is humanized or dehumanized."

—HAIM GINOT

The basic premise of this book is that each child bears a potential that asks to be lived. Not even the darkest life is empty of some shining spot. In previous chapters, we have been discovering in our own and our children's differences what those bright places might be. It is with this last asset—thinking talents—that the pattern of gifts begin to shine, as if we have been looking at individual stars and now the whole constellation can emerge.

One root meaning of the *sapiens* in *Homo sapiens sapiens* is "wise." We are the wise species with the capacity to be aware of being wise. It is this unique ability to think and be aware that sets us apart. As a young child, I never understood why when the word *talent* was used, it referred only to someone in the performing arts or sports. It seemed to me that people who could think the best would be considered talented as well. Fifty years later, I believe the same thing.

Each child—and each parent, for that matter—has unique and specific ways of thinking, such as analysis or thinking ahead or feeling for others or humor, in which he or she excels. If all these talents could be assembled, like the shards of light my grandmother spoke of, they would compose the true brilliance and wisdom of our species.

In an orchestra, it is the individual excellence of each musician combined together in harmony that results in a fine collective performance. Similarly, on a baseball team, it is the blending together of each individual's separate and specific abilities to perform different tasks that determines a winning team.

When I worked with corporate leadership teams, it was their collective capacity to think well together, or not, that determined whether the company would succeed. But rarely did anyone pay attention to this. Thinking to them was like water is to a fish. It was transparent and its condition was largely ignored. Everyone tried to think in the same way as everyone else—analytically and in bullet points. If one person used images in his conversation, for example, the rest of the team would consider his thinking weird. If another asked questions, she would be considered indecisive. There were unstated norms of how you were supposed to think that people inferred and followed implicitly. The result, more often than not, was collective mediocrity.

I have experienced the same phenomenon in classrooms and families. One little boy was referred to me as having ADD (attention deficit disorder) because he kept staring out the window and didn't do his homework properly. He had been asked to write a definition of "infinity." What he put down on the paper was a Cream of Wheat box. When I inquired what he had meant by that, he described to me how, in the picture on the front of the box, you could see a man holding up a Cream of Wheat box. In that picture, if you could have seen it, there would be another man holding up the same box, and so on. That's what he thought infinity was. To his teacher, there was one way of thinking that was considered "right." It excluded this boy's unique, three-dimensional imagery, which if recognized and developed could be a significant gift to the rest of us.

In Marybeth's family, her parents and sisters all thought in very linear and procedural ways. She, on the other hand, was highly attuned to others' feelings and had a unique capacity to think into the future. She was considered the "odd one," and was teased, even humiliated for being too soft and too impractical.

What I am calling Thinking Talents are natural ways of thinking that a person excels at, and feels energized when using. They are so intrinsic that if they were to disappear, the person would be unrecognizable as him- or herself. Like a rough-cut diamond, they may appear to be as ordinary as a rock to the person, but when cultivated and polished, their unique value to the rest of us becomes apparent.

If we all have these bright gifts, and exercising them feels so good, why don't we always know how to identify and use them? One reason, as I've previously pointed out, is the deficit orientation of psychology and education. Many of us heard negative and pathological attributions about our natural talents as we grew up. When she was a child, Oprah Winfrey's natural self-assurance was described by her family members as being "too full of herself." An architect I worked with was described by the other members of his firm as a "lost soul." I followed him around one day and noticed that he spent far more time in the hallways talking to various employees than at his drafting table. At board meetings, he was bored, but during breaks and lunch, in conversation with others, he came alive. I asked him if he noticed the difference.

"Oh, yeah, I just like listening to people tell me about their problems, that's all."

"You actually *like* to hear people tell you about their troubles?" I asked incredulously.

"Well, yeah, I do. I guess I've always liked connecting with people on that level. Even as a kid, I used to be everybody's 'shoulder to cry on,' you know?"

I was flabbergasted. "I do know, but, well, did you ever think about going into human resources or becoming a counselor? You seem to have a natural gift of empathy and attentiveness."

He looked away, embarrassed. "Nah. My dad always told me that was girl stuff, and that if I kept it up, I'd end up on a shrink's couch. My high school guidance counselor told me all the aptitude tests I took showed that I should be an architect." He shrugged and his chest shrank. His basic assumption was that his gifts were a curse, not a blessing. He acquired skills and training as an architect, but his soul was lost following someone else's stars.

A second reason that recognizing our own and our children's Thinking Talents can be such a challenge is that they come so easily to us that we don't even know we have them or that they make us exceptional. In the ordinary light of day, stars are not apparent. An eleven-year-old girl I met in one of our workshops uncovered her natural talent of humor. She had always known she was able to make people laugh, but considered it more of a handicap than a gift. The rest of us listened incredulously as she described how she had always thought of her brilliant sense of humor as "that old thing." She insisted it could not be a gift because it had gotten her into so much trouble. Teachers and her parents all told her she was "trying to be a smart-ass."

A third reason for the difficulty we experience in recognizing gifts and talents is the absence of language or navigational charts that could help us explore this fertile terrain. In this chapter, I'd like to offer two approaches that are like maps of the constellations in the night sky and will help you uncover the pattern of your own and your child's spots of brilliance. The first will give you an overall sense of the territory and the second focuses it down into specific detail.

Redefining Intelligence

"Our survey data prove that intelligence comes in at least four different forms. Typical tests of intelligence measure only two thoroughly, and disregard the other two almost completely. . . . When we assess talent without considering the entire spectrum of intelligences, we mismatch education, careers, and jobs. The consequences are particularly painful when loving but uninformed parents attempt to help their children make educational choices."

—NED HERMANN, ORGANIZATIONAL PSYCHOLOGIST

It was a frozen white afternoon in mid-December when the phone rang. I was writing and had no intention of answering it, but before thought could interrupt, my hand picked up the receiver. A man's voice asked if I was the woman who had written *How Your Child IS Smart* and *The Open Mind.* Within minutes I was engaged in a fascinating conversation with Ned Hermann. He told me he was very excited by what I had written about Mind Patterns, and that he also had spent most of his life researching the expansion of human capacity, first as director of training at General Electric and then as the head of his own organization.

When his book *The Creative Brain* arrived a few days later, I was humbled to discover that he was well into his seventies and an expert in the field of human development, brain dominance, and learning. In subsequent conversations, it became clear we were each traveling along different banks of the same river. He put it this way: "My experience in working with tens of thousands of people supports the conclusion that most if not all of us are capable of finding some island of potential brilliance still hidden in our mental seascape."

Hermann's model, based on over 130,000 brain dominance surveys (HBDI), proposes that there are four different aspects of intelligence, four different preferred ways of knowing and approaching problems that function together as a whole brain: analytical, procedural, relational, and innovative. He identified the first two as left-mode dominant processes and the latter two as right-mode dominant. In the same way that we develop preferred hand, eye, ear, and foot dominance, he said that we also develop brain dominances that are expressed in how we think about, understand, and express what we know. Although Hermann believed we are born with the capacity to use all these different mental processing modes, he said that as we mature we tend to develop preferences, habitual ways of thinking about the world. You might think about these as different ways of being smart.

As our lives shape us, the way the wind shapes a tree, we tend to develop particular preferences and avoidances of these different ways of knowing. Our preferred mode of knowing is the one we are most likely to use when faced with the need to solve a problem, and correlates strongly with what we prefer to learn and how we go about it. For the sake of clarity, I call these "mental preferences," to distinguish them from Mind Patterns or learned skills. Herman's findings were that 7 percent of adults have one mental preference, 60 percent favor two, 30 percent favor three, and 3 percent have equal preferences for all four.

Let's take the children in one particular family and look at their assets through this lens. For the sake of simplicity, we'll suppose that each has only one mental preference, and we'll make them all boys.

Mel, the oldest son, prefers thinking logically. He often asks, "What are the facts?" He enjoys theories and naturally seems to analyze a problem by breaking it down into pieces. He considers himself very logical and wants things to be proven.

Jeff, the second son, strongly prefers procedural thinking. In essence, he is concerned about the form of something. It is very important to him that he be in control, that things are consistent. He prefers doing things the way they have been done before.

Andy, the third son, prefers relational thinking over any other way of approaching a problem. He often wonders how people are feeling as well as how one thing relates to another.

John, the youngest son, prefers innovative thinking. He frequently thinks into the future, and comes up with one new idea after another.

If a child or adult avoids any one of the four particular ways of thinking, it might show up like this:

Mel avoids relational thinking. He overlooks the way people could be feeling about a given situation and is often described as "cold" or "a bean counter."

Jeff avoids innovative thinking. He thinks about the past and dislikes having to think about the future or trying something new.

Andy avoids analytic thinking. He may overlook the data and can be considered too touchy-feely for his own good.

John avoids procedural thinking. He therefore overlooks details and the way things have been done in the past. He may be seen as flighty and be bored by history.

Since the majority of us prefer two or three ways of thinking, it becomes a bit more complex, but also more interesting. If Jane prefers procedural and relational thinking, for example, she may be in a constant inner tug-of-war between the "part" of her that wants things organized and the "part" of her that feels. If Martin uses both innovative and analytic thinking, his civil war may be between the aspect of his thinking that comes up with new ideas and the one that shoots them down because there isn't enough data to make a case for them.

Research has not clearly indicated at what point these preferences form and when they "track" in. I have observed very young children with clear preferences and others who seem to shift this way and that through puberty.

The more mental preferences we have, the longer it may take us to mature, because we are complex. Belinda is a case in point. She described herself as jumping around from one thing to another, a jack of all trades and a master of none. She had all four mental preferences, could not choose a major in college, and was slow to make decisions in general. Her mind was like a barbershop quartet that had to learn to think in harmony. She was a natural leader, however, because she understood and could integrate the different perspectives of various people on the outside as she lived that struggle internally.

The other side of the coin is the 7 percent who have a single dominant mental preference. They have the benefit of living a harmonious internal life. However, the vast majority of people around them perceive the world differently than they do. Getting along in life requires some ability to understand the way another person thinks. This can be quite difficult for someone with a strong single preference. It's just hard to imagine there could be more than one way of thinking about a problem if your inner perspective is always aligned.

My conversations with Ned Hermann and years of working with his model reaffirmed what my grandmother and my own life experience had already taught me: that every person has a mind in which there is an "island of brilliance," some particular area of optimal functioning that can provide that person with an experience of enormous fulfillment, competence, and joyful activity. Uncovering that brilliance in one's child and helping develop it is one of the most gratifying things any parent can do.

Inspiration

Ned shared with me the true story of Mary Lempke, known as May, a middle-aged Canadian woman who felt challenged by the plight of an apparently hopeless case, a baby named "Leslie," who was born blind and with severe cerebral palsy. Doctors predicted her death within months, but May said, "Nothing ever dies that comes to me," and adopted the little boy, expecting that he would be able to walk and talk. She persisted with her belief, unconditional love, and encouragement. Finally, at twelve years old, he could indeed walk. In his early teens, while watching him play with a piece of string, May had an intuition to expose him to music. She brought a piano into the house, and filled their rooms with music from a phonograph. Three years later, Leslie was playing the piano. A few years after that, he began to sing, and eight years later, he began to talk. He was twenty-five.

His musical skills were so developed by that time that he began to give public concerts, astounding audiences. He could play back perfectly any music he heard after hearing it for the first time. Ned Hermann's explanation was that Leslie's right-mode musical abilities were brilliant even though his left-mode capabilities were minimal—that is, his innovative and relational modes were exceptional, while his analytical and procedural modes were barely functional. Some people described Leslie as an idiot, but Ned said of him, "Imagine what it would be like to grow up never seeing the light of day and occupying a body whose every limb seemed to have a mind of its own! But that's not the whole story. Another part is the extraordinary faith, love, and dedication of May and her positive assumptions about what he could become. She demonstrated that Leslie's hidden mental potential could be accessed and put to use."

Conversations of Discovery

Once you begin to see a particular constellation in the sky—say, the Big Dipper—you may wonder how you could have ever not been able to find it. In my experience, this information about mental preferences has a similar impact. Just spend some time noticing your own and other family members' way of approaching a particular problem or experience. How do you do it? How do they? Analytically, procedurally, relationally, innovatively, or a combination?

The chart that follows may be a useful reference.

As we teach, we also learn. Spend a bit of time explaining this notion to your child. You can compare notes on favorite movie stars, sports heroes, television programs—the list is endless—and guess what their mental preferences are.

Analytical	Innovative
[Why are we doing this?] Concerned with facts, logic, and rationality.	[What are all the possible ways to do this?] Concerned with doing new things, seeing new patterns, bringing things together in a new way.
Procedural	**Relational**
[How will we do this?] Concerned with doing things in a sequential, orderly fashion.	[Who will we do it with?] Concerned with people and feelings, intuitive knowing.

If your child has a strong preference in an area that you might avoid—innovative thinking, for example—ask for his or her help when you have to come up with a new idea. Likewise, encourage your child to go to someone in the family who is very strong in a domain he or she may be avoiding.

Smart Family Practice

For a family activity, each person writes on a piece of paper what he or she values about their own "analytic self," "procedural self," "relational self," and "innovative self."

Each person shares what he or she has written and then discusses the major differences between family members, and how those differences could be used to help one another.

Recognizing Thinking Talents

"We are always more anxious to be distinguished for a talent which we do not possess, than to be praised for the fifteen which we do."
—MARK TWAIN

If Ned Hermann's whole-brain model is like an AAA road map of the United States, then the next model I'd like to share with you is like a topographical map of specific territories within each state. My associates and I have been using this information in recent years and have found it extremely effective in helping parents and children recognize their specific thinking assets.

Four things distinguish Thinking Talents from skills, personality traits, or other capacities: (1) They are innate ways of thinking—that is, you've always been really good at doing them, even if you never had any training in them, and you always will be really good at them. One of mine, for example, is storytelling. As far back as I can remember, I was telling stories. And when I am a little old lady laid out in a coffin, I will probably push up the lid and declare, "This reminds me of a story about . . ." (2) You get natural pleasure and energy from using your Thinking Talents. You can't burn out when using them. (3) You excel in using these talents and you would enjoy developing skills or capacities in them. (4) They are your default way of thinking, mental lenses through which you understand and relate to the world.

Recent research on excellence by the Gallup Organization shows that by the time we are adults, most of us use five Thinking Talents out of a possible thirty-four. They were interested in finding out why some organizations were more productive than others and what were the determining factors. They did a computer analysis of 198,000 questions, and found five that were the most highly predictive of organizational profitability and productivity. The question that interested them the most was a true/false one where people stated whether they had the opportunity to use their strengths every day at work. The more people who answered "yes" to this single question, the higher the success of the organization. Gallup became very interested in why this was true and in what those strengths were. Thirty years of research into individual and organizational excellence (a sample of two million people from sixty-three countries) resulted in the discovery that there were thirty-four of what they called specific "signature strengths" in their sample population. They stated that most adults have five. This means that there is one chance out of thirty-three million of finding someone else with the same five strengths as you have.

My colleagues and I, based on the latest findings in neuroscience and our own experience in working with children and families, synthesized a new way of recognizing and defining these mental assets. We call them Thinking Talents and describe thirty-six of them.

The way our particular Thinking Talents are combined determines our uniqueness. Like notes in a musical chord, "smart" means being able to blend the ones you have together in harmony. The more Thinking Talents a person has, the more he or she has to learn how to use them in such a way that they don't work against one another. Monique, for example, a high school senior, has eight Thinking Talents: the capacity to think logically, feel for others, think ahead, think about the past, concentrate, innovate, be optimistic, and the talent for "fixing it."

Whenever she tried to make a decision about what to do after high school, she couldn't make up her mind. It was as if her capacity to think about the past, facts, concentrate, and fix it were on one side of a teeter-totter and her capacity to feel for others, think ahead, and innovate were on the other side. It took her much longer to come to a decision than it would have for someone who had only five Thinking Talents.

It isn't clear at what age Thinking Talents develop, or whether we are born with them or, like the oak tree in the acorn, they emerge over time. Because we use this model with children, we don't limit the number to five, and we've included thirty-six of them. It doesn't mean you're smarter because you have more. When children are young, they often seem to have many Thinking Talents. As they go through puberty, the brain begins to "shed" or prune many of its neural circuits. More and more of the cells that "fire together, wire together." Some become like superhighways. Some of the circuits that haven't been used are shut down.

It isn't necessary to search frantically for the "right" Thinking Talents. It's far more useful to be curious about which talents have always been there for you, come the most naturally, and energize you the most.

What we know from extensive research by Ned Hermann and the Gallup Organization as well as our own experience is that *the closer the alignment between an individual's Thinking Talents and the mental requirements of a task or job, the more likely success and satisfaction will occur.* For example, one young teenager in Vermont, John, had the following thinking talents: innovation, thinking ahead, goal-setting, humor, and standing out. He suffered through his math classes, almost failed most of his science labs, barely made it through history. In addition, he was always explaining to his teachers how they could present the information in new and interesting ways, which didn't exactly endear him to them. At home, his father and older brother both had mostly procedural and analytic Thinking Talents. His need to stand out and accomplish something was constantly thwarted until he joined his high school newspaper. Suddenly there was an avenue for his gifts. As he became recognized for his humor, vision, and innovative ideas, his sense of self-worth began to grow. He finally felt as if he belonged to the human race. Two decades later finds him excelling as a magazine editor and successful entrepreneur.

Following are the thirty-six Thinking Talents we have discovered in adults and children. Which ones do you excel at and give you energy?

The next chart, Thinking Preferences, has the thirty-six Thinking Talents arranged into the four corresponding Hermann quadrants.

THINKING TALENTS

Thinking and doing with others
Enjoys working things out in a
group rather than alone.

Sticks to a single goal or activity
Thrives when focusing on something for
a long period of time.

Making new friends easily
Enjoys the challenge of meeting and
dealing with new people.

*Wanting things to be
fair for everybody*
Needs to know that everyone involved is
being treated equally.

*Understanding others'
emotions and needs*
Instead of thinking about oneself,
thinks of others.

*Knowing what's wrong and
finding solutions*
Likes to make things better.

Willing to change
Goes with the flow and what is
best for others.

Collecting facts, ideas, or objects
Enjoys gathering interesting things.

Getting it done
Impatient for action rather than contemplation.
Must make something happen.

Usually looking for a challenge
The daily drive to accomplish something
and meet a goal.

Making people laugh
Enjoys finding what is funny about
situations and sharing it.

*Likes to make everyone feel
part of the group*
Always trying to find a way to include
people in a group.

Thinking of new ideas, and doing things in new ways

Loves to create and to do things that have never been done before.

Making a few close friendships; uncomfortable with strangers

Likes to be close and genuine with just a few people.

Connecting people or ideas

Combines different ideas or people into something new or larger.

Always needing to learn something new

Energized by learning itself.

Searching for ideas that explain things

Fascinated by new ideas, theories, and concepts.

Sorting or arranging

Enjoys putting many things into the best form. Organizes what's messy.

Helping others learn and grow

Recognizes possibilities in others and
wants to help them succeed.

Thinking positively

Looking on the bright side. Always on the lookout
for the positive; contagiously enthusiastic.

Wanting people to get along

Prefers agreement and harmony, does not
like fighting or argument of any kind.

Noticing people's differences and needs

Easily sees what makes each person different,
and what their qualities are.

*Doing things in an exact
and orderly way*

Enjoys making detailed order from confusion.

*Dependable, wanting
to do things right*

Thrives on being responsible.

Trying to make everything great
Driven to do the best with the least.

Confident about what you can do
Naturally trust yourself, and feel sure of yourself.

Wanting to be noticed
Likes to be recognized when he/she
makes a difference.

Wanting to write or tell stories
Needs to explain things by using metaphors and
telling a tale to bring an idea to life.

*Strategizing many ways to
think about something*
Enjoys thinking about all the possible options:
"If this happens, then we could do this or that or that."

Likes to direct or give orders
Enjoys taking over and telling others what to do.

Usually looking into the future
Fascinated by thinking "what if…"

*Needs to think something over
by him- or herself*
Usually reflecting and thinking things through solo.

Usually looking to the past
Enjoys thinking about history and what has happened.

Wanting the facts
Wants to know the reasons and logic.
Needs specific data.

Strong sense of right or wrong
Uses strong beliefs as guide to behavior; people
know where he or she stands.

Usually needing to be first
Thrives on competition and comparing self to others.

Thinking Preferences

ANALYTIC

TALENTS IN

PROCEDURAL

INNOVATIVE

 INNOVATION
 TAKING CHARGE
 LOVE OF LEARNING
 THINKING AHEAD

 STANDING OUT
 STRATEGY
 FLEXIBILITY
 LOVING IDEAS

ADRANTS

 THINKING ALONE

 GOAL-SETTING

RELATIONAL

 OPTIMISM
 INCLUDING
 CONNECTION
 INTIMACY

 PEACEMAKING
 ENROLLING
 STORYTELLING
 PERSONALIZING

 VALUES
 MENTORING
 FEELING FOR OTHERS
 COLLABORATION

Inspiration

Oftentimes, children's Thinking Talents, because they are unrecognized, become disguised as what I call "near gifts." Here are a few true stories of "near gifts" that were uncovered by resourceful parents.:

Jo, age six, was described by her parents as stubborn and difficult to motivate unless they forced her into doing what they wanted her to do. This produced too much wear and tear on all of them. One day, during gymnastics, her mother noticed that Jo refused to participate unless several girls were involved in a particular movement. Then she willingly entered in. After the class was over, Jo's mom stayed and talked to the teacher, who told her that her daughter loved to compete. Whenever there was a contest or any kind of an opportunity to be first, Jo would be fully engaged.

Although she had always tried to encourage Jo's collaborative skills, when mom began to encourage her daughter to be the best or be first, Jo jumped right in with no further motivation necessary. "I'll bet you can't clean those dishes before your sister can." "I wonder if you can do your homework faster than you did it last night." "First one into the car wins."

Sure enough, when recognized as a Thinking Talent, wanting to win opened the door Jo needed to motivate herself to excel.

Sonjo was described by his eighth-grade teachers as withdrawn and isolated. The school suggested he be medicated for an anxiety disorder. At home, he often went off on his own for long periods of time, wandering in the fields near his family's South Dakota farm. He was part of a large family—six brothers and two sisters—where everybody chipped in on both work and play.

Sonjo's grandfather refused to allow him to be medicated. Instead, he asked to go for a walk with his grandson. Sonjo was silent for the first fifteen minutes, which was just fine with his grandfather. Then they found a tree and both sat down under it. His grandfather asked why Sonjo liked to be alone so much. His reply was surprising: "I just need to think things over, that's all. I need quiet and a long view. Everyplace I go—school, home, church, the bus . . . everyplace is filled with people yammering. When I'm out here on my own, I can hear myself think. Sometimes ideas are all swirling in my mind until I start to sit here in the quiet. Then they get untangled. Things just start making sense to me. I guess that's why I like to be alone, Grandpa. Do you think that means there's something wrong with me? Nobody else seems to need this."

Although he didn't have a name for it at the time, his grandfather recognized Sonjo's need for time to think alone and knew how difficult it was for him to get the space he needed in a crowded family. He became his champion and Sonjo flourished in the spaciousness that now was his.

Nan, aged fifteen, and her older sister, Terry, did not get along. Terry complained that Nan was always criticizing the way she did things and was extremely negative. Nan complained that Terry only cared about herself and had a "one-track mind." Their mother, Elizabeth, said she couldn't stand their continual bickering.

As I sat in their living room on a Monday night after dinner, I became aware of Nan criticizing her sister for leaving the dishes half washed in the sink. After a short period of time, I realized that she had a natural "rearview mirror." Nan's particular Thinking Talent of "Fixing It" was surfacing over and over again, pointing out the best way any particular problem could be solved.

An hour later, listening to Terry talk to her friends on the phone, I realized that she had "Concentration" as one of her Thinking Talents. Once her mind found a "groove," thinking about the English paper she had started before dinner, for example, that's all she could think about until it was complete. Doing the dishes was irrelevant until she had completed that paper.

In addition, Terry had "Optimism" for another Thinking Talent. In any situation, she came up with the best possible explanation for why it had occurred. It was this optimism and Nan's need to "fix it" that tangled like a cat and dog in a late-night alley.

Both of her daughters described Elizabeth as a wimp. In fact, it was her Thinking Talent of "Peacemaking" trying to emerge. She was a mediation counselor and her whole life was dedicated to creating harmony between people, not because she was a wimp, but because she really enjoyed making harmony happen. The constant bickering made Elizabeth feel totally inept, because she couldn't give to her own daughters what she gave so freely to everyone else.

Once the three of them recognized the Thinking Talents hiding beneath their "near gifts," they could understand what each of them needed and negotiate more successfully to get those needs met.

Conversations of Discovery

- Listen in to a conversation your child has with someone else or with several other people. Instead of paying attention to the content of the conversation, notice what Thinking Talents could be talking at any given moment. What is the central concern? Where could he or she be coming from?
- With your child, go through the five bubble diagrams that follow and help each other uncover what each of your thinking talents could be. Come back to the conversation after a couple of days and notice if you've changed or refined your choices.

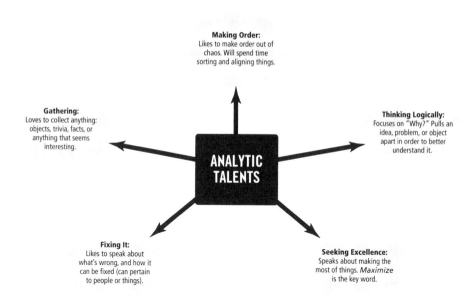

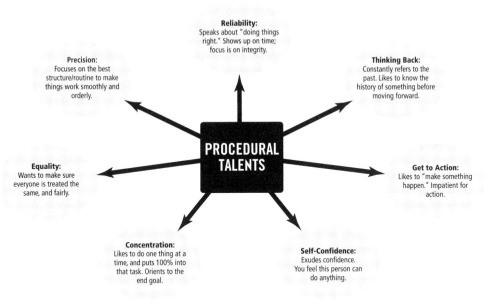

Reliability: Speaks about "doing things right." Shows up on time; focus is on integrity.

Precision: Focuses on the best structure/routine to make things work smoothly and orderly.

Thinking Back: Constantly refers to the past. Likes to know the history of something before moving forward.

PROCEDURAL TALENTS

Equality: Wants to make sure everyone is treated the same, and fairly.

Get to Action: Likes to "make something happen." Impatient for action.

Concentration: Likes to do one thing at a time, and puts 100% into that task. Orients to the end goal.

Self-Confidence: Exudes confidence. You feel this person can do anything.

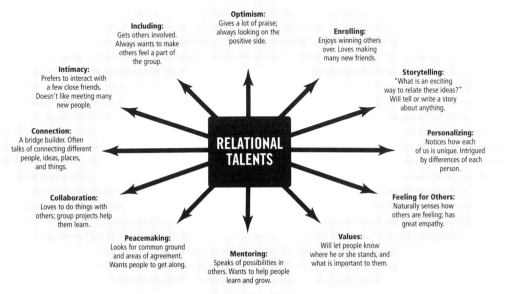

Optimism: Gives a lot of praise; always looking on the positive side.

Including: Gets others involved. Always wants to make others feel a part of the group.

Enrolling: Enjoys winning others over. Loves making many new friends.

Intimacy: Prefers to interact with a few close friends. Doesn't like meeting many new people.

Storytelling: "What is an exciting way to relate these ideas?" Will tell or write a story about anything.

Connection: A bridge builder. Often talks of connecting different people, ideas, places, and things.

RELATIONAL TALENTS

Personalizing: Notices how each of us is unique. Intrigued by differences of each person.

Collaboration: Loves to do things with others; group projects help them learn.

Feeling for Others: Naturally senses how others are feeling; has great empathy.

Peacemaking: Looks for common ground and areas of agreement. Wants people to get along.

Mentoring: Speaks of possibilities in others. Wants to help people learn and grow.

Values: Will let people know where he or she stands, and what is important to them.

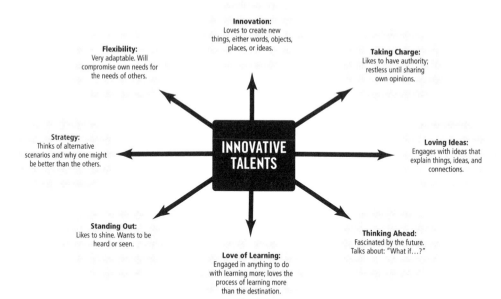

Innovation:
Loves to create new
things, either words, objects,
places, or ideas.

Flexibility:
Very adaptable. Will
compromise own needs for
the needs of others.

Taking Charge:
Likes to have authority;
restless until sharing
own opinions.

Strategy:
Thinks of alternative
scenarios and why one might
be better than the others.

INNOVATIVE
TALENTS

Loving Ideas:
Engages with ideas that
explain things, ideas, and
connections.

Standing Out:
Likes to shine. Wants to be
heard or seen.

Thinking Ahead:
Fascinated by the future.
Talks about: "What if...?"

Love of Learning:
Engaged in anything to do
with learning more; loves the
process of learning more
than the destination.

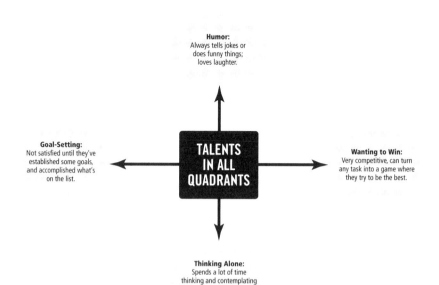

Humor:
Always tells jokes or
does funny things;
loves laughter.

Goal-Setting:
Not satisfied until they've
established some goals,
and accomplished what's
on the list.

TALENTS
IN ALL
QUADRANTS

Wanting to Win:
Very competitive, can turn
any task into a game where
they try to be the best.

Thinking Alone:
Spends a lot of time
thinking and contemplating
on their own.

Smart Family Practices

Post Thinking Talent stickies on the refrigerator, a different color for each member of the family. Remember, a Thinking Talent is a way of thinking that gives a person energy, and has always been easy to do. For Mason, as an example, we would put up a sticky for "Strategy," for Carol one for "Including," and a "Storytelling" sticky for Joan.

Let each child design a play time for the rest of the family based on his or her Thinking Talents. Mason might have the whole family plan scenarios for the next vacation. Carol might interview each family member about the ways they are smart, then make a big chart that anyone could add to. Joan might tell stories at dinner on Tuesday nights about talents she noticed in each family member during the week.

SECTION THREE

Handholds in the Darkness

The time was long ago during a war that only some of us can remember. The place was far away, but close enough for some of us to know. Many children were orphaned. They lived alone in abandoned attics or basements, hiding in whatever corners they could find, scrambling for scraps of something to eat. Hunger was the worst of it; that, and having nothing to hang on to in a world where fear had fragmented whatever was fragile.

Relief came finally. People with kind eyes and open hands gathered the children one by one and brought them into orphanages, where they could huddle together and be cared for. Their stomachs stopped aching. But hope had vanished and sleep would not come to the children.

The caregiving people tried everything. They rocked the children. They sang to them. They whispered that morning would come and their bellies would be filled again. Nothing helped. The children could not sleep.

One of the women had an idea. She went from child to child, and as she tucked a blanket around each thin body, she placed into their hands a piece of bread.

It worked. The children clutched at their piece of bread as if it were a rope let down in the darkness, a private corner of hope, a tiny promise that there would be food in the morning, a handhold to carry them through the darkness. The children slept.

Utilizing and Developing Your Child's Gifts

"Meaning is not something you stumble across, like the answer to a riddle or the prize in a treasure hunt. Meaning is something you build into your life. You build it out of your own past, out of your affections and loyalties, out of the experience of humankind as it is passed on to you, out of your own talent and the people you love, out of the values for which you are willing to sacrifice something. The ingredients are there. You are the only one who can put them together into that unique pattern that will be your life. Let it be a life that has dignity and meaning for you."

—John W. Gardner, author and activist

No parent can prevent or eliminate the challenges a child will face in his or her life. Our brains are programmed to learn, to adapt, to be flexible. An asset-focused approach does not mean ignoring or denying challenges. The conversations and inquiry you are involved in with your child will help transform how he or she is experiencing and relating to those challenges. Remember what it is like to teach a child to ride a bike for the first time without training wheels? You can hold on for only so long. You cannot prevent the spills and falls that are an inevitable part of the process. What you can do, however, is arrange the conditions and give the support, encouragement, and tools that will make it possible for your child to learn through those challenges.

In my own struggle to learn my way through cancer, I realized that there are three specific beliefs that diminish our trust in ourselves, leaving us feeling helpless when we are challenged. They are that (1) a problem is permanent ("This is chronic and will always be this way"); (2) a problem is part of our personal nature ("I am my diagnosis"); and (3) a problem is pervasive ("I am not knowledgeable enough to change this"). When our children struggle with a challenge, therefore, if we wish to help them have an orientation of possibility, we must help them create life-expanding beliefs.

This section is written to help you provide the bridge between limitations and possibilities, as well as the faith that your child can learn to cross it. This is no small thing. When most of the culture is focusing on what is wrong, you will be focusing on how to help your child utilize and develop what is right and create communities to support it.

Like the orphans in the preceding story, when our children are focused in fear on what may not be possible, it is our responsibility to place into their hands the nourishment that their natural assets provide so they can trust themselves as they struggle through the unknown. In this case, the "piece of bread" takes the form of an inquiry that will help them find what they need.

When others are pointing out what's the matter with your child, you will be asking, "What really matters about this given situation?" When others are pointing to what hasn't worked, you'll be inquiring into "What has been possible in the past and what did it take to accomplish it?" When others are suggesting ways to fix the problem, you'll be asking your child, "How can you use what has worked and is working to move beyond what isn't?" And when others are predicting a limited future, you and your children will be creating alliances with others who are asking, "What else could be possible and what are the steps we can take to make that possibility a reality?"

Sound like a challenge? It is. But think of one time you've already done this, even in some small way, since you've begun reading this book. That moment can be your own piece of bread.

Chapter Ten

Utilizing What's Right to Overcome What's Wrong

"When inspired by a great purpose, a wonderful project, your thoughts shatter their bonds; your mind travels beyond limitations; your consciousness extends in all directions; and you discover a new and exciting world. Hidden forces, talents, and faculties spring to life and you find yourself to be far greater than you ever dreamed you could be."
—PATANJALI, YOGI

The word *utilize* means to employ something for its inherent and natural purpose. In this chapter, we'll be exploring many different ways of employing children's assets to learn their way through challenges. Rather than trying to live their lives according to someone else's imagination, utilization empowers children's authenticity and inherent sense of self-worth by encouraging them to use the gifts they were born with as if they were the sail of their own boat.

Each asset we discuss in this chapter will have a slightly different focus, but in any domain, what you'll essentially be exploring with your child is: What has made past successes work, and how that could be used to move beyond what isn't working in the present.

Your inquiry will be helping your child's brain "decompartmentalize" its resources: Take an asset used in one situation and transfer it to another. Think of it as cross-referencing. My grandmother did this when she made braided bread every Friday afternoon. She was very short and had many tall sons who frequently fought with one another. As her nimble fingers would entwine the hanks of dough, she'd mumble, "Let Bill and Sam be like this. Let Allie and Izzy be like this."

A CEO I worked with used to get very nervous when he had to make a presentation before the board of directors. He was proficient and confident when playing golf, however. I suggested that he decompartmentalize by planning his presentations while holding his putter.

Rather than always searching outside themselves for answers and direction, utilization enables children to decompartmentalize their inner assets—what they already know—and use them in domains where they feel clueless or stuck. Thus, it deepens their trust of themselves and their capacity to deal with difficulty step by step, day by day.

Utilizing Successes

"There is always a moment in childhood when a door opens and lets the future in."

—GRAHAM GREENE, AUTHOR

Robin had to make an oral presentation to a very important teacher. Her whole grade hinged on saying "the right thing," which, of course, terrified her. Her father asked her to describe a time when she had successfully convinced someone else that she knew what she was talking about. Her face lit up as she told a story about a time she had convinced him to give her the keys to the car. Then she whined, "But that doesn't count, because I knew you'd agree if I told you I'd be in on time."

Her father put his hand on her shoulder and replied, "So knowing what the other person's criteria are makes it easier for you to articulate what you know?"

Robin looked quizzically at him, "Well, of course, but how can I know what Mrs. Johannssen's criteria of success would be for me?"

He waited a few seconds and then said quietly, "What if you asked her?"

Without hesitation, Robin replied, "You mean just *ask* right up front, like, 'Mrs. J, how will you know if I know this? What will you be listening for?' "

Her father smiled but said nothing.

Robin chewed on her thumb and then said, "Is that fair? I mean, why not? I could go in tomorrow and just ask her that very question. Then I'd know whether to give her facts or history or maps. Dad, you're brilliant!"

Robin's dad's brilliance was merely helping her remember her own success, and then figure out how to apply it where she was stuck. The most important component in helping children do this is asking questions that will bring their awareness to what the conditions were in the past when they met a similar challenge. Tigest, for example, did brilliantly in French but was having problems understanding biology. Her godmother asked her what it was that made biology so difficult. Tigest was quick to explain that her mind kept snagging on words she had never heard before. Her godmother asked her how she had learned all the French words so well. Tigest showed the flash cards she had made, and then the lightbulb went off. She realized she could made similar flash cards for biology. In a month, her grades and self-confidence rapidly climbed.

If a situation arises when your child has never had such a successful experience, then you can ask if she knows of anyone else who has ever succeeded in a similar circumstance, inquiring into that pattern and wondering together how to apply it to the current challenge. If, for example, a child has to take piano lessons and has never succeeded at playing a musical instrument, you could take him to a concert that features a young and obviously joyous pianist and at the end ask what your child observed, and how he could use that as a guide.

Utilizing Mind Patterns

"The law of flotation was not derived by studying that which sinks."
—WAYNE DYER, PH.D., MOTIVATIONAL SPEAKER

The information that follows was adapted from an earlier book I co-authored with Anne Powell, *How Your Child IS Smart: A Life-Changing Approach to Learning.* It will support you in helping your child utilize his or her particular Mind Pattern to think through challenges. I suggest you also share it respectfully with mentors, teachers, and tutors, bearing in mind that each of us also has unique ways of presenting material.

The Coach: Helping Children Who Use the AKV Mind Pattern

Children whose minds use this pattern present what can be a confusing academic challenge for today's parents and teachers. They can easily learn and express what they know verbally. Their verbal prowess creates an expectation of easy academic success. They often have very intense or revved-up physical energy. They can also be seriously challenged by tasks that require their visual theta mode to focus in detailed ways, most notably reading and writing. Until recently, there has been little flexibility in how these essential skills are taught, so children with this Mind Pattern are sometimes thought of as both "gifted" and "learning disabled."

As parents, you can help your child monitor his or her physical energy, coming to recognize when it is demanding they move or play with something in their hands. He could tell you that at breakfast, for instance, it's a calm number three, but when waiting for the bus and fighting with his brother, it's a number seven. You can help him realize that every time it climbs above five, he needs to do something physical: "Oops, I'm at a seven now. I'd better do some push-ups before I do my homework."

You can most effectively support the development of your children's reading and writing skills working with the strengths of their style. They remember easily what they have heard and/or talked about. They usually love to be read to, so make this a regular practice, if possible. As their interest in reading builds, stop short of reading familiar lines or phrases and have them fill in the blank verbally. They will begin to put together the word on the page with the word they have spoken. Review words they recognize out loud with them frequently. Their desire to read and their personal experience will provide an important link between auditory and visual channels. Follow their excitement.

Once they've begun to read independently, children with this style may benefit from tracing the words on the page with their finger or reading aloud. Combining movement with reading may help them stay alert. For example, sitting in a rocking chair or pedaling on a stationary bike may provide enough motion to keep them from spacing out while they are reading. Invite them to tell you or to act out what happens in the stories they read. Their ability to remember and evaluate what they've read (or seen) will come from their speaking about it. They may choose large-print picture books or magazines for some time. Support them in selecting these books, which are easier on their eyes. Their interest and comfort should be the most important considerations in book selection.

The physical task of writing can be difficult for them. Provide big paper and lots of space for younger ones to write big as they learn their letters. Help them to remember how to form the letters with a rhyme like "A stick and circle makes a P, add one on the bottom and it's a B." Personal meaning will also make this practice more enjoyable. Encourage them to write letters to friends and relatives. Invite them to write stories of their experiences. Have them dictate at first, with you or another family member or friend as their scribe. Encourage them to do more and more of the writing themselves. Older children can use this dictation method with a tape recorder. Train them early in the use of a keyboard and computer. Understand that all written material, both what they create and what they receive, means a lot to them. Avoid scribbling on it or treating it casually.

In general, schoolwork is very visually focused. Find out what they like to do to rest their eyes or how they can ease into a restful daydream. Help them become conscious of this need for balance. Discover together pleasurable ways to do this—watching clouds and sunsets, or walking in wide-open places.

These children memorize by repeating material verbally; they are natural rap stars. Have them record, "lip sync," and create movements for what they must memorize. Teach them to put a rhythm to spelling words, or make up a song or cheer. Encourage them to repeat the rhythm softly to themselves when they are writing their words. Have them bounce a ball or do familiar dance steps while they repeat what they must learn.

If you are trying to help these children learn a new skill, invite them to teach you what they already know and expand from there. They generally will learn best by talking about it first and then doing what they've just heard. Encourage them to speak each of the steps as they do it. Written instructions can be confusing to children who learn this way. If you must use them, have your child read them out loud.

Children whose minds use this style organize by telling themselves or someone else what they are going to do. These children will probably not be inclined to write down their assignments. If they become forgetful, have them tell you what they are going to do on a daily basis. Listening to music of their own choice will help these children to concentrate.

The Communicator: Helping Children Who Use the AVK Mind Pattern

These children rarely have trouble succeeding in school. Their verbal ability can take them far in the academic world. Unfortunately, this can make them especially impatient with the physical skills that they learn more slowly. Provide gentle encouragement at home so they can learn with their hands and bodies at their own pace.

Children who use this Mind Pattern rarely get all the verbal airtime they need at school to solidify their learning. They have an intrinsic need to say what they understand in their own words. Parents can support them by setting aside time to listen, by having them tape record what they have to say and listening to it themselves, or by giving them opportunities to sing, be involved in plays, etcetera.

Seeing and experiencing what they are learning about can have a profound impact on these children. Help the learning come alive for them: If they're studying the fifty states, suggest they keep track of how many you visit or who you know who might live in each one. If they are interested in politics, take them with you to a community meeting, where they can witness or even get involved in local social action.

Help these kids develop their expertise by asking them their opinion on a wide range of topics, from the point of a television show to the reason they prefer vanilla to chocolate ice cream. Tell them what you are curious about, whether it's writing comedy, African drumming, or auto mechanics. Involve them in discussions about decisions that affect them.

Support any way these children want to be physically active, but don't force them to play team sports. Allow them to make choices in this regard and encourage them to learn physical activities privately and in small steps.

Children who use this Mind Pattern organize by talking about what needs to be done and jotting notes. They memorize by saying material repeatedly. They may also do well recording and listening or "lip syncing" to things they must memorize. The level of quiet at home may be an important factor for them while studying. Some find extraneous noise very distracting and need to have complete quiet to concentrate; others can concentrate well with background music or outside sound.

Encourage these children to plan variety into their timelines. They will get easily bored doing the same task for a long period of time and the quality will suffer. In working on projects, they can talk about what they want to do in elaborate detail, but they may try to plan something their hands cannot create easily. Encourage them to plan simple presentations.

The Mover-and-Shaker: Helping Children Who Use the KAV Mind Pattern

Some children with this Mind Pattern may have a very difficult time in school because they need to be moving to concentrate. Their abundant physical energy is sometimes labeled as "hyperactive" by slower-moving adults. When they "space out" in class, it is often triggered by the heavy visual input of most learning environments. Even for those who have not been so labeled, the visual demands and physical restrictions of traditional classrooms can make their experience a frustrating one. You can support them by providing what is only minimally offered at most schools: opportunities to use their bodies to learn and their eyes to create.

These children remember most easily what they've handled or experienced. Supplement reading and writing assignments with chances to get physically involved with whatever they're studying. Let them attach wires from batteries to test bulbs and complete a circuit themselves so they can help a demonstration or book diagram come alive. Field trips are significant for these children so that information has personal meaning.

Making models will reinforce class discussions and textbook chapters. Acting out the stories in their book or the word problems in math will increase their comprehension and skill development.

Encourage children with this Mind Pattern to play outside or participate in sports before doing homework. This will help balance out the sedentary nature of the typical school day and will make concentration easier when the time comes to sit down and work.

Find ways to ease the pressure and the difficulty of the reading and writing process. It may be hard for them to read without spacing out if they are not jiggling or moving. Sitting in a rocking chair or pedaling a stationary bike may provide the stimulation they need to concentrate while they are reading. Following along with their fingers on the page of print may help, too. Invite them to tell you about what happens in the stories they read. Ask them questions to help them discover how their feelings and experiences may be similar to the characters they are reading about. This will reinforce their comprehension. They may be most comfortable choosing large-print picture books or magazines.

The eye-hand coordination required by writing can be difficult for some children who learn this way. Get an easel, a chalkboard, or tape large paper to the wall so they can practice with their whole bodies while learning. Understand that their way of writing may not be neat and standardized.

The content of their writing should come out of their experience whenever possible. Encourage them to write stories of times they remember, or to send letters to friends about what they are doing. At first, it might help for you to take dictation so they can have the pleasure of creating without the struggle of trying to visually remember the formation of the letters.

Encourage these children to find ways to express their dreams and inner images. Help them explore the more creative aspects of their visual channel to balance the more focused aspects emphasized in school. Suggest dabbling at home with different kinds of art supplies—paints, clay, pastels, craft materials, or wood.

After being asked to concentrate in a visually detailed way for much of the school day, children who use this Mind Pattern may need opportunities to "space out" and take in the world more "widely." Help them discover what visual images are soothing and pleasant to look at. Invite them to take a walk with you and watch the clouds together, for example.

These children are very aware of their environment. Help them create study places where they can both move around and be comfortable. Discover together what works well with regard to furniture, light, warmth, fresh air, and moisture in the environment. "Neat" to them may mean making piles rather than making it "look" neat.

The Investigator: Helping Children Who Use the KVA Mind Pattern

Typically, these children are most enthusiastic about the parts of school that allow them to express their physical energy and coordination: gym, art, woodshop, and lab sciences. The traditional visual and auditory ways of learning do not fully satisfy the needs of most children who use this Mind Pattern. School often leaves them either lulled and withdrawn or ready to explode with unreleased energy. These children want to be actively engaged and involved in everything; they want to do, they want to know how, they want to be skillful. They also need quiet to integrate information fully. School lets them down on both counts. Their natural capabilities are frequently misunderstood and largely untapped.

You can most effectively support them at home by offering them both physical activities and solitude. Directing their energy into a sport or other activity in the hours after school will increase their ability to concentrate on homework assignments later. When these children arrive home, understand that they may need a lot of quiet time to balance out the typical highly verbal school day. Provide opportunities for them to be out in nature or in their rooms where they can choose silence or their own music.

Whenever possible, provide opportunities for them to experience what they are learning about; field trips and hands-on experiences are often their best teachers. When helping them study, as often as possible follow the pattern of "experience, see, hear" and "do, show, say." To study spelling words, for example, trace words on their backs so they can feel them and see the word in their mind's eye before you tell them. Then have them write and say the word themselves to complete the loop.

Children who use this Mind Pattern should be taught to read and write with a "whole language experiential approach" if possible. Encourage them to tell you stories from experiences they've had that they want to remember. Their motivation will be much higher if it is their own words they are reading and writing. Encourage them to be in motion while reading. Stationary bikes or rocking chairs may provide just enough motion so they can concentrate. Encourage them to imagine themselves taking part in the stories or actually invite them to act them out. Illustrating the story or taking notes may help them remember what they've read. When they must give oral presentations, encourage them to use notes, props they can hold, or to move around. Reviewing concepts for a test or studying spelling can often be easier with visual games or flash cards. A wall-mounted chalkboard or easel may be a useful, fun study tool.

Most children who use this Mind Pattern are well aware that they space out when people are talking. Experiment with them to find the best ways for them to move their bodies or hands so they can stay alert while listening.

Help them create a study place for themselves where they can both move around and be comfortable while sitting.

The Connector: Helping Children Who Use the VKA Mind Pattern

School can be a "mixed bag" for children with this Mind Pattern. They are often very good readers who have a difficult time accessing and articulating what they have learned verbally. They can be very competent, even creative, writers. Unfortunately, the educational emphasis on lecturing and listening diminishes their confidence in their ability to learn. You can most effectively support this child at home by respecting their auditory sensitivity, and helping build on visual strengths. When they arrive home from school, understand that they may need a lot of quiet time to balance out the typical, highly verbal school day, or they may need to be listened to. Home may be the only place they feel comfortable speaking so they can put together the experiences of their day. Be patient with their pauses and the circular pattern of their words. Take notes for them so they will have a visual model of what they have said. Encourage them to add to your notes later.

Children who use this Mind Pattern have good visual memories for words. Encourage them to use flash cards to help them learn the look of unfamiliar words. Point out visual similarities among word families that will help them learn whole groups of words at once. Encourage these children to make pictures in their minds of the stories they read. This is a natural skill for them, one that will help them with comprehension and retention. Otherwise some will get stuck in the process of sounding out the words. Encourage them to follow along in the book with their finger so they can touch what they see. Children of this pattern usually love to be read to.

Provide a special public place to display your child's interests and accomplishments. These children can be very creative with their hands, so include art projects, scientific inventions, and decorations, as well as photos of special places and events, trophies, certificates, special notes, cards, or letters they've received. Having a place where these important things can be seen may mean more to your child than verbal congratulations.

Children who use this Mind Pattern remember best what they have seen or experienced. Relating new concepts to something they have lived through or finding a visual image will really help them grasp things. Find ways to help them do something with what they are learning. Make math concepts obviously useful with practical applications, such as building, cooking, or gardening. Find opportunities for them to be with people who are using what they are learning so they can watch.

Avoid long verbal explanations when helping these children. They respond best to being shown how to do something and then being given the space to try it themselves. When the use of words is all that is available, relate what they are learning to an experience they have had, use visual images, or touch them.

Oral presentations can be among the most anxiety-producing experiences for these children. Encourage them to prepare written notes to help focus what they will say. The use of props that they can talk about will also help them trust that they can remember their words. Listen while they practice and give them feedback about what they do well. Help them find lively images and experiences they can bring to mind and talk from, especially if they get stuck.

Children who use this Mind Pattern may not be able to think with visual clutter. Help them set up a study area they can keep relatively neat, with just enough color or things to look at without being distracting.

The Storyteller: Helping Children Who Use the VAK Mind Pattern

These children tend to do well in school primarily because traditional elementary teaching styles, which are largely "show and tell," matches theirs and therefore meet their most basic educational needs. It may be, however, that their learning process does not go deeply enough. They can easily cram for a test, score well, and over time not retain what they have "learned." What's missing too often is what makes learning come alive for all of us—the kinesthetic, experiential component.

You can most effectively support the complete integration of your children's learning at home by finding ways for them to get enthusiastically involved in what they are studying. If you take an interest in what they are learning, they can generally work independently on most typical assignments. Read together. Read to them or have them read to you out loud. With older children, occasionally read a book they've been assigned along with them and discuss it together. Take time to listen to what these children have written. It helps them to edit effectively if they can hear the flow of their words out loud.

Children who use this Mind Pattern may not be able to think with visual clutter around them. Help them set up a work space they can keep relatively neat. Encourage them to include just enough color and things to look at without being distracting. Provide a special place to display their accomplishments, doodles, winning score sheets from a card game marathon, or photos. They need to be encouraged in their natural proficiency for teaching and storytelling. Talking out what they think will help them discover what's true for them.

These children can easily get overwhelmed with time management because they often cannot judge accurately how long a specific task will take, and will therefore procrastinate. In working on projects, these children can imagine in elaborate detail something their hands cannot create easily. Encourage them to plan simple presentations. Help them break down projects or papers into smaller tasks and to set realistic deadlines.

In the more experiential subjects, especially science, upper-level math, physical education, and technical subjects, these children need to be shown and talked through new skills before trying a task themselves. It may be difficult for them to learn structured physical activities. They may need a lot of specific, patient attention when learning to use their hands or bodies. When learning physical skills, they first need to be shown what they are going to do and told why it is an important thing to know, particularly how it fits into a larger set of skills or content. Then they need to be given a metaphor for each step in the process, a visual image that will represent what their body will look like while doing it. For example, you might say, "Pretend your body is a clock. To begin this warm-up exercise, your arms are like the hands at two and ten." Next, they need to be talked through the skill one small, slow step at a time, using the same metaphor: "Now move your arms so they are at three and nine on your clock." At this phase, they also need verbal feedback about what they are doing right, and they need to practice on their own, as privately as possible, so they can build confidence.

In the pages that follow, there is a "before and after" example of how one family bridged their communication gaps after they understood the differences in their Mind Patterns.

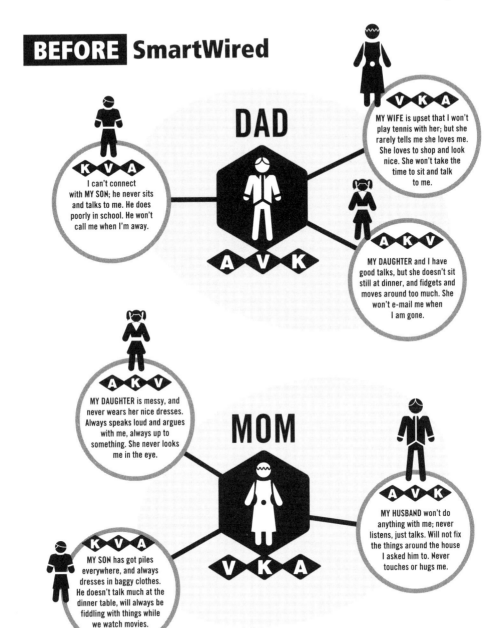

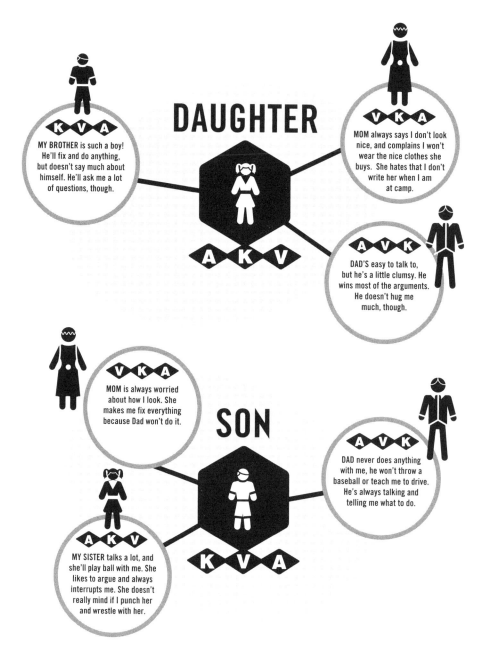

DAUGHTER

MY BROTHER is such a boy! He'll fix and do anything, but doesn't say much about himself. He'll ask me a lot of questions, though.

MOM always says I don't look nice, and complains I won't wear the nice clothes she buys. She hates that I don't write her when I am at camp.

DAD'S easy to talk to, but he's a little clumsy. He wins most of the arguments. He doesn't hug me much, though.

SON

MOM is always worried about how I look. She makes me fix everything because Dad won't do it.

DAD never does anything with me, he won't throw a baseball or teach me to drive. He's always talking and telling me what to do.

MY SISTER talks a lot, and she'll play ball with me. She likes to argue and always interrupts me. She doesn't really mind if I punch her and wrestle with her.

AFTER SmartWired

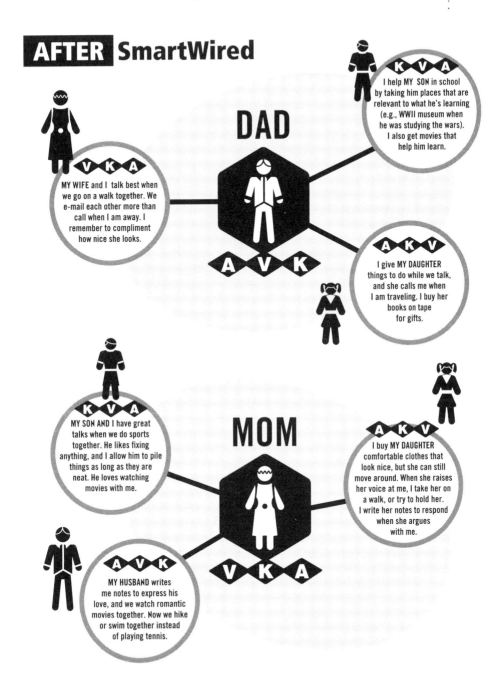

K V A
I help MY SON in school by taking him places that are relevant to what he's learning (e.g., WWII museum when he was studying the wars). I also get movies that help him learn.

DAD

V K A
MY WIFE and I talk best when we go on a walk together. We e-mail each other more than call when I am away. I remember to compliment how nice she looks.

A V K

A K V
I give MY DAUGHTER things to do while we talk, and she calls me when I am traveling. I buy her books on tape for gifts.

MOM

K V A
MY SON AND I have great talks when we do sports together. He likes fixing anything, and I allow him to pile things as long as they are neat. He loves watching movies with me.

A K V
I buy MY DAUGHTER comfortable clothes that look nice, but she can still move around. When she raises her voice at me, I take her on a walk, or try to hold her. I write her notes to respond when she argues with me.

A V K
MY HUSBAND writes me notes to express his love, and we watch romantic movies together. Now we hike or swim together instead of playing tennis.

V K A

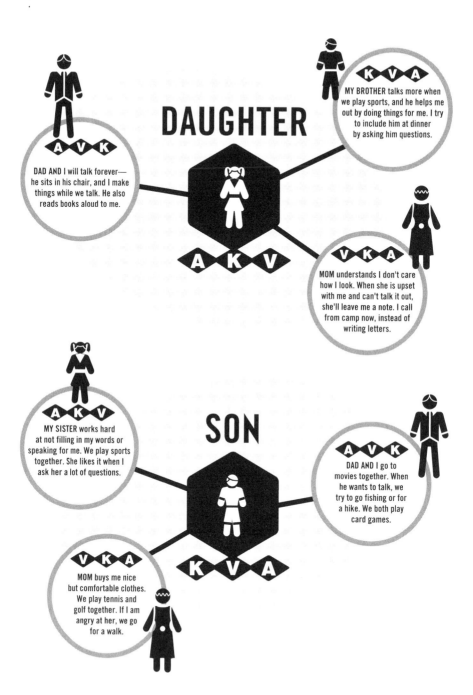

DAUGHTER

MY BROTHER talks more when we play sports, and he helps me out by doing things for me. I try to include him at dinner by asking him questions.

DAD AND I will talk forever—he sits in his chair, and I make things while we talk. He also reads books aloud to me.

MOM understands I don't care how I look. When she is upset with me and can't talk it out, she'll leave me a note. I call from camp now, instead of writing letters.

SON

MY SISTER works hard at not filling in my words or speaking for me. We play sports together. She likes it when I ask her a lot of questions.

DAD AND I go to movies together. When he wants to talk, we try to go fishing or for a hike. We both play card games.

MOM buys me nice but comfortable clothes. We play tennis and golf together. If I am angry at her, we go for a walk.

Utilizing Attractions

"Don't ask why [the child] is the way he is; ask for what he would change."

—MILTON ERICKSON, M.D.

Attractions are natural motivators. They can, therefore, be easily utilized by connecting them to what is difficult for a child. The human brain shapes and develops itself by making connections and associations. Sometimes these are explicit and we are consciously aware of them, as when you travel to China for the first time and say, "Oh, this reminds me of Paramus, New Jersey." Sometimes they are implicit and we are triggered into feelings that seem to arise from no place, as when someone you've never met before just gives you the creeps. Understanding the power of these associations and connections can help your child utilize his or her attractions to overcome challenges.

Let me tell you about one such experience we had with our friend Brian. We were in Hawaii with Brian and his family. He was a "tweenager," sometimes magnificently coordinated and sometimes awfully awkward. He was passionately involved in windsurfing, and had become quite proficient at it on the lake near his home in Massachusetts. His walls were covered with posters of huge waves and tightly muscled young men flying across them. He had been waiting to sail in Hawaii for months. He talked about it incessantly during the eight-hour plane flight. His younger brother, Jeff, got bored listening and put on headphones to watch the movie. With no one to listen, Brian was forced to watch also. The movie was *Jaws*.

We landed late at night, but Brian was awake at first light of day, ready to ride. Andy accompanied him as he rented board, sail, and harness. They drove out to Anini Beach, where all the local board sailors were already flying from the top of one wave to the top of the next. The wind was up. The surf was up. And Brian stood frozen in fear at the shoreline. By the time I arrived, he had been immobilized like that for thirty minutes. Andy stood next to him silently, with his hand on Brian's shoulder. Evidently, Brian's brain had wired together being at the edge of the ocean with *Jaws 2*, starring Brian and a monster shark.

I was just close enough to hear Andy softly ask Brian what he was feeling in his body. The reply was a very accurate description of total terror. Andy then asked, "Pretty big fear, hmm?" Brian nodded. "And what is there that you want even more than your fear?" Brian shook his head, then refocused his eyes from the wide horizon to the board sailors skimming the tops of the waves. He pointed to them. "I want to be able to do that."

Andy then asked, "Is your want bigger than your fear?" Brian hesitated for just a moment and then nodded. Andy continued, "Can your want be a companion, like an older brother, to your fear?" Brian looked up at Andy and then over to Jeff. He had been older-brothering for eleven years. He knew he was good at it, and he truly loved Jeff, despite the occasional punch here and there. Then he looked out at the board sailors again, shook his head as if popping a soap bubble, and shouted to Andy, "Let's fly, dude!" Off they went.

You can also use the brain's associative capacity to link attractions and challenges, even though they might not seem "logical." For example, David, a Dallas Cowboy addict from the time he could crawl, had severe and frequent asthma attacks that began when he was six. We often ended up with him wheezing in the emergency room of the local hospital.

One night he awoke in the middle of one such attack. As his chest heaved he gasped out a dream he had been having of suffocating under a mountain of slime. I asked him if there was any way he could get out from under it. He shook his sweaty head negatively. I asked if he had ever faced a monster or challenge as scary as that one. Again, he shook his head. I asked if he knew of anyone strong enough and smart enough to help him confront such a challenge. He was quiet for several moments, and then he wheezed, "Roger Staubach." Staubach was the Cowboys' quarterback, and David's hero.

"Well, I wonder what would happen if you closed your eyes and imagined that Roger Staubach came into your dream and helped you out of that mess?" I said calmly. David sat with his chest heaving, but he did close his eyes, and in several minutes his breathing eased. I could feel his body get heavy. I laid him down gently on the pillow, where he slept breathing easily for the rest of the night.

The next morning, he bounded into the kitchen and asked me if we had any Red Rose tea. I gave him a bag and he took the label and slipped it into his back pocket.

"What's that for? And by the way, what happened in your dream last night?"

"Well, it was very cool. Staubach came in a helicopter, which let down a big hook. It pulled that mountain of slime right off of me. Then Rog said that because I was so brave in facing the danger and in asking for help, I deserved a present.

When I reached out, there was a cup of Red Rose tea. Rog said I should imagine I was smelling the flower and that the dark, hot liquid was seeping into my chest. That's the last thing I remember, but I figure that now that I've got my tea bag," he patted his back pocket, "I won't be having any more asthma attacks."

I wanted to caution him about being too optimistic, but he was out the door before I could say anything. In the thirty-two years since, I just haven't had the heart to tell him it was only a dream. And he also hasn't had another asthma attack.

You can help your child utilize his or her attractions as if they are the trunk of a very large tree. In any challenging storm, when the wind blows, remind them to scramble down from the topmost branches and hang on to something they love. The trunk is where, in their world, they can be most stable and grounded.

Utilizing Resources

"Driven by the force of love, the fragments of the world seek each other that the world may come into being."

—PIERRE TEILHARD DE CHARDIN, PHILOSOPHER

The secret to utilizing resources effectively is taking what is plentiful in a system and mating it to what is scarce. The challenge in doing this is that our culture teaches us to focus on and crave what is scarce. This is good for the economy. Your imagination, however, can be a great ally in utilizing resources because it naturally makes new patterns through association and connection. If, for example, when worried about not having enough money (focusing on what is scarce), you engage your imaginative capacity by asking yourself, "What is my *real* wealth?" you will find yourself utilizing resources you may have been previously ignoring.

The following story is about creating this same kind of connection on a larger scale. When I worked with migrant children in central Florida, what was plentiful was old people abandoned by their families, and children whose families had to abandon their homes so they could work. What was scarce was the love necessary to recognize how much they needed each other.

Jerome told me that he had never known his grandmother. I could not imagine who I would have been without my grandmother's love to help weave me into the larger story of how I belonged to the world. I wanted to ask him who rocked him with lullabies, who read to him, who told him stories, whose cool palm rested on his forehead when he was sick. I didn't ask, of course. I knew enough to understand that he had never experienced those tender mercies.

Every morning I drove past the nursing home on my way to the school. They were the two buildings that could have been easily mistaken for a prison by a visitor from outer space. The old people sat and rocked silently, staring into worlds I could never visit. I looked at them in those rocking chairs and I began to wonder.

It was the week before Christmas vacation and the principal was in an unusually generous frame of mind. Knowing this was a rare occurence, I asked her if I could bring a few rocking chairs into the school cafeteria for the week. I didn't mention the old people who came with them, just the chairs. She shrugged, which I took as an unconditional yes. The next day, a rocking chair was in each corner of the cafeteria. In it was, of course, a potential grandmother or grandfather disguised as an ordinary old person. And in the lap of that elder there was a child. And a book. The cafeteria had never been so nourishing before. The rocking chairs were, to say the least, a grand success. As were the elders, the books, and the love that made it all happen.

If you want to help your child utilize the resources available to help him or her face a challenge, it is questions that will lead you. The first one is about what resource would help the child succeed with the challenge being faced.

"Jeri, I know you're terrified to go visit your friend in the hospital. What resource would most help you make that visit a success?"

Jeri shrugs. She's never had a sick friend in the hospital. She barely knows what a resource is, anyway.

"Have you ever been scared to do something like this before and then gone ahead and done it and felt really good afterward?"

Jeri shakes her head. "No."

No available inner experience to resource? Let's try an outer resource.

"Okay. Do you know anyone who could do something like this and do it really well?"

Jeri shakes her head again. "No."

No specific outer resource available? Let's try fictional.

> "Okay. Have you ever read about someone or seen someone in the movies who could do something like this and do it really well?"
>
> A pause.

If at this point Jeri says no, go rent a video or go to the library together. But let's say she says,

> "Well, yeah, Junie B. Jones could do it."

I'm searching for what resource Junie has that Jeri doesn't—yet.

> "How come she could succeed?"
>
> Jeri giggles and then replies, "Because she's not afraid to do new things. And she's very funny. She makes people laugh with the things she says and does."

Aha! The resource. Now let's just connect it to Jeri's imagination with a question.

> "Jeri, imagine that Junie goes into the hospital to visit her friend. Imagine you read a whole story about this. I'll be really quiet and then you tell me what the title would be."
>
> We're looking for some kind of a symbol or icon or song that will make it possible for Jeri to carry that resource around with her.
>
> Jeri is quiet for a minute or two and then opens her mouth and lights up as she says, "I know. I know. It would be called Junie B. Jones, Sass-Mouth."

Okay, there's the symbol. Now a question to connect it to Jeri.

> "Jeri, what do you imagine it would feel like to have a 'sass-mouth'? What would you feel in your body? How would you talk and how would you walk?"
>
> Jeri giggles. She parades around the room wiggling her butt and humming. "I wouldn't be afraid to say whatever I wanted, like Junie isn't. And I wouldn't be worried all the time about getting into trouble."

Now it's time to have her practice someplace totally safe—in her imagination.

> "Jeri, would you be willing to imagine as you go to sleep that you have a sass-mouth and you go to school and then you go to visit your friend in the hospital? Just imagine it and then tell me tomorrow morning what happens."

The imagination is a wonderful practice field to generate possible futures by utilizing resources. This is what our dreams do naturally. And the process Jeri and I just went through is also a natural process. It's what happens in our minds when we envy someone else, or watch an actor and fantasize ourselves on the screen. It's envy done well, because in the imagination, there is no limit to resources. They are abundant and overflowing and there's more than enough to go around.

When you wonder about helping your child utilize external resources, consider asking what are the environments, people, and places that bring out his or her best. Sami's mother realized he needed to build his self-confidence, but it wasn't easy in their city environment. She arranged for him to receive a scholarship to Outward Bound, where he learned to sustain himself in the wilderness as well as cooperate with others in the pursuit of a common goal.

Utilizing Thinking Talents

> *"There is only one real deprivation . . . and that is not to be able to give one's gifts to those one loves most."*
>
> —MAY SARTON, POET

When we or our children are "stuck" in a situation, the chances are that we are disconnected from our Thinking Talents and not using them on our own behalf. Getting stuck usually means our brains are searching in the same habitual way over and over, expecting different results. We may be stuck in one way of think-ing or one kind of attention. Or we may be stuck giving to everyone else what we most need to give to ourselves. In the same way that children learn to imitate our unconscious habits of posture and speech, they also learn to imitate our uncon-scious habits of thinking.

Let's say, for instance, that every time I lose my car keys, I mumble, "What's the matter with me, why am I so careless?" and I repeatedly search in the same coat pocket. The chances are, my child will say and do exactly that when he or she loses something. But what if I take several deep breaths, and widen my periphery? What if I resist telling myself the same old story and use my gift of storytelling on my own behalf? What if I say to myself, "Ah, a chance to slow down and be aware of where I am now. Good. I need to be full of care when life goes so quickly. I think I'll just stop and get grounded"? The chances are that telling myself this story will help me see and feel more, heightening the possibility that I'll find my keys, as well as supporting my child not losing his self-worth each time he loses his keys.

In addition, when I call on my Thinking Talent of "Linking," I'm more likely to be able to rise above the situation and get a sense of where my body and mind were when last I was holding my keys. If I call on my Thinking Talent of "Strategy," I'll be able to consider many possible futures instead of the dead end of having to call a locksmith or being unable to move.

Utilization, therefore, helps us reconnect to the widest possible bank of resources we have at our disposal. Instead of being stuck on a single track going nowhere or stuck between either/or, our brain disengages and has many more options available to it. We give this gift of freedom to our children when we have conversations of discovery with them that help them to use all of their Thinking Talents on their own behalf.

A friend of ours is a great blues musician. He once told me a story of growing up as an only child in the worst part of a city. His loneliness led him to join a gang, where he found membership, but not the sense of belonging that he was aching for. His father was also a musician and, although he didn't have the language for it, understood intuitively that his son had "Thinking Alone," "Collaboration," and "Peacemaking" as Thinking Talents. Late one night, he inquired of his son, "You've told me what all those guys in the gang are asking from you, but what's your soul asking of you?"

The father got very quiet and waited through his son's silence until he began to speak, haltingly at first, and then in a torrent. He spoke of feeling more lonely when he was with the gang than when he was alone.

The father listened and then finally, when the words ran out, put one hand on his son's shoulder and passed him an old beat-up guitar with the other, saying, "I can't give you everything you need now, but this can be your friend forever. You can pour out your heart to it. Share the best feelings and the worst. It will always listen and it will always accept you. You can make harmony between notes and that'll teach you how to make it between people. Someday it'll lead you to others who will understand and want to join in. That's when you'll know where you really belong."

Our friend has been doing exactly that for over fifty years. He's traveled around the world, been part of several bands, and composed great music that brings peace to the hearts of audiences who find understanding for their feelings that have no words.

I often suggest to kids that they give each of their Thinking Talents a name, as if it were a friend, such as Bessie Brilliant, logical thinker. Then I explain that all their Thinking Talents together are like a tribal council or gang that will always live inside their mind waiting to help them when they're stuck. We've made drawings, magazine collages, and collections of symbols or icons representing the tribe. One eight-year-old girl made a charm bracelet she wears daily, one charm for each of her seven Thinking Talents. When she goes through a challenging situation, she fingers them, wondering what advice each could give her.

Sometimes children will tell me that one of their "tribe" is being too bossy and has taken over. I ask them how the others can have an equal voice—the playful, the fierce, or the tender ones who represent Thinking Talents that may not be utilized as fully as possible. All they usually need is being asked this question. Then they remember to respect their own capacity to leap over the hurdles that seemed like obstacles before.

In the pages that follow are suggestions for relating to each of the Thinking Talents. Please use them as a guide and support to your own connective imagination.

Relating to Children's Thinking Talents

Collaboration
- Encourage this child to think and play with others.
- Understand that this child is a natural social director and always searching for ways to bring people together.
- Find examples of other famous people who have this Thinking Talent— such as choreographers, orchestra conductors, the head of the U.N., and so on.
- Know that what the group accomplishes will be more important than what he accomplishes.

Concentration

- Set goals with timelines and then let him figure out how to achieve them.
- Ask if and when she wants you to check in on her progress on a task—it can be thought of as not trusting her to get the task done on time.
- Put this child with others who are struggling to get something done. He can help focus the whole group.
- She may have problems in a group, in a conversation, or with a task if it is not clear what the purpose or goal is. You might hear: "What is the point of this?" Help her figure out the goal, then step back.

Connection

- This child will likely have social issues that he will defend strongly. Listen closely to know what these issues are.
- He is likely to have a strong faith. Your knowledge and acceptance of his spiritual position is important.
- Encourage this child to build bridges to different groups in school or after-school programs. She should excel at showing different people how each relies on the other.
- He likes to feel part of something larger than himself.

Enrolling

- Try to give this child a chance to meet new people every day. Strangers energize him.
- Find activities where she can be a goodwill ambassador—for a school, a church, an after-school activity.
- Look for chances for this person to sell something he believes in.

Equality

- When it comes time to recognize a group or team after the completion of a project or activity, ask this child to pinpoint each person's contribution.
- Be supportive of her during times of great change because she is most comfortable with predictable patterns that she knows work well.
- With situations where rules must be applied equally and absolutely and no favoritism must be known, ask him to step in and make suggestions.

Feeling for Others

- Ask this child to help you know how others in the family or the classroom or after-school event are feeling.
- Before making a decision that affects her, ask how she feels about it. For her, emotions are as real as other, more practical factors and must be weighed when making decisions.
- Do not overreact when he cries. Tears are part of his life. He may sense the joy or tragedy in another person's life more poignantly than even that person does.
- Test her ability to make decisions instinctively rather than logically. "What is your gut feeling about what we should do?"
- Arrange for him to be with positive, optimistic people. He will pick up on these feelings and be motivated.

Fixing It

- Ask this child what might go wrong with an idea or a plan.
- Offer your support when she meets a particularly thorny problem. She may feel personally defeated if the situation remains unresolved.
- He may come across as negative when pointing out what could go wrong. Help him learn to communicate insights in a positive way.
- When she resolves a problem, make sure to celebrate the achievement.
- Ask him in what ways he would like to improve. Agree that these improvements should serve as goals for the following six months.

Flexibility

- She will be most productive on short-term school or after-school assignments that require immediate action.
- He is energized by changes in routine. When balls are dropped or plans go awry, invite him to make suggestions about how to cope.
- She will need help when it comes to things like planning for the future long term (such as going to college or figuring out, in January, what to do for the summer).

Gathering

- Ask him to collect information about a topic of importance to your family, school, or after-school program.

- Help her develop systems for storing what she collects.
- Make a point of asking him for information. Look for opportunities to say something positive about his recall of facts.

Get to Action
- This child wants to do, do, do.
- Let him know that you know he is a person who can make things happen and that you will be asking him for help at key times. Your expectations will energize him.
- When she complains, talk about what she can do right away.

Goal-Setting
- When there are times that require challenging extra work, call on this child.
- Recognize that she likes to be busy and is motivated by a concrete goal to work toward.
- Whatever he is doing, there needs to be a way to measure progress and success.
- When this child finishes a task, she will be much more motivated if you give recognition for past achievement and then a new goal that stretches her.
- Ask questions such as "How late did you have to work to get this done?" He will appreciate this kind of attention.

Humor
- Look to this child to lighten a situation. Include her in group or team situations where the humor can be an asset.
- Be aware that he can't help joking, so don't take it as a challenge to your authority.
- Encourage her to use humor in constructive ways—it can be a valuable medium in written communication, making speeches, and many social and athletic settings.
- Offer opportunities to showcase his talent (in class, at the dinner table, during snack) so he will have appropriate outlets for it.
- Although they may be overshadowed by the constant jokes, don't forget that this child has several additional Thinking Talents—look for ways to utilize those other strengths as well.

Including

- This child is interested in making everyone feel part of a group. Ask her to take the lead in welcoming new people into an activity, group, or class.
- When there are group functions or sports-team selections, ask him to make sure everyone is included.
- Encourage her to learn inclusive games to use in developing this talent.
- He is sensitive to those who are left out. Encourage him to join groups that fight for social justice, civil rights, etcetera, where this talent can shine.

Innovation

- This child tends not to look back. When you want her best thinking, say, "Imagine it is a year from now and you have gotten exactly what you want. What will have happened? How have you gotten from A to B?"
- When he is stuck, ask, "What are all the ways you could do this?"
- Recognize that it may be challenging for her to follow standardized ways of doing things because she quickly loses interest if it's not new. Challenge her to continue to find ways to keep things interesting.

Intimacy

- Understand that meeting and greeting new people may be challenging.
- Help him to stay connected to the people he is close to, even if far away.
- Help her understand that others don't necessarily have a need to stay connected.

Love of Learning

- Explore new ways for him to learn and remain motivated. It is the *process* of learning, not the result, that energizes him.
- Help her track her learning progress by identifying milestones or levels that she has reached. Celebrate these milestones.
- Ask him, "What have you been learning about X?"
- Ask her to lead discussion groups or presentations at school or after school, and to share with the family what she has learned.

Loving Ideas

- This child has creative ideas. Be sure to value them.
- Try to feed her new ideas, and ask what she has been thinking about recently.

- When decisions are made, take time to show him how each decision is rooted in the same theory or concept.
- Give her books, audiotapes, lectures, performances that will offer new ideas.

Making Order
- Give this child a chance to arrange things—people, flowers, table settings, rooms.
- He will thrive in situations where he has many things going on at the same time and there is a need to arrange them in the right order.
- When she is stuck, ask, "What order is it best to do this? How else could this be arranged?"
- Find a productive use of this child's ability to sequence things and events.

Mentoring
- Ask this child to tell you about his friends: what they are learning, how they are growing.
- Give her opportunities to mentor and coach.
- Set him up as the one to give recognition to others.
- Be aware that she may protect a struggling friend or problem pal long past the time when others would have given up.
- Notice when and how you may need to relieve him of the responsibility for another's growth.

Optimism
- This child brings drama and energy wherever she goes. Help her find ways to use that in school, home, and after-school activities: as the head of the booster club, working in a nursing home, etcetera.
- The glass is always half full for this child. Help him to see potential pitfalls in a situation and strategize how to respond. He is just not aware of them.
- She likes to celebrate. When milestones of achievement have been reached—a big school project, for instance—ask her for ideas on how to celebrate the achievement.

Peacemaking
- As far as possible, steer this child away from conflict.
- If people are disagreeing or fighting, ask this child how to make peace. He is good at helping others find areas where they agree.

- Don't expect her to disagree or stand up for herself. For the sake of harmony, she may nod her head or go along no matter what.
- He wants to feel sure about what he is doing. Help him find expert opinions for the actions he wants to take.
- Include music or painting in her life as a way of exploring how notes and colors can "make peace with each other."

Personalizing
- When you are having difficulty understanding someone's perspective or getting what you need from someone, turn to this child for insight.
- Ask him to mentor or teach. He will have a knack for spotting how each person learns a little differently.
- She is a resource on what people like, what's important to them, how they are unique.
- Count on this child to come up with ideas for presents for family members, friends, teachers, and so on.

Precision
- If an event or organization is chaotic, ask him to take the lead in planning and organizing it.
- Don't expect her to last long in a physically cluttered environment unless she has a chance to put it in order.
- Always give him advance notice of deadlines and try not to surprise him with sudden changes in plan and priority. Surprises are distressing.
- When there are many things that need to get done in a set time period, remember her need to prioritize.
- If forced to be in a situation that requires flexibility and responsiveness, encourage him to devise a set number of routines, each appropriate for a certain situation.

Reliability
- This child defines herself by her ability to live up to her commitments. It will be intensely frustrating to be around people who don't.
- He defines himself by the quality of his work. He will resist if you force him to rush so much that quality suffers.

- Be aware that she may be uncomfortable trying something new—she wants to do it *right*. Ask her to identify what the worries or concerns are and help her work through them.
- Periodically ask him what new responsibility he would like to assume.
- Help her not to take on too much.
- He can let go of a task and move on to something new (if this is needed) only if you can assure him that it will be done right by someone else.

Seeking Excellence
- Ask how she can personally become excellent in a subject or a sport or in an area of self-improvement.
- Discuss with him how he knows when he has done an excellent job.
- Children with this talent dislike inefficient designs and processes. Ask her how you can make something better—a school bag, a process in a group, a team.
- Invite him to help develop procedures for class projects that would make clear the standards for excellence.
- She is always trying to do many things at once to maximize efficiency. Ask her to give you the most efficient way to do three chores at once.

Self-Confidence
- He is at his most effective when he believes he is in control of his world.
- Create strong outside boundaries and then allow for a lot of leeway within those when it comes to actions and decision making.
- Understand that she may have beliefs about what she can do that might not relate to her actual strengths. If she overclaims or makes some major misjudgments, be sure to point these out immediately.

Standing Out
- He thrives on meaningful recognition for his contributions. He loves awards, honors, ribbons.
- Give her the opportunity to stand out, to be known. She enjoys the pressure of being the focal point of attention. Arrange for her to stand out for the right reasons, or she will try to make it happen herself, perhaps inappropriately.

- Because he places such a premium on the perceptions of others, his self-esteem can suffer when others do not give him the recognition he feels is deserved.
- Behind wanting to stand out is the desire to make a difference in the world. Help her find ways to make a concrete difference in her family or community. Then be sure to recognize her for it!

Storytelling

- Understand that this child is not lying—he is creatively using facts to fit the story.
- Explore how her storytelling abilities can be developed.
- Ask him to help some other students make more engaging presentations.

Strategy

- This child has the ability to anticipate problems and their solutions. In a group project at school, or in an after-school program, ask her to sort through all the possibilities and find the best way forward.
- Give ample time to think through a situation before asking for input. He needs to play out a couple of scenarios in his mind before voicing an opinion.
- Give her some financial and/or other constraints and ask her to come up with three vacation options, after-school activities, chores, or other activities.
- Use role-playing and simulations to allow this child to utilize this talent in school.
- Ask him to help you with a real challenge you have. For instance, what is the best strategy for deciding which car to buy next?

Taking Charge

- Look for situations where this child can give orders and tell others what to do.
- She will not like to be supervised too closely.
- If he starts bossing siblings, friends, parents, meet him head-on. Confront directly with specific examples.
- Never threaten unless you are 100 percent ready to follow through. You most likely will end up in a power struggle.

- Understand that her assertiveness is part of what makes her powerful—as long as she remains assertive rather than aggressive or offensive.

Thinking Ahead
- Keep in mind that he lives for the future. Ask him to share his vision with you—his vision about career choices, summer vacation, the state of the world, and so on.
- Talk with this child often about what could be. Ask lots of questions. Push her to make the future she sees as vivid as possible.
- When a group or a family needs to embrace change, ask for this person's help. He can help others rise above their present uncertainties and become almost as excited as he is about the possibilities of the future.

Thinking Alone
- Don't expect this child to make snap decisions. Give her time to think through all the pros and cons.
- Whenever possible, give notice far in advance that some action or decision will need to be made.
- Encourage him to take alone time when he can simply muse.
- Engage this child in discussions about her strengths. She will enjoy the chance to think about herself.

Thinking Back
- When you ask this child to do something, take time to explain the thinking that led to your decision. He needs to understand the context for a course of action.
- At home or school, turn to her to review what has been done and what has been learned up to now.
- When he's stuck, ask him to recall when he was in a similar situation. What did he do then that could help now?

Thinking Logically
- When a decision that affects this child is being made, take time to think through the issues with her. She will want to know all data and supporting facts affecting the choice.
- When speaking to this child, remember to lay out your logic very clearly.

- Recognize and praise his reasoning ability.
- This child can see patterns in data. Always give her the opportunity to explain the pattern in detail to you.
- Understand that because the accuracy of work is so important to him, getting a task done correctly may be more important than meeting a deadline.

Values
- Discover her deepest beliefs and tie them to the work to be done.
- Understand that he will have rock-solid commitments to family and friends. You will need to understand, appreciate, and honor these commitments, and he will respect you for it.
- She may place more value on opportunities to provide service than on opportunities to do well academically.
- You do not have to share his belief system, but you do have to understand it, respect it, and apply it.

Wanting to Win
- Use competitive language with this child. From her perspective, achieving a goal is winning and missing a goal is losing.
- Measure him against other people, particularly other competitive people.
- Set up contests that pit her against other competitors.
- Find places where he can win. Remember, in the contests that matter, he doesn't compete for the fun of competing, he competes to win.

Inspiration

As I was writing this chapter, I watched a segment of *60 Minutes* that blew through my heart and mind like a strong, warm wind. It featured a professional British viola player named Rosemary Nalden who, twelve years ago, went to Soweto, the sprawling black township in South Africa where the struggle over apartheid was born, to teach children to play the violin. Without naming it, she incorporated every practice of utilization with the children, many of whom had never even seen a violin. "What goes on in their lives, when it's painful, comes out in their music as absolute truth," she said.

In 1992, Nalden, then forty-eight years old, heard a BBC radio program featuring a small group of young novice musicians playing a piano and a few violins from a Soweto lavatory. She rounded up her colleagues from symphony orchestras and had them "busking," playing at railway stations all across Britain for money. She took the $10,000 they raised to Soweto, unaware that the energy and motivation she found there would cause her to make the commitment of her life.

She founded a school teaching music composed by dead white Europeans to poor young Africans. Nalden recognized the power of the assets she found in the children: Music was deeply embedded in their life, as was dancing and movement. Judging from the South African music called *"kwela,"* I suspect that many of the children used the KAV, KVA, and AKV Mind Patterns. She tucked the instruments under their chins, and told them to start moving and keep moving. "The fact is that the instrument is just part of the moving force of their body and their inner rhythmic sense."

She was tough on them, very tough, but most of her students had nothing else happening in their lives except hunger, trauma, and violence. Nalden got the best from them and took them to perform before audiences in Johannesburg, and then before Nelson Mandela and the queen of England. Eventually, she took them to California, where their talent and vitality were immediately recognized.

Two of her top students are now attending music school in England, and she has seventy-five others, some as young as four years old, under her tutelage. But Nalden has had to turn away thousands. The children refer to her as "Mother," because she came to Soweto as a music teacher but, utilizing all the talents she found in its children, gave birth to so much more.

(For more information, contact www.buskaid.org.)

Conversations of Discovery

My grandmother never followed a recipe for the fabulous braided bread she made every Friday. My father once bought her an electric mixer, which she promptly gave away, asking, "A machine kneading the bread? A recipe? How could the love get in?"

I have shared many ingredients and processes throughout this chapter, and will summarize them here, but they are only meant as a general guide to the process of utilization. It is your love that will yeast the dough, and your faith in your childern that will take you through the hard work of kneading and braiding their assets with the challenges they face to bring out their potential.

- *Utilizing Successes:* Ask questions that will bring awareness to what the conditions were in the past when they went through a similar situation successfully. Increase curiosity about how to apply what worked then to the current challenge.

- *Utilizing Mind Patterns:* Take a guess at your child's Mind Pattern and experiment using its strengths to meet a small challenge in your home, such as having a child who uses the AKV pattern create a rap song while washing the dishes. Discuss and build on what works.

- *Utilizing Attractions:* Use what your child loves as a natural motivating force to do something difficult, such as practicing addition and subtraction of fractions while making cookies. Discuss and build on how he or she could do that in other ways.

- *Utilizing Resources:* Inquire as to what resource would make it possible to succeed in the challenging situation. Then ask him/her to reflect back to a time in the past or someone else who used that resource. Create a symbol of it. Ask your child to imagine embodying the symbol and to practice using the resource in the future in his or her mind.

- *Utilizing Thinking Talents:* Have a conversation with your child about which Thinking Talents would be best for accomplishing a particular task. Find someone who has one of those talents or a similar way of working through problems and ask for his or her help.

  Conversely, talk together about how the Thinking Talents he or she has can be used in this situation, employing the suggestions for relating to each talent from this chapter as a guide for you both.

Smart Family Practices

Begin a joint study of the causes of positive events with your child. When he was studying for that math exam, what made it possible for him to get such a great score? What was it that made you feel so excited about what happened at work? What made it possible for your daughter to learn to play soccer so readily:

Was it watching someone else, or being told how to make a particular play before she had to do it? How did he and she resolve that fight instead of beating up on each other?

Do a family Boredom Study: Have family members study their own minds when they are "bored," and report at dinner what they discovered about what boredom feels like in their body, how to turn boredom into daydreaming, what triggered their boredom, what happens when they use a Thinking Talent in a task that has always bored them?

Have Family Focus meals: Each dinner can be a time when the entire family focuses attention on one person, asking questions about their latest hero or heroine, what activity made them happiest that week, what three things went well, or how they've used their Thinking Talents to face a challenge.

Chapter Eleven

Developing Your Child's Potential

"The greatest events of this world are babies, for each child comes with the message that God is still expecting good-will to become incarnate in each human life. And so God produced a Mandela and an Eleanor Roosevelt, and protecting today's children is fostering tomorrow's Mother Teresa."

—MARION WRIGHT EDELMAN, CHILDREN'S ADVOCATE

There is an ancient story told about an old man named Zusya. He spent the last ten years of his life trying to be generous, loving, kind, perfect. As he aged, he became more and more depressed because he was so fallible. Finally, his wife called in the village wise man. He came and sat by Zusya's side and listened deeply to him complain. "I've done my best to be like Moses, but I'm a wretched failure at it."

The wise man was quiet for a long time. Then he said, "But my friend, you have not failed. When you die, God will not ask you why you weren't more like Moses. You will only be asked why you weren't more like Zusya!"

Our children are being pressured to be unique in the same way as everybody else. When a deficit focus prevails, we all become afraid to offer the gifts that we bear. What helps is open acknowledgment of those gifts and respect for our responsibility to contribute them. In this book, I have been reminding you that, as parents, you need to recognize, utilize, and develop these gifts in yourself and your children so you can support their minds taking the shape that is truly their own.

A deficit focus makes our children victims. If we parents change our thinking, we can help children conceive of their lives as a hero's journey. Not a superhero battling monsters from another world, but a journey to realize his or her own destiny. Following one's own calling by using the talents each is given to face the challenges life brings has been noble and daring enough to capture the human imagination for all its history.

Heroes, like athletes, need cheering bystanders to encourage them to enter the game in the first place, and then, like the fans in Boston did year after year for the Red Sox, to stand by them, shouting blessings louder than any curses, as they develop their talents to play the game like champions. You can help this development by becoming what author Julia Cameron calls "believing mirrors" for your children by reflecting back to them how you specifically perceive them to be competent and capable. You can make sure they have what they need to bring out their best. You can create a network of support for them to give them what you cannot.

It's a lot easier to shrug than it is to cheer. It's a lot easier to be too busy to care than it is to believe despite the curses that would limit us. But if we wanted life to be easy, we wouldn't have become parents in the first place. Parenting is always a matter of faith. Faith is always a matter of communication and connection. It requires that we be willing to ask for support, and that we be willing to receive it. Then it comes, bit by bit, piece by piece, event by event. We are led, guided, shown. All of evolutionary intelligence is behind us. Every mother who has ever birthed a child, every father who has ever held one in his arms, vowing to protect it. Every grandmother who has ever prayed for a child, every grandfather who has every dreamed of one stands behind us.

The Two Faces of Development

"Given the right circumstances, from no more than dreams, determination, and the liberty to try, ordinary people consistently do extraordinary things."

—DEE HOCK, FOUNDER AND FORMER CEO, VISA INTERNATIONAL

Searching for the whisper of potential and encouraging it to speak is not easy. How do we recognize its voice through the interferences and static that make us hard of hearing? Developing a child's assets involves both taking away and adding to. Taking away requires removing threats from the learning environment such as shaming, humiliation, sarcasm, or bullying. "There is not one shred of research or evidence that these threats are effective in fostering learning," writes Eric Jensen in *Teaching with the Brain in Mind.*

To think about what needs to be taken away, let's return to the formula from Timothy Gallwey: $p = P - i$—possibility equals potential minus interference.

Given what you now know about your child's gifts, how can you minimize what is interfering with the development of his or her strengths and talents so he or she can perform as well as possible?

Asking that question increases awareness without also increasing negativity. For instance, your child is having trouble with his homework, you might ask (with genuine curiosity), "Simon, I'm aware that you've been staring out the window for some time now. How many minutes do you think you've been doing that? To do this homework, do you need to concentrate, sort through what you know or imagine? What would help you get there?" You might ask for a conference with Simon's teachers and initiate a similar inquiry: "I'm aware Simon is having trouble with his homework. What could happen here and at home to minimize what's interfering with his natural ability to learn well?"

Development also means adding what's needed to create a rich learning environment. The human brain is born with well over a trillion connections and then builds them at a furious pace until the age of six, when they are at their densest. It is thought that half of those are shed or pruned during puberty. A child's experiences determine which synapses are strengthened and which are discarded. This is why, for example, it is easier to learn to play an instrument or learn another language without a foreigner's accent before the age of ten.

That's also why it's important that your child's learning includes novelty, challenge, feedback, physical activity, art, and music. The more multisensory and multidimensional a child's environment, the more there will be the possibility of learning that is wide and deep. That means engaging the eyes, the ears, and the whole body in as many experiences and relationships as possible. For instance, children in one school who were learning about water in a science program were engaged with videos, field trips to local rivers, and Web site conversations with experts. They tested the drinking water in their own neighborhoods, wrote a report that was published on the Internet, and taught younger children in their school what they could do to help conserve water.

Multisensory learning means that if one perceptual channel is blocked, switch to another. If listening to lectures about world history doesn't work, support your child watching movies or making models. The goal is to learn about history, not to learn to listen to lectures about history.

Multidimensional learning means integrating the three criteria that determine success at work or in school: learning, performance, and enjoyment. Think about it for yourself. If you are working and performing well, but not learning anything or enjoying your work, would you consider that successful? Will you want to continue or will you "burn out"? If, on the other hand, you are learning but not performing well or enjoying yourself, will you want to continue? For how long? Many adults have decided to "be satisfied" with performance alone as a success criterion. The Gallup Organization found that 74 percent of American workers are disengaged clock-watchers who cannot wait to go home. Even they want more for their children.

No one can deny that when people are learning, performing well, and enjoying what they are doing, interferences to developing their full potential are minimized. What would happen if, for a week, you kept a pad of paper on your desk and measured all three elements at the end of every day? What if your child did the same thing? What kind of conversation could you have about how to increase enjoyment *and* learning *and* performance?

Given that what we want for our children is to help them realize their potential and become successful members of society, test scores alone are too narrow a measure. Children need to bring the full scope of their capacities to solve problems encountered at work and in relationships; they need to know how to care for themselves and their families; they need to learn how to generate a positive future; they need to learn what is necessary so they can become contributing, motivated members of society.

Many of the corporate leaders I worked with attributed their success to their own effort and ability. They forgot or ignored all those who stood behind them, the innumerable random acts of kindness, the support they received from networks of family, librarians, kin, teachers, coaches, and mentors. This misperception, these omissions influence much of our educational and governmental policy. These communities are shrinking. It's not just ability, hard work, and good fortune that results in a successful member of society. It is the network of connections that help a child develop into one.

When this infrastructure isn't naturally there, we as parents have to faithfully join with others in creating one. This doesn't mean dragging our children from one lesson to another. Listen to the description of how one mother did it for her children. The story is told by James P. Comer, M.D., professor of psychiatry at the Yale Child Study Center:

> When she had to leave school at sixteen, my mother declared that if she ever had children, she would make certain they all got a good education. And then she set out—very, very, very carefully—to find a husband, a person of like mind and purpose. Her caution paid off. My father, with six or seven years of education, worked as a steel mill laborer, and my mother, with no education, worked as a domestic. The two of them eventually sent the five of us to college, where we earned a total of thirteen degrees.

Our family was enmeshed in an African-American church culture that provided the necessary social, ethical, and emotional context. My parents took us to everything educational they could afford; they talked and interacted with us in a way that encouraged learning and promoted overall development. Working for and respected by some of the most powerful people in our community, my mother observed and acquired mainstream success skills and made useful social contacts. Most of the summer jobs that helped us pay our way through college came from those contacts. And I enjoyed caviar brought home after parties before my working-class friends knew that it existed. Indeed, many European, black, and brown immigrants "made it" through similar experiences.

My three best friends were as intelligent as anybody in our family and in the predominantly white working- and middle-class school we attended. On the playground and the street corner, they could think as fast and as well as students who were more successful in school. But all three went on a downhill course: one died early from alcoholism, one spent time in jail, and one was in and out of mental institutions until he died. My parents had the same kind of jobs as their parents did, and we all attended the same school. Why the difference? It was the more useful developmental experiences we were provided.

Despite massive and rapid technological, scientific, and social change, children have the same needs they always did: They must be protected and their development must be guided and supported by the people around them. Problems don't exist *in* people but *between* them. It follows, then, that the search for ways to develop the best in children doesn't exist in you alone or in your child or the educational system. What you can do is, like Dr. Comer's mother, create a connective infrastructure *between* the allies who will nurture the development of your child's resources.

Thinking with Others on a Child's Behalf

"The range of what we think and do is limited only by what we fail to notice."

—R. D. LAING, PSYCHIATRIST

I began this book writing about the live oak trees that surround our home. I end it thinking about the ancient redwood trees that grow at the end of our road.

They are so tall that to even look up at them can be disorienting. Huge as they are, I've been told that, unlike the oak trees, they have a very shallow root system. Nonetheless, they cannot be blown over by even the strongest wind. The secret of their stability is the interweaving of each tree's roots with those that stand by it. In this way, a vast network of support is formed just beneath the surface. In the wildest of storms, these trees hold one another up.

Begin to think about creating this network with those in your own backyard. What follows are two different kinds of support networks you can create for yourself and your child outside of school. They both are wonderful ways to help yourself by helping one another.

Thinkubators

This is a way to get support from a group that incubates your asset-focused thinking in a warm and positive environment. It can be just one other person, your whole family, or a group of a few friends and neighbors. It can be a group of kids, eight and older, you teach how to do it. Here's how it works:

- One person is the focal person. He or she names as many assets as possible of a child who is struggling with a challenge. (It can be you talking about your challenge, your child talking about his or her challenge, or someone else in the group talking about his or her challenge.)
- The focal person describes the challenge, limitation, or difficult situation. This should take no more than five minutes. Everyone else just listens in silence. (Be sure the focal person doesn't try to persuade everyone else that the situation is impossible or they won't be able to think on your behalf!)
- Then the focal person takes out a pen and paper. The rest of the group brainstorms ideas for how the described assets could be used in this situation. The focal person says nothing, just writes down what everyone else is saying without responding. The pace must be slow enough that the focal person can capture each idea, but lively enough to keep ideas flowing. This is not a debate or discussion. The purpose is to generate as many ideas as possible so the focal person can break through the limitations of their own thinking.
- Later, the focal person can read the list and decide which suggestions to use. More ideas may also start bubbling in his or her own mind.

- Switch roles. If doing this in a small group or with your family, each person takes a turn as focal person.

SmartGroups

Most revolutions did not begin at the top of an organization or government. They began when small groups of "ordinary" people gathered in living rooms or kitchens to think together about what really mattered to them. Let the revolution begin! The purpose of SmartGroups is to have a regular place that reinforces and supports the positive development of our only renewable resource: our children. Some guidelines we have found that helped other parents are:

1. Keep the group small so everyone has a chance to speak and be heard.
2. Group get-togethers should be for a specified length of time—for example, six weeks—with an option to continue if people so choose.
3. The group should meet weekly, or every other week, for an hour, so that everyone can stay committed.
4. No money should be charged.
5. All members of the group decide on the ground rules so that each person feels completely safe—for example: confidentiality, the right not to speak if you don't want to, no criticizing.
6. The group decides where it will meet, who will be the leader, and if they will rotate leadership.
7. The host or hostess is responsible for making sure the ground rules are followed, keeping time, and staying on task.
8. Members are invited to bring a photo of their child or children to place in the center of the circle.
9. From the second meeting on, the members begin to share their success and what they learned from the previous week.
10. There is an opportunity at every meeting for each person to be the focal person as in a Thinkubator, as well as a discussion about how people could support one another. For example, several parents could accompany a group member to a parent-teacher conference. Parents could also broaden one another's knowledge of available resources—tapes, books, classes.
11. At the end of every meeting, there is a brief period of acknowledgment where each person names what he or she and others specifically did to contribute to the meeting's success.

On the Same Side: Establishing Partnerships with Teachers, Mentors, and Coaches

"Since we can't know what knowledge will be most needed in the future, it is senseless to try and teach it in advance. Instead, we should try to turn out people who love learning so much and learn so well that they will be able to learn whatever will be needed."

—JOHN HOLT, EDUCATOR

Teachers, mentors, and coaches contain the pressures of so much these days. They are balancing the increasing push toward standardization and shrinking resources on the one hand, and their real care and concern for children on the other. Some of them intuitively sense that each child learns differently and that a child learns best by understanding his or her strengths and using them to overcome challenges. Too often they find themselves lost in the educational forest of powerlessness and despair. How can we partner with our children to help them become all they can be?

Your observations of your child's assets are incredibly valuable for any classroom teacher. Communication between home and schools, however, is all too often reduced to logistical information or coping with crises. In order to bring out the best in children, we must gather and share all that we know about the assets of every child in our mutual care. Their lives and futures depend on it. *We all need to focus on the right questions:* How can each of you help this child learn to trust his or her own mind? How can you together help him or her love learning, and do quality work?

Once in a while, I hear a teacher say, "But *we* are the professionals, not the parents. How can their opinion count as much as our trained observations and our data?" At those moments, I can only breathe and remind them that a professional is meant to be someone who professes faith in something or someone. Both parents and teachers need to do this in order to bring out the best in our children.

Every one of us is, in fact, a teacher. We all teach people something—how to work the stamp machine, plant bulbs in a garden, mend socks, etcetera. When you go to a conference in your child's school, remember that there is a teacher within you who will help you to value what you have to offer. Children are also teachers, but they are usually absent from these conferences, even though it is their learning, lives, minds, excitement, and difficulties that are being discussed. Consider bringing them and doing what you can to create a respectful partnership on the child's behalf. The common denominator you all share is *how* this child is smart, and the most important question to focus on is: How do we access and develop his or her abilities? The product of education is not better schools, but students who are learning better.

Find the simplest way to open the lines of communication. If your child has been having trouble in math, and you've made some new discoveries, you might want to write a note to his teacher that says, "I know Lincoln often gets confused doing multiplication. Here's what's working at home. If we use some kind of objects to lay out the problem so he can work it in his hands, it really helps. He can do about four problems in a row and then it's best if he gets up and walks around." Or you might say to her coach, "We've found that Missy can swim her best if she's given verbal advice before the race rather than yelling at her during it. Would that work for you?"

Tell your child's teachers, coaches, and mentors what you are working on. Enlist their support in observing your child for more ideas. One parent told us how helpful it was to find out from a teacher that her child went to lie down on her mat to read. It was something they had never tried at home.

A special note on selecting tutors, mentors, and coaches: We often have more choice when it comes to selecting tutors or mentors for our children than we do when it comes to teachers or coaches. Since very few adults truly understand how to individualize learning to match a child's Mind Pattern or maximize their assets, it is crucially important that you find someone who either has the same pattern of learning or who is very flexible and willing to learn what you have to teach them. Over and over, I have seen "well-intentioned" reading tutors, athletic coaches, dance teachers, and such shrink a child's self-worth by insisting there is only one right way to learn—the adults'.

Understanding that there *are* learning differences takes us only so far. We need to work together to build our repertoire of new ways to learn and teach. We need to know what works for someone else so that we have more options to try with our children. Experience has taught me that people generally like to talk about how they do things. Many of the ideas we need so much are still undiscovered, still under the surface, or kept in secret. Sometimes we develop ways that we don't even think about that could be really useful to someone else. We never know what will click for someone else. Please don't keep what you are learning to yourself.

But what happens when you're at a school meeting and a teacher tries to convince you your child has a learning disorder because he needs to wiggle to read or looks out the window to pay attention? What if they will just not understand that developing a love of learning and developing your child's gifts can be as important as perfect test scores?

It is said that trees that are strongest at the top are those that are blown by the most powerful winds. Let different opinions be just like a strong wind in the branches of your mind. Let your belief in your child and your intention rest in the heartwood of the trunk, where it is firmly rooted in respect and faith rather than being swayed by another's lack of understanding.

Inspiration

This time, you get to star in the "inspiration section" by learning something really revolutionary: how to influence instead of control. When parents, teachers, and children struggle with one another, it is often because they feel helpless in their ability to *influence* what is happening and so they resort to *control*. What's the difference between the two? To answer that question, I'd like to offer you an experience that may help put your fate back in your own hands. I learned this powerful little practice from Sensei Lloyd Miyashiro, a teacher of both a martial art form called Ki Aikido and high school students in Kauai, Hawaii:

> Have someone extend one arm and make a fist. If there's no one around, do it with one of your own arms. First try to control it by attempting to move the fist.
>
> You will probably notice, in a very short time, that the more force you use, the more resistance or rebellion there will be on the part of the fist.
>
> Now, try another way: influence. Place your thumb and index finger (of your other hand if you are doing this by yourself) on either side of the extended wrist as lightly as a butterfly. The lighter, the better. Don't try to do anything, just breathe and notice where movement already exists. Unless you are working with a corpse, there will be some very slight movement.
>
> Notice how you can move with that fist for a while and then extend the direction of the movement whichever way it is naturally going. Lightly.
>
> After a few minutes, it will probably be obvious to you that you can influence the direction of the movement, especially if you don't push. As soon as you get controlling, there will be resistance or rebellion. The more aware you are, the more possibilities there are for influence. It feels like a dance, and almost everyone would rather be danced with than pushed around.

I could do this practice a thousand times and still learn something new each time. You might imagine, as you are doing it, that the butterfly is you and the fist is your child's teacher. While you are doing it, you can allow yourself just to wonder, "What if this is how I was relating to her? I wonder how I'd be talking? What would my tone of voice be? What would I be doing? What is the best way to tell her what I know?" You won't need to "get" answers. They will just emerge, pop into your mind.

Here's another possibility: What if you behaved toward your own mind, when it got stuck or stubborn, when it was confused or frustrated, the way you were with the fist?

While we're at it, you might want to imagine that the fist is your child. Wonder your way through some struggle you are having now by trying to control him or her. For example, "If this is Simon when he refuses to do his homework, and this is me, I wonder how I could influence him? What could I show him? How could I encourage him?"

Did you notice that when the fist was being pushed around, your attention shifted to wanting to fight against the hand pushing it? In a like manner, when there is force, children tend to shift focus from taking responsibility for their own behavior to fighting against "the boss." They have many weapons—acting out, dropping out, drugs, depression, suicide, pregnancy. Like the fist, they resist: "You can't make me!"

Teachers and parents cannot communicate effectively with each other when they are attempting to control the way the other person thinks, or force them into agreeing with their point of view. They cannot serve as mentors, enhance learning, or encourage children to become more responsible when they resort to control or coercion. A sword striking a sword produces a clash. But what happens if the sword strikes and hits water?

To some of you this all can seem like Martian, since it may not be how your parents and teachers treated one another or you. Most people feel awkward when they first begin to practice influence instead of control. But awkward is part of learning something new, isn't it? Remember your first kiss? I wonder how you can make mistakes while learning something new without making yourself wrong.

The human race is supposed to evolve, to become more effective, more humane, more compassionate. Our culture is riddled with the sickness of violence and abuse. If we always do what we always did, we'll always get what we always got. Between an impulse and an act, we have a choice as to how we respond. I wish my parents and my teachers had been more willing to choose to be awkward butterflies than lethal swordsmen. Let's hope our children don't end up wishing the same thing about us.

Remember also to think with other parents. Together, you can discover solutions rather than despair alone because there are problems. You can break through the isolation that too often keeps the despair in place. We all—children and adults, guardians, teachers, coaches, and mentors—can help kindle one another's flames.

Developing a Partnership with Yourself

"Self-care is never a selfish act—it is simply good stewardship of the only gift I have, the gift I was put on earth to offer to others. Anytime we can listen to our true self, and give it the care it requires, we do so not only for ourselves, but for the many others whose lives we touch."
—PARKER PALMER

A child learns, before he or she walks, to imitate the posture of the adults around him or her. Similarly, if you are someone who views life as a constant opportunity to bring out the best of who you are, develop it, and offer it to the rest of the world; this will inspire your child to want to do the same. The only way to teach respect is to give it—to your children and to those who support your children, including yourself.

One of the ways we do this is by respecting our own assets and needs. We can stop in the moments we're feeling most worn down and impatient, take several deep breaths, and bring our minds back to our own SMART assets:

- Successes: Think about a time you've been successful with this child. What were you doing? What was going on? Can you use that now?
- Mind Patterns: Is this a situation where you need to say to your child, "You really want some good focused attention right now, but I'm distracted. Come back in half an hour."
- Attractions and Interests: How could what you are doing become more interesting or fun for you? Or do you need a five-minute break to do something that would interest you?
- Resources: What resources are available to you in the moment? What are you giving to your child that you need to be giving to yourself?
- Thinking Talents: What are *your* Thinking Talents? Which one could be most helpful in this situation?

Being a guardian is a crucial and important job and there is little support in society for it. There is a simple way you can support yourself and your child that requires no money, special equipment, or skills. Stop for one minute and take a joy break. Return to your senses. Take a deep breath and enjoy this child as you did when he or she was an infant. See, hear, and feel for one minute the miracle of uniqueness that is this child. This one brief moment of enjoying what is will help you with twenty difficult moments of worrying about what is not.

You can also shift your attitude by recalling this story: Two men were hauling huge stones up a hill. One was sweating and complaining, the other whistling and smiling. The smiling man was asked what made the difference between the two. "Well," he said, "I remember that I'm building a cathedral." Like the happy worker, when we remember the purpose of our labors with our children, it makes it easier to enjoy them, ourselves, and the process itself. As John Breeding writes in *The Wildest Colts Make the Best Horses*, "Always remember that this job of caring for and supporting the development of our young people is profoundly significant, important and valuable."

Enjoying our children is good for them as well as for us. "When we feel valued and cared about, our brain releases the neurotransmitters of pleasure, endorphins and dopamine. This helps us enjoy our work more," writes Eric Jensen in *Brain-Based Learning*. Jensen goes on to say that these neurotransmitters also increase the possibility that we will learn well and be less likely to be bored or give up.

Considering what a small portion of our mental capacity we use, it is obvious that all of us underestimate who we really are. The greatest gift you can give your child is yourself. By making the commitment to live your own life fully, to work at continuing to grow in self-awareness, you will create a contagion of curiosity. By recognizing and becoming acquainted with your own gifts, you will be better able to accord a similar acceptance to them. By being in search yourself, you will recognize and support your children's search.

The asset-focus approach described in this book is just that—an approach, a way of thinking about yourself and your children that can help you maximize potential. The more you practice, the more you will learn. But because this requires thinking in a way we haven't been trained to, it can be challenging. We adults have been so focused on fixing what's the matter, moving from minus ten to zero, that we forget to build on what really matters, moving from zero to plus ten.

Be gentle with yourself as you change your focus. It is a bit like shifting to night vision. At first you may feel totally inept in the dark. But gradually new shapes and forms begin to emerge that were not apparent at first. We actually use less photons to see more.

Smart Family Practices

For one week keep track of how many moments you actually enjoy your child. Help your child develop the skill of self-evaluation, which places the focus on what and how he or she is learning rather than on grades or other assessments that come from the outside. Regularly ask your child open-ended questions that help your child recognize, utilize, and develop his or her assets, such as: "On a scale of one to ten, how would you rate your learning today? Why do you give that rating? What do you like most about the work you produced? What are you most proud of? What was the hardest part? When did you get stuck? How did you help yourself get unstuck? How did you have fun? What did you learn that you wanted to? How did you show what you've been learning? What have you learned about yourself?"

Create a Satisfaction Stop. Some of us run from one thing on our list to the next without ever stopping to learn from our experience about what we've done well and what conditions increase our effectiveness. You can create Satisfaction Stops frequently. They can be very brief. For example, at the end of math home- work, a child can be asked, "What do you like most about what you just did?" and then tell him or her to run up and down the stairs three times before going on to spelling.

Find fun ways to track what your child is learning. Get a map of the world and, using her favorite color, flag all the places your child knows something about and wants to visit. Make a timeline of the growing list of people he admires. Make a tape or CD of all the books he's read or the songs she can play on the clarinet.

In moments of frustration with your child, stop and ask yourself, "What has worked in the past? What has been effective before?"

Now What? Learning Is Discovering
That Something *Is* Possible

"In my dream the angel shrugged and said, 'If we fail this time, it will be a failure of imagination.' And then she placed the world gently in the palm of my hand."

—BRIAN ANDREAS, ARTIST AND POET

Children should not fail. If they do, it is we who have not yet learned how to help them succeed. There is a new song in the air, enticing us toward something more worthwhile than better test scores or better salaries. We're all a little weary of the ways the world is treating its children. We all want something better for them and for the world they will inherit. Following that song is what matters. In recognizing, utilizing, and developing your child's assets, you share with them two precious treasures: the belief that they are lovable and that the universe is a place worthy of exploration where they belong. In exchange, your children share with you their precious presence. As the moon shines with light reflected from an invisible sun, their gift can return you to who you were truly meant to be.

It's time for us all to move forward. It's time to help create a revolution in the way our children are being perceived. It is time to look at assets more than deficits. You began helping your child move forward when he or she was an infant and took those first faltering steps toward your outstretched arms. You wondered *when* your child would walk, not *if.* You encouraged your child to risk that reach toward what you knew would be a great accomplishment.

Learning is discovering that something is possible. Guardians and schools are meant to serve the gifts our children bring, to name them, bless them, help aim them. This is the dream we can all make real.

Imagine a world in which every child understands what his and her natural strengths and talents are, how he or she learns and communicates most effectively, how she or he thinks most effectively with others. If you can imagine it, then you can help create a world worthy of your children.

Resources

Smartwired is a worldwide movement dedicated to the ideal that the uniqueness and diversity of young people, our greatest natural resource, must be recognized, valued, and empowered. It accomplishes this through the creation of multimedia learning adventures that connect children of all ages and adults to themselves, their talents, and others in meaningful ways so they can generate positive futures. For more information, contact www.Smartwired.org.

Ackerman, Diane. *An Alchemy of Mind: The Marvel and Mystery of the Brain.* New York: Scribner, 2004.

Albert, David. *And the Skylark Sings with Me: Adventures in Homeschooling and Community-Based Education.* Gabriola Islands, B.C., Canada: New Society Publishers, 1999.

Armstrong, Thomas. *The Myth of the A.D.D. Child: 50 Ways to Improve Your Child's Behavior and Attention Span Without Drugs, Labels or Coercion.* New York: Plume, 1997.

Breeding, John, Ph.D. *The Wildest Colts Make the Best Horses.* Fort Collins, Colo.: George Weir & Co, 2003.

Buckingham, Marcus, and Donald O. Clifton. *Now Discover Your Strengths.* New York: Free Press, 2001.

Cameron, Kim S., Jane E. Dutton, and Robert Quinn, eds. *Positive Organizational Scholarship: Foundations of a New Discipline.* San Francisco: Berrett-Kohler, 2003.

Comer, James P. *Leave No Child Behind: Preparing Today's Youth for Tomorrow's World.* New Haven: Yale University Press, 2004.

Cooperrider, David, Diana Whitney, and Jacqueline Stavros. *The Appreciative Inquiry Handbook: The First in a Series for Leaders of Change.* San Francisco: Berrett-Kohler, 2003.

Dennison, Paul E., and Gail E. Dennison. *Brain Gym: Teacher's Edition*. Ventura, Calif.: Edu Kinesthetics, 1995.

Edelman, Gerald. *Bright Air, Brilliant Fire: On the Matter of the Mind*. New York: Basic Books, 1993.

Erickson, Milton, M.D., and Sidney Rosen. *My Voice Will Go with You*. New York: W.W. Norton, 1982.

Frankl, Victor E. *Man's Search for Meaning*. New York: Pocket, 1997.

Freed, Jeffrey, and Laurie Parsons. *Right-Brained Children in a Left-Brained World*. New York: Simon and Schuster, 1998.

Gallwey, Timothy. *The Inner Game of Work*. New York: Random House, 2000.

Glasser, William. *Quality School: Managing Students Without Coercion*. New York: Perennial, 1998.

Goertzel, Ted, and Ariel M. W. Hansen. *Cradles of Eminence: Childhoods of More Than 700 Famous Men and Women*. Scottsdale, Ariz.: Great Potential Press, 2004.

Griffith, Mary. *The Homeschooling Handbook*. New York: Prima, 1999.

Hall, Edward. *Beyond Culture*. New York: Anchor, 1977.

Hannaford, Carla. *Smart Moves: Why Learning Is Not ALL in Your Head*. Arlington, Va.: Great Ocean Publishers, 1995.

"Hardwired to Connect: The New Scientific Case for Authoritative Communities." New York: Institute for American Values, 2003.

Hartmann, Thom. *Attention Deficit Disorder: A Different Perception*. Grass Valley, Calif.: Underwood Books, 1997.

Herrmann, Ned. *The Creative Brain.* Gainesville, Fla.: Brain Books, 1995.

Hillman, James. *The Soul's Code: In Search of Character and Calling.* New York: Random House, 1996.

Hirsh-Pasek, Kathy, Ph.D., and Roberta Mischnick Golinkoff, Ph.D. *Einstein Never Used Flash Cards: How Our Children Really Learn and Why They Need to Play More and Memorize Less.* Emmaus, Pa.: Rodale Press, 2003.

Jensen, Eric. *Brain-Based Learning: The New Science of Teaching and Training.* San Diego: The Brain Store, 1995.

Kabbat-Zinn, Jon. *Coming to Our Senses: Healing Ourselves and the World Through Mindfulness.* New York: Hyperion, 2005.

Kohl, Susan Issacs. *The Best Things Parents Do: Ideas & Insights from Real-World Parents.* Berkeley, Calif.: Conari Press, 2004.

Markova, Dawna. *I Will Not Die an Unlived Life: Reclaiming Purpose and Passion.* Berkeley, Calif.: Conari Press, 2000.

———. *The Open Mind: Exploring the 6 Patterns of Intelligence.* Berkeley, Calif.: Conari Press, 1996.

———. *Think-Ability.* Park City, Utah: Professional Thinking Partners, 2002.

———, ed. *Random Acts of Kindness.* Berkeley, Calif.: Conari Press, 2002.

Markova, Dawna, and Anne Powell, *How Your Child IS Smart: A Life-Changing Approach to Learning.* Berkeley, Calif.: Conari Press, 1992.

———. *Learning Unlimited: Using Homework to Engage Your Child's Natural Style of Intelligence.* Berkeley, Calif.: Conari Press, 1998.

Palmer, Parker. *The Courage to Teach: Exploring the Inner Landscape of a Teacher's Life.* San Francisco: Jossey-Bass, 1997.

———, *A Hidden Wholeness: The Journey Toward an Undivided Life*. San Francisco: Jossey-Bass, 2004.

Paul, Annie Murphy. *The Cult of Personality: How Personality Tests Are Leading Us to Miseducate Our Children, Mismanage Our Companies, and Misunderstand Ourselves*. New York: Free Press, 2004.

Ratey, John J. *A User's Guide to the Brain: Perception, Attention, and the Four Theaters of the Brain*. New York: Vintage, 2001.

Remen, Rachel Naomi. *My Grandfather's Blessings: Stories of Strength, Refuge, and Belonging*. New York: Riverhead Trade, 2001.

Rosen, Sidney. *My Voice Will Go with You: The Teaching Tales of Milton H. Erickson*. New York: W. W. Norton, 1982.

Ryan, M. J. *Trusting Yourself: How to Stop Feeling Overwhelmed and Live More Happily with Less Effort*. New York: Broadway, 2004.

Siegel, Daniel. *The Developing Mind: How Relationships and the Brain Interact to Shape Who We Are*. New York: Guilford Press, 1999.

Siegel, Daniel, and Mary Hartzell, M.Ed. *Parenting from the Inside Out: How a Deeper Self-Understanding Can Help You Raise Children Who Thrive*. New York: Tarcher-Putnam, 2003.

Taffel, Ron. *Parenting by Heart: How to Stay Connected to Your Child in a Disconnected World*. New York: Perseus Publishing, 1991.

Waldman, Jackie. *Teens with the Courage to Give*. Berkeley, Calif.: Conari Press, 2000.

Wesselmann, Debra. *The Whole Parent: How to Become a Terrific Parent Even If You Didn't Have One*. Cambridge, Mass.: Da Capo Press, 1998.

Acknowledgments

Gratitude

To those who stand behind me
To the hidden hands that hold me
To those who stand beside me
To those who stand before me and will walk where I cannot go

And in particular,

Andy Bryner

Angie McArthur

Donald McIlraith

Caroline Sutton

Mark Vancil

Stephen Roloff

Vicki Saunders

Anne Powell

Joan and Lew Sapiro

Sgt. Major Alford and Rita McMichael

David Wiley

Milton Erickson, M.D.

Daniel Siegel

Bea Mah Holland

John Hofmeister

Visions of a Better World Foundation

Paul Houston

Jerome

Marina and Lew Graham

Julia Johnston

The Burke family

Simone Amber

Mary Jane Ryan

David Peck

Ana Li McIlraith

The Random House folks

Robin Rankin

Will Glennon

Richard Ford

Peris Gumz

Elaine Goudy

General James L. and Diane Jones

Linda Booth Sweeney

Rachel Naomi Remen, M.D.

Peter Senge

Michael and Justine Toms

Karen Otazo

Royal Dutch Shell

Stephen Sokolow

Clayton

Brenda Cooper

Lisa Caine

Tina Donbeck

Tom Hadfield

Richard Kuboyama, Sensei

John Vieceli

Connor and Ryan Judge

Katie Brass

Lloyd Miyashiro, Sensei

Christina Duffy

Logan and Hunter Kessler

Anna Piepmeyer

Nate Senge

About the Author

DAWNA MARKOVA, PH.D., is internationally known for her groundbreaking research in the fields of learning and perception. She serves as the president of SmartWired, the CEO of Professional Thinking Partners, and a research member of the Society for Organizational Learning, founded by Peter Senge of the Sloan School at MIT.

In the past forty years, Markova's work has expanded into the boardrooms and corporate headquarters of companies in America, Europe, Asia, and Africa. She now reaches hundreds of thousands of people around the globe through seminars, keynote speeches, and her eight books, which have been translated into seven languages.

Dr. Markova was recently honored with the Visions to Action Award, "for people who have made a profound contribution to the world." She lives in northern California.

Bring SmartWired to Your Family and School

SmartWired, the company Dr. Markova founded in 2003, is devoted to creating a worldwide asset-focused revolution in teaching, learning, mentoring, and parenting. Utilizing both live programming and cutting-edge online processes and technology, SmartWired supports groups and organizations as well as individual children and their families.

To obtain information about SmartWiring your child's school or to purchase a set of cards designed to help you discover and utilize your child's SMART assets, go to www.smartwired.org.

About the Type

This book was set in Bodoni, a typeface named after Giambattista Bodoni, an Italian printer and type designer of the late eighteenth and early nineteenth century. It is not actually one of Bodoni's fonts but a modern version based on his style and manner and is distinguished by a marked contrast between the thick and thin elements of the letters.